CompTIA Cloud+ Certification Guide (Exam CV0-004)

A comprehensive guide for
Cloud+ CV0-004 certification

2nd Edition

Gopi Krishna Nuti

bpb

www.bpbonline.com

Second Revised and Updated Edition 2026

First Edition 2023

Copyright © BPB Publications, India

ISBN: 978-93-65890-594

LIMITS OF LIABILITY AND DISCLAIMER OF WARRANTY

To View Complete
BPB Publications Catalogue
Scan the QR Code:

Dedicated to

The light of my life, Padma
and
The apple of my eye, Dheeraj

About the Author

Gopi Krishna Nuti is an experienced professional with 23 years of experience in the IT industry. He has done his B. Tech in computer science from Andhra University, M.S. in business analytics from State University of New York at Buffalo, and an executive MBA from Amrita University, Bengaluru. He has worked extensively in analytics and software development projects and has delivered award-winning products and solutions. He has authored a few books and has multiple patents and research papers to his name. He is also a faculty at various training events and a guest faculty at various engineering colleges in Andhra Pradesh and Telangana. He is a member of the board of studies for Geetanjali Institute of Science and Technology. He is currently working as a data science manager at Autodesk, Bengaluru. He also volunteers for MUST research and is committed to democratizing AI for all. An incorrigible foodie, he is a passionate teacher and is obsessed with demystifying AI for the next generation of Software developers.

About the Reviewers

❖ **Kevin Hebron** is a results-driven IT manager with extensive experience in systems administration, cloud infrastructure, cybersecurity, and technical support. With certifications including AZ-104 and Security+, Kevin has successfully led hybrid migrations, streamlined IT operations, and implemented scalable solutions in fast-paced environments. He is passionate about empowering teams, improving IT documentation, and driving efficient transitions from MSP models to in-house IT structures.

❖ **Joshua Charles** is a self-taught cloud and DevOps engineer with a strong focus on building scalable, reliable, and automated infrastructure. He has hands-on experience across major cloud platforms, including AWS, Azure, and Google Cloud, and specializes in Infrastructure as Code using tools such as Terraform, Pulumi, and CloudFormation. His expertise also extends to Kubernetes, CI/CD pipeline design, and configuration management with Ansible and Helm.

In addition to his engineering work, Joshua writes extensively about DevOps practices, cloud-native tooling, and automation strategies. He is passionate about helping individuals and teams adopt modern infrastructure workflows and has contributed to technical books and online publications in the DevOps and cloud computing space.

When not architecting cloud solutions or writing technical content, he enjoys exploring distributed systems, mentoring aspiring engineers, and contributing to open-source projects.

❖ **Nicholas Bell** is a technical support engineer with over 7 years of experience in IT infrastructure, virtualization, and cloud technologies. He specializes in supporting mission-critical systems in healthcare and holds multiple CompTIA certifications, including Network+, Cloud +, and CloudNetX. Nicholas is passionate about automation, VoIP, and scalable system design and actively maintains a homelab for hands-on learning and experimentation. In his spare time, he enjoys challenging himself with progressive rock and metal guitar and trying out new recipes.

Acknowledgement

First and foremost, I want to express my heartfelt gratitude to my mother, Gnanaprasunamba.

Next, I want to express my sincere thanks to my wife, Padma Latha, and my son, Dheeraj, for sacrificing their share of my time and encouraging me to keep writing this book. I owe them a lot and hope to be worthy of their affection.

I would also like to acknowledge the valuable contributions of my colleagues and coworkers in these past two decades, who have graciously taught me so much.

I am also thankful to BPB Publications for their guidance and patience in dealing with my eccentricities.

Finally, I would like to thank you, my readers, for your support and feedback.

Preface

Cloud computing plays a crucial role in today's world across various sectors and industries. Imagine a cloud as a vast network of remote servers connected through the internet, where you can store, manage, and access data and applications instead of relying solely on your local computer or device. Such a system offers innumerable benefits to enterprises. Starting from accessibility to scalability, cost savings, collaboration, productivity gains, security, data backup and recovery, and innovation, the benefits are simply too many to ignore. Consequently, cloud computing is fast becoming a default approach for enterprise computing. This necessitated a skilled workforce that can understand the different flavours of cloud computing with sufficient knowledge of the concepts to help enterprises plan and implement their cloud strategy. It is crucial to be able to differentiate the workforce possessing the knowledge and skills to enable an organisation's cloud journey. CompTIA has introduced the Cloud+ certification for this purpose and is now in iteration 4 of this certification.

This book aims to guide and provide a comprehensive reference to readers in their journey to achieving the CV0-004 certification exam. The topics are carefully covered to provide an in-depth discussion on all the topics that can be expected in the exam. The chapters are designed to match the topics that are covered by the CV0-004 exam, which are up-to-date skills needed in the market.

Chapter 1: Introduction to CV0-004 Exam- Introduces the examination, pattern of questions, and provides complete details of the information needed to take the exam. By the end of this chapter, you shall be in a position to decide if CV0-004 exam is apt for you, how to approach the book, and how to prepare for the exam.

Chapter 2: Overview of Cloud Computing- Covers the topics of cloud computing right from the basics. Starting with a brief intro to the history of cloud computing, this chapter covers cloud service offerings, delivery models, and common cloud jargon.

Chapter 3: Managing Virtual Machines- Provides a comprehensive discussion of virtual machines. It covers the technology of virtualization, its inner workings, advantages, types, and why it is crucial to cloud computing.

Chapter 4: Managing Storage- Discusses everything about storage. Starting with the traditional storage mechanisms and advancing to aspects like NAS and SAN, this chapter discusses all cloud storage topics like object storage, replication, and disaster recovery.

Chapter 5: Networking Fundamentals- Covers all the fundamental aspects of networking. These fundamentals originated with traditional datacenters and have evolved to cloud, and are important even today. This chapter covers OSI 7 layer architecture, 4 layer IP architecture, and introduces various network topologies and networking components.

Chapter 6: Managing Networks- Expands on the previous chapter. It gets into significant details of IPv4 and IPv6 and discusses various protocols used over the internet. State of the art topics like network virtualization, address translations, and Software Defined Networking are covered in complete detail.

Chapter 7: Managing Security- Discusses security aspects of computing. IT discusses the approaches to IT security, cryptography, and encryption, and discusses the network security threats that are common in the IT industry. It also discusses the common approaches for protecting against such threats and discusses the security implementations that are common to cloud computing. This chapter also serves as a basic introduction to the CCSP certification exam.

Chapter 8: Identity and Access Management- Introduces the concepts of identity management, authentication, and various approaches for authorization and access control. The state of the art approaches, like SAML, OAuth, OpenID are discussed in this chapter.

Chapter 9: Migrating to cloud- Puts all the topics together. This chapter discusses how a traditional IT system can be migrated to a cloud and the different migration strategies available for accomplishing this. This chapter also explains the life cycle of a migration project and discusses how to prepare a roadmap for enterprise application migration.

Chapter 10: Orchestrating Cloud Applications- This chapter discusses the administrative and development aspects of a cloud. The topics of automation, orchestration, and their relationship are discussed in detail. Latest topics like Infrastructure as Code, runbooks, and runbook automation are covered in detail.

Chapter 11: Troubleshooting in Cloud- Discusses CompTIA's troubleshooting methodology. It also discusses how to troubleshoot problems that occur in cloud applications. It discusses the tools and approaches available for developers and cloud administrators for troubleshooting applications. It also discusses the best practices for cloud application development.

Chapter 12: Disaster Recovery and High Availability- This chapter discusses the disaster scenarios that can impact a cloud application, the need for business continuity, and the methods for withstanding and recovering from disasters. Various metrics to be used for measuring the effectiveness of disaster recovery, approaches for backup, and the facilities available in cloud for high availability are discussed.

Chapter 13: DevOps- This chapter discusses the development and operations processes, which aim to improve efficiency and reduce time to market. It also covers the tools used for this and discusses Infrastructure as Code, which is fast gaining traction in the industry.

Chapter 14: Vendor Specific Solutions- This chapter provides some information on the various cloud service offerings provided by the major cloud service providers. This chapter provides auxiliary information to provide additional information to readers.

Chapter 15: Practice Questions- Provides a set of questions that are not found elsewhere on the internet. These Q&As provide a simulation of the examination and give the reader a mock examination experience.

Coloured Images

Please follow the link to download the
Coloured Images of the book:

https://rebrand.ly/3f0c94

We have code bundles from our rich catalogue of books and videos available at https://github.com/bpbpublications. Check them out!

Errata

We take immense pride in our work at BPB Publications and follow best practices to ensure the accuracy of our content to provide with an indulging reading experience to our subscribers. Our readers are our mirrors, and we use their inputs to reflect and improve upon human errors, if any, that may have occurred during the publishing processes involved. To let us maintain the quality and help us reach out to any readers who might be having difficulties due to any unforeseen errors, please write to us at :

errata@bpbonline.com

Your support, suggestions and feedbacks are highly appreciated by the BPB Publications' Family.

At www.bpbonline.com, you can also read a collection of free technical articles, sign up for a range of free newsletters, and receive exclusive discounts and offers on BPB books and eBooks. You can check our social media handles below:

Instagram   *Facebook*   *Linkedin*   *YouTube*

Get in touch with us at: business@bpbonline.com for more details.

Piracy

If you come across any illegal copies of our works in any form on the internet, we would be grateful if you would provide us with the location address or website name. Please contact us at business@bpbonline.com with a link to the material.

If you are interested in becoming an author

If there is a topic that you have expertise in, and you are interested in either writing or contributing to a book, please visit www.bpbonline.com. We have worked with thousands of developers and tech professionals, just like you, to help them share their insights with the global tech community. You can make a general application, apply for a specific hot topic that we are recruiting an author for, or submit your own idea.

Reviews

Please leave a review. Once you have read and used this book, why not leave a review on the site that you purchased it from? Potential readers can then see and use your unbiased opinion to make purchase decisions. We at BPB can understand what you think about our products, and our authors can see your feedback on their book. Thank you!

For more information about BPB, please visit www.bpbonline.com.

Join our Discord space

Join our Discord workspace for latest updates, offers, tech happenings around the world, new releases, and sessions with the authors:

https://discord.bpbonline.com

Table of Contents

CHAPTER 1
Introduction to CV0-004 Exam

Introduction

The purpose of this chapter is to introduce the CompTIA® Cloud+ certification examination to readers. This chapter covers the purpose of the examination, who can attempt the exam, how to register for it, and what is expected from one who clears the examination. It also provides guidance on how to approach this book and how to prepare for the examination.

Structure

In this chapter, we will cover the following topics:

- About CompTIA
- About CV0-004 exam
- Who should take this exam
- About this book
- Exam readiness checklist

About CompTIA

The **Computing Technology Industry Association (CompTIA)** is a leading vendor-neutral, independent source of information, education, training, and certification for the global IT workforce. They offer training and certifications on emerging technologies. Their membership and certification holders span the range of technology companies from established Fortune 500 leaders to small and medium-sized tech businesses. By remaining vendor-neutral, their certifications aim to evaluate the test takers on the concepts that are relevant to the industry without being confined to a single vendor. More details about CompTIA, like their board of directors and membership details, can be found on their website **http://www.comptia.org/**. Much of the information in this chapter is taken from their website as is.

About CV0-004 exam

CompTIA's Cloud+ is a global certification that validates the skills needed to deploy and automate secure cloud environments that support the high availability of business systems and data. It is a performance-based IT certification that views cloud-based infrastructure services in the context of broader IT systems operations, regardless of the platform. CompTIA Cloud+ validates the technical skills needed to deploy, optimize, and protect mission critical applications and data storage.

There are no prerequisites for attempting the examination. CompTIA recommends five years of total IT experience, including two to three years of networking or systems administration experience, but it is not mandatory. The exam itself contains 90 questions, which are mostly multiple choice questions. A few performance-based questions are also included, where the candidate should understand a given exhibit and answer questions based on it. In a time of 90 minutes, the candidate should score 750 marks out of 900. Being a vendor-neutral examination, the questions will not be specific to any cloud vendor.

From the date of acquiring, the certificate is valid for three years. After this period, candidates can renew their certificate by following the CompTIA's Continuing Education program. Candidates can renew their certification by collecting and reporting 50 Continuing Education Units within three years.

The Cloud+ certification examination is continuously updated by CompTIA to ensure it meets the latest industry requirements. CV0-004 is the latest version of the Cloud+ certification. It includes questions across six domains as mentioned in the following table:

Domain	Examination questions in CV0-004	Examination questions in CV0-003
Cloud Architecture Design	23%	13%
Security	19%	20%
Deployment	19%	23%
Operations & Support	17%	22%
Troubleshooting	12%	22%
DevOps fundamentals	10%	-

Table 1.1: Distribution of questions in CV0-004 exam

Compared to CV0-003, the latest exam added DevOps fundamentals and adjusted the percentage weightage for others. Specifically, the share of questions on Cloud Architecture increased, and those on Troubleshooting are reduced significantly.

Who should take this exam

CompTIA Cloud+ is ideal for cloud engineers who need to have expertise across multiple products and systems. As per CompTIA®, the following job roles are primary and secondary beneficiaries of obtaining a Cloud+ certification. This content is taken as-is from CompTIA's website here **https://www.comptia.org/blog/the-new-comptia-cloud-your-questions-answered**. Most of these roles exist in the traditional data centres as well. However, with the advent of cloud, their job profiles have undergone a significant change. Let us see in the following table the traditional data centre roles and how they can benefit from cloud knowledge and from Cloud+ certification.

The following table shows the beneficiaries for CompTIA Cloud+:

Traditional role	Responsibilities	Cloud role
Network administrators	The people in this role generally develop, maintain, and troubleshoot the network connections. They are responsible for maintaining the firewalls, switches, routers, gateways, VPNs, and other network devices.	Cloud Administrators
Systems administrators	Sys admins procure, install, manage, and monitor hardware and software on which organisations' business applications and services are deployed. They are generally tasked with activities like user identity management, backup management, and the like. They are sometimes the first responders for any system incidents as well.	Cloud Administrators
Systems engineers	These roles work very closely with developers and provide guidance to them in architecting, building, and maintaining the business applications and services. It is not uncommon to see this role being merged with development team.	Cloud Engineers and DevOps
Systems Architect	Cloud engineers are responsible for maintaining the cloud to meet the organisation's expectations. They build and maintain the cloud infrastructure.	Cloud Architects
Security Analyst	Security analysts are responsible for the physical and cyber security of the organisations computing assets. They assess and evaluate the security risks to organisations assets. They devise means to protect and recover from malicious attacks.	Cloud Security analyst
Project manager	Project managers set timelines for projects and keep the group in scope and on budget.	Project Manager
Infrastructure team	This team is one of the most heavily impacted because of cloud migrations. All the activities involving physical assets are being moved into the cloud these resources must be reskilled to suit the cloud requirements.	

Table 1.2: Beneficiaries of Cloud+ certification

Anyone wanting to showcase their knowledge of the cloud computing concepts and targeting the above-listed roles can attempt the exam and benefit from it.

About this book

This book is meant as a comprehensive guide for all the information needed to successfully complete the CV0-004 examination. The book does not assume any prior knowledge of cloud computing. However, a basic knowledge of the IT industry and the way of working of IT professionals is assumed.

Exam readiness checklist

Test takers are recommended to read the book thoroughly before scheduling the examination. Questions provided at the end of every chapter should be thoroughly practiced. Of particular importance is *Chapter 15, Practice Examination,* which is a mock practice examination. It is highly recommended for the candidates to practice those examinations in a timed manner and test their knowledge against the answer key provided. It is suggested to aim for a 90% correctness in these mock tests before appearing for the actual CV0-004 examination. Once you are confident of your scores, you should visit **http://www.comptia.org/** and schedule your examination as per the instructions on CompTIA's website. The following table is a checklist to verify your preparedness for taking the exam:

S. No	Item	Completed Yes/No
1.	Practice questions at the end of every chapter	Yes
2.	Mock tests in *Chapter 15*	Yes
3.	Timed Mock tests in chapter 15 with 90% correct answers	Yes

Table 1.3: *Exam readiness checklist*

Conclusion

In this chapter, we have learnt about the CV0-004 examination, the preparation needed for it, and who will benefit from it. We have also discussed how this book approaches it.

In the next chapter, we shall start with the topics that are directly relevant for the examination. We will start with the basics of cloud computing and shall proceed to cover the more advanced topics.

CHAPTER 2
Overview of Cloud Computing

Introduction

This chapter shall provide an introduction to the concept of the cloud. We will look at how the idea of virtual machines started from the earliest days of computing, that is, the MULTICS operating system, Unix. We will discuss how innovations in networking and computing have made computing ubiquitous and affordable to all. We will also briefly discuss the economic drivers, such as economies of scale and Capex/Opex considerations, that have driven cloud adoption in the enterprise.

Moving on, we will discuss the basic terminology of cloud computing. An eagle's eye view of cloud-based application development will highlight the salient differences between traditional application development (that is, standalone/desktop applications) and cloud-based applications.

Structure

We will look at the following topics in this chapter:

- History of cloud computing
- Cloud service offerings
- Cloud delivery models

- Common cloud jargon
- Cloud developer beginner questions

Objectives

The objective of this chapter is to understand how cloud computing came into being and how it has evolved over the years. The chapter also discusses the different cloud delivery models and introduces the common jargon. Finally, it covers some of the questions a beginner in cloud computing development might have.

History of cloud computing

The earliest computers were costly machines and very slow in computing speed. As the computing power of the systems increased, it was observed that all programs did not utilize the entire CPU. The concept of time-sharing emerged in the 1960s with the idea of using the idle time of CPUs and improving the cost-efficiency of computing. Improvements in hardware and software algorithms have allowed enterprises to rent out their computing power to third parties and monetize the idle time of their systems. This gradually became a business model where large organizations procured expensive computing power, and third parties used and paid for it **on demand**.

Salesforce pioneered the revolution when it released its enterprise software as a subscription model known as SaaS. Amazon started offering storage and virtual machines over the internet and revolutionized the computing world with its IaaS model. Google offered a PaaS offering named Google App Engine, which provided a platform for application development over the Internet. Coupled with significant hardware advances like hypervisors, hardware-assisted virtualization, and software innovations like Docker containers, software-defined networking, and so on, cloud computing redefined the software development paradigm and became the next big *it* thing.

Innovations in networking

It would be remiss if we did not consider the advances in networking that have contributed to the cloud computing phenomenon. When the concept of time sharing was in its infancy, the USA's Department of Defence invested in other research at its Advanced Research Projects Agency. Computer networking is one of the many stellar inventions that came out of this place. It evolved into the internet and proved to be a major game-changer for humanity. Evolution in networking, like TCP/IP protocols, DNS, LANs, and improvements like Coaxial cables, fiber optics, routers, switches, and so on, contributed to a steep reduction in data transfer cost while allowing for increasing complexity in computer networks. Innovations like software-defined networking have brought about significant maturity in cloud computing.

Innovations in computing

Several improvements in software have also contributed to the cloud computing phenomenon. Virtualization is the foundation of cloud computing, and software development has gradually moved away from monoliths to modular architectures. Improvements like client-server architectures, microservices, APIs, protocols like HTTP, REST, and so on, and disciplines like DevOps and extreme programming have all made cloud computing possible.

Cloud service offerings

In the previous paragraphs, we talked about SaaS, PaaS, and IaaS offerings from Salesforce, Google, and AWS, respectively. In this section, we will discuss them in detail. We will demystify the terms and discuss the differences and similarities between these offerings in layman's terms. The most important differentiator between service offerings is the flexibility for the customers and the responsibility distribution between the customer and the service providers.

Software as a Service

In a **Software as a Service (SaaS)** model, the application is installed on a remote server. End users access the application typically via a web browser. The entire infrastructure complexity is hidden from the end user in this model. If you have ever used web-based email services like Gmail and Yahoo, then you have used a SaaS cloud offering. This approach provides maximum control to the application developer and places minimum constraints on end-user environment requirements. Salesforce was the first company to offer its CRM software as a SaaS offering. Customers pay for the services only to the extent they use those services. Applications like OneDrive and GDrive are all examples of SaaS products.

Platform as a Service

In a **Platform as a Service (PaaS)** model, the service provider does not provide application software. They deliver the framework needed for building an enterprise-grade application. For example, you might want to host a web application. Using a PaaS provider, you need not build web servers and other infrastructure. You can upload only your application code, and the PaaS provider shall take responsibility for deployment, capacity provisioning, load balancing, and so on. Developers no longer need to worry about maintaining the underlying building blocks, reducing the amount of code to be written. Building a highly scalable application has become simpler than an altogether homegrown solution. Providers charge only for the services used. So, if the user demand is not high, then the organization's finances will not get locked into purchasing expensive hardware and infrastructure.

Infrastructure as a Service

In an **Infrastructure as a Service (IaaS)** model, the cloud provider delivers raw infrastructure to the users. These can be virtual CPUs, RAM, GPUs, storage, network interfaces, and so on. Cloud service providers own the physical devices and ensure their upkeep. Users have complete flexibility in configuring and using these machines. Providing redundant machines and power supplies is the responsibility of the service provider. Organizations pay for these resources for actual usage, which is typically significantly cheaper than the cost of procuring physical devices. Admins can commission and decommission virtual machines quickly, improving the organization's agility. Organizations can considerably reduce their capital expenditure requirements with the **pay-as-you-go** model.

It is essential to understand the different models adequately. All other cloud service models are essentially a variation of these three models. For example, Machine Learning as a Service is a PaaS model dedicated to artificial intelligence, and **Communication as a Service (CaaS)** is an intriguing combination of SaaS and PaaS.

Table 2.1 explains the differences between the different service offerings in generic and non-technical terms. We will revisit these differences in significant and technical detail again in *Chapter 9, Migrating a Business Application to Cloud*, when discussing cloud migrations.

	IaaS	PaaS	SaaS
Service delivered	Computing infrastructures	Frameworks as APIs	Enterprise application
Intended users	Systems administrators	Developers	End users
Flexibility for cloud developers	Near total	Limited; use the available APIs to build a custom application	Almost none; use what is available
Cloud service provider responsibility	Maintaining the service levels for infrastructure only	Maintaining the service levels and KPIs for the framework	End-to-end
Service customer responsibility	Configuring the infrastructure, troubleshooting, building and maintaining the enterprise application	Building and maintaining the enterprise application	Almost none

Table 2.1: Comparison of Cloud Service Offerings

Desktop as a Service

Desktop as a Service (DaaS) is also called a **CloudPC**. It is essentially a variation of SaaS. The end user gets a complete desktop virtually, which eliminates investment in purchasing a PC of their own, yet provides the facilities of a personal computer at a low price point.

Anything as a Service

In **Anything as a Service (XaaS)**, X stands for **Anything**. XaaS means that anything shall be delivered in a service model. The service provided could be a **Database (DBaaS)**, **Business Process (BPaaS)**, **Communications (CaaS)**, or even a laptop.

Cloud delivery models

We have seen the different business models for cloud service offerings. Now, we will look into the cloud delivery models. Choosing the cloud service offering is a design decision for an enterprise application developer. However, choosing the cloud delivery model is an organizational decision involving multiple aspects of the business. When selecting a cloud delivery model, organizations have to weigh decisions regarding administrative, data safety, legal, financial, and other such concerns.

In typical data center-based enterprise application development, organizations procure high-performance hardware and build redundancies and fault tolerance. The choice of a cloud delivery model redistributes this responsibility between the cloud service provider and the organization. The standard cloud delivery models are private clouds, public clouds, hybrid clouds, and community clouds.

Private cloud

In a private cloud, the computing systems that host the virtual machines and enterprise software are owned, operated, and maintained by the organization's IT department. This approach is comparable to maintaining traditional data centers. The IT support team function expands to support virtualization, but otherwise remains the same. This model is helpful if the organization has already spent a considerable amount of money setting up its own data centers and on upkeep. However, the financial benefits of a private cloud are the lowest as compared to those of all the other delivery models.

Public cloud

The cloud service provider is a distinct organization catering to multiple cloud customers in a public cloud. CSP provides the IaaS/PaaS services consumed by the customer organization's developers and administrators. The organization can choose to use them to build either a development environment for internal use or an end-user-facing SaaS application. The CSP provider uses the same hardware to create a virtual platform for multiple client organizations and distributes costs across multiple clients. By doing so, CSPs can bring down the price point for each customer. This is known as **economies of scale** and is a significant driver for adopting public clouds among startups. During the early days of the cloud computing revolution, large organizations faced stiff resistance from their internal IT teams and legal departments regarding the risk of data breaches. Subsequent improvements in hardware and software have allayed these fears.

Hybrid cloud

A hybrid cloud is a combination of private and public clouds. Organizations mix and match the capabilities of their internal cloud capabilities along with those of public clouds. Organizations can achieve a wide range of capabilities without compromising on non-negotiable business or legal constraints when using a hybrid cloud approach. For example, an organization may choose to use their private cloud only for storing data and the public cloud for hosting their application software. This allows them to retain complete control of sensitive data while providing flexibility like low latency, auto-scaling, and so on.

Community cloud

A community cloud offering is similar to a public cloud, with one crucial difference. A community cloud is a custom-built cloud that meets the requirements of a specific group of companies or teams with similar infrastructure requirements. A public cloud is open to all individuals or organizations (unless prohibited by legal concerns). On the other hand, the community cloud has specific functionalities built to cater only to a set of organizations. For example, all banks have similar requirements regarding the availability of their systems, data backups, and retention, and so on. So, it might be beneficial to build a community cloud only catering to FinTech customers. Such a community cloud might not be helpful for college students who only want to understand web application development. *Table 2.2* provides an overview of the differences between multiple delivery models:

	Private Cloud	Hybrid Cloud	Public Cloud	Community Cloud
Cloud service provider (CSP)	Organisation's own IT team	Third-party org and organisation's data center	Third-party org AWS, Azure, Google and so on	Third-party
Responsibility of maintaining the cloud service agreements	Organisation	CSP and Org	CSP	CSP
Availability of tailor-made functionality for cloud customers	High	Medium	Low	Low
Cost-benefit for customer	Low	Medium	High	High

Table 2.2: Comparison of cloud delivery models

Figure 2.1 depicts how benefits differ for each delivery model:

Private Cloud	Community cloud	Public Cloud	Hybrid Cloud
• Limited to a single organisation • Allows utilization of CapEx already invested • Helps in managing OpEx	• Caters to organisations with similar business needs • Helps reducing CapEx and OpEx • Government cloud offerings from major public cloud service providers	• For generic organisations of all sizes • Moves CapEx to OpEx • Risk of Vendor Lock-In • AWS, Azure, Google Cloud, and so on	• Combination of Private cloud and public or community clouds • Allows adjustment of CapEx and OpEx • supports portability of features

Figure 2.1: *Benefit differences for cloud delivery models*

Common cloud jargon

As with any other business or technical domain, cloud computing has evolved to encompass several concepts. These concepts might often look like jargon to those unfamiliar with them, but as with most jargon, the underlying ideas are straightforward and easy to understand. The following is a list of terminologies one can expect to encounter when working with cloud computing. There are certainly many more, but these should give you a general understanding of the concepts and help you engage in meaningful conversation:

- On-premise hosting is the traditional way in which organizations host their data centers. Virtualized machines are hosted by the hardware "on the premises" of the organization. This is like a private cloud.

- Off-premise hosting refers to hosting the virtual machines elsewhere, not in the organization's own data centers. It is similar to public or community clouds.

- Orchestration refers to the automation of the day-to-day administrative activities performed by IT teams in the cloud. Any business will have policies and procedures for tasks to meet its service-level agreements. Automating these tasks is crucial to achieving organizational agility.

- Orchestration platforms provide automated tools to perform the tasks. They reduce a significant workload for IT administrators. For example, an orchestration platform might provide a template for creating virtual machines. Administrators need only fill up the template, and the platform will take care of building, spawning and maintaining the virtual machine based on that template.

- Scalability is a cloud feature that allows data centers to handle larger workloads by adding additional physical machines (scale-out) or replacing the device with another higher configuration (scale-up).

- Elasticity refers to a characteristic of a cloud that allows the organization to pool all its resources and utilize the idle resources without having to invest in additional hardware. The elasticity of the cloud permits developers to scale-up/scale-out their virtual machines on short notice.

- On-demand service is a significant characteristic of cloud computing. It refers to a facility by which computing resources are made available to the user on an **as-needed** basis. The user pays only for the actual usage of resources. It is also known as the **pay-as-you-go** model.

- Pay-as-you-grow is a different way of marketing on-demand services. Using a CSP allows the start-up to scale-up/scale-out as their business expands. Start-ups need not invest in expensive hardware upfront, but can increase their infrastructure as they grow.

- Ubiquitous access refers to cloud capabilities being available anywhere to their users. Whether the user is using a PC from within their company's network or via a home Wi-Fi or internet kiosk, the cloud's resources are available in the same way. Individual organizations might place administrative constraints to restrict such access, but that is not a restriction for the cloud service provider itself.

- Chargeback originates from an accounting concept known as activity-based costing. An organization typically has multiple teams using the cloud resources to different extents. The management needs to know how much each team's usage has contributed to the overall cloud costs. This knowledge allows them to judge the return on investment and other such factors in a more informed manner. Distributing the cloud costs to individual resources or teams is called chargeback.

- Metering is measuring the usage of cloud resources by each customer. Customers might place quotas and upper limits on cloud resource usage to prevent unintended costs from exhausting the budgets. The limits can be on CPU usage time, memory, network usage, and uptime.

- Multi-tenancy is an architecture wherein multiple tenants, that is, clients, are served by a single application server. However, one tenant cannot access or modify the data belonging to another tenant. Gmail and Yahoo Mail are good examples of multi-tenant SaaS. The same server serves multiple email users, but no user can read another user's email. In PaaS, the same platform serves as the building blocks for different customers, but one customer cannot access or modify another customer's data. Extending to IaaS, the same physical computer runs multiple virtual machines for different customers, but one virtual machine cannot share the data of another virtual machine. In single-tenant architecture, a virtual resource is limited to one tenant. Compared to multi-tenancy, single-tenancy can be more straightforward in terms of security but more expensive.

- Cloud bursting is a technique employed in hybrid clouds, where the application typically runs on the private cloud but **bursts** onto the public cloud to meet higher demands for computing resources. For example, a retail company might have its own data center to host their applications, but might want to use cloud servers for special sale days where shopping traffic might be very high. This technique is known as cloud bursting.

- Autoscaling is a technique used by combining many of the concepts mentioned above. CSPs provide a way for the application to run on multiple VMs when the demand is high, using elasticity. This flexibility of scaling out virtual machines is known as autoscaling.

- Cloud elements are different elements that make up a cloud environment. While it is very common to think of a cloud as only virtual machines, it is only partially accurate. Many resources are available via the cloud, and many other resources are necessary for setting it up. Examples of this can be virtual resources like vCPUs, GPUs, RAM, storage, and network interface cards. These are collectively called cloud elements.

Cloud developer beginner questions

In this section, we will discuss some of the most frequent questions asked by developers who are starting their cloud journey:

- *Does an application require changes to its coding when moving to the cloud?*

  To a certain extent, yes. If an application is migrating from its own data center to an IaaS cloud, the necessary changes are fewer than those required when migrating to a PaaS cloud. Migrating to a PaaS cloud might require a complete rewrite of the application. Migrating to IaaS requires changes only to the components accessing the virtual infrastructure.

- If an application is run on the cloud, *will it automatically get the benefits of autoscaling?*

  Yes. However, it should be migrated after considering storage access, latency, and other requirements.

- *Can various public CSPs be mixed and matched?*

  Technically, yes. The complexity of managing such a situation generally exceeds the complexity of a single cloud provider.

- *Will other tenants of the CSP be able to access the data?*

  No. Multi-tenancy comes with a strong commitment from the CSPs to prevent accidental data leakage across tenants. The possibility of an intelligent hacker bypassing the security limitations always exists, but the stringent administrative and systemic checks make the probability negligible.

- *Will cloud computing replace the internal IT teams?*

  It will not entirely replace them, but it will undoubtedly need the internal IT teams to change their skill sets. In the traditional data center, skills like cabling were essential. In a cloud environment, particularly in the absence of private clouds, skills like software-defined networking take higher precedence. Due to this, traditional IT teams shall certainly reduce in size but are unlikely to vanish completely. By adding cloud skills, traditional IT teams can make an excellent addition to an organization's capabilities to offer cloud-enabled services.

A detailed review of cloud migration strategies is provided in *Chapter 9, Migrating to Cloud*.

Conclusion

Cloud service providers have multiple delivery models and service offerings for their customers. All these models and services aim to shift the administrative burden from the customers to the service providers. Cloud computing also helps service providers achieve economies of scale and pass on the benefits to the customers, reducing their financial burden. However, organizations should choose the service offering and delivery model after weighing various factors and risks.

In the next chapter, we shall discuss virtual machines, how virtualization technology forms the backbone of cloud computing, and how to manage virtual machines.

Join our Discord space

Join our Discord workspace for latest updates, offers, tech happenings around the world, new releases, and sessions with the authors:

https://discord.bpbonline.com

CHAPTER 3
Managing Virtual Machines

Introduction

In this chapter, we will discuss a critical technology named virtual machines, which made cloud computing feasible. It is fair to say that cloud computing would not have been as successful without virtualization.

Let us consider a scenario. Suppose you have purchased a powerful desktop machine and installed Linux on it. You are happy using the available apps, but you want to run a Microsoft Windows on the same machine for a few applications. The old way of achieving this was to format the disk and install Windows. This gives you the ability to use Windows, but you will lose the functionality of Linux. This is not the best solution. An alternative was the dual boot. When booting the system, the user can choose between Windows and Linux. While this removed the problem of completely losing one OS, it was still an either-this-or-that solution. You could not manage if you wanted to run heavy-duty computing work in Linux and an excellent code editor in Windows. It would be nice to run both OSes simultaneously. This is precisely the issue that virtualization addresses. It has a major impact on the way developers design their applications. It is crucial to understand the virtualization technology and the inner workings of virtual machines.

Structure

We will cover the following topics in this chapter:

- Overview of virtual machines
- Benefits of virtualization
- Exam topics
- Virtualization on a host machine
- Virtualization on a virtual machine/guest machine
- Virtualization as the building block of cloud computing

Objectives

This chapter shall focus on the history and evolution of virtual machines, their usage in cloud computing, and their advantages and disadvantages. It will also cover how computing components like memory, storage, and networks work in a virtual environment. Finally, it will discuss how virtualization offers cost benefits and how both CSPs and users benefit from it.

Overview of virtual machines

Imagine a Linux application that simulates bare-bones hardware and allows you to install the Windows operating system onto this simulated hardware. Such an application will run the Windows operating system as an application on Linux. This facility enables the user to run both operating systems simultaneously and choose applications simultaneously.

The Linux machine, as described in the scenario we discussed, is called a host machine/ host OS. The simulated hardware is called a virtual machine. The Windows machine is called the **guest OS**, and even vice versa is possible. Your host operating system can be Windows. You can install a Windows application to simulate hardware and install Linux onto the simulated hardware. The concept is the same.

Extend the idea further. The simulated hardware does not need to be the same as the host machine. It is a simulation, anyway. Virtual machines hit on this idea precisely. The virtual machine's configuration need not be similar or comparable to the host machine. You can create a virtual machine with a configuration of your choice, and the application shall simulate that for you. For example, your host machine may have 64 GB RAM and a 2 TB hard disk on a quad-core Intel i5 processor. However, you can configure your virtual machine to be 8 GB RAM and 500 MB hard disk on a duo-core Intel i2 processor. Even better, you can have multiple virtual machines on the same host, each with a different configuration. They all run as separate applications on the host OS. **Virtual machines (VMs)** bank on the multi-tasking capabilities of the host OS to run multiple VMs. Virtualization software simulates various physical machines available for the end users, who can remotely login to each one. If you created 4 VMs, you have 4 VMs + 1 host = 5 devices for the end users. You have accommodated five users without investing in additional hardware.

Consider storage, network, and similar aspects. Virtual machine simulators have a solution for that. As mentioned in the earlier example, the 500 MB configured for the VM will be stored as a physical file on the host machine. This is called a **virtual disk**. Virtual disks contain the guest OS installation, additional software (like code editors), and user files. The host and guest OS can access each other's files and clipboards with additional configuration.

This concept is beautiful because the virtual disk can be moved between different host machines. All that is needed is for the host machine to simulate the virtual machine hardware, which can run on that hardware seamlessly. The VM's end user is often unaware that the host hardware has changed.

That is how VMs work. The idea of VMs has been around for some time. In the earliest days of mainframe, it was often observed that a lot of computing power was being left idle. To improve the utilisation, VMware popularised the idea of VMs and achieved significant success. IBM's mainframes introduced virtualization, but VMware brought it to x86 architecture in the late 1990s. As mainframes fell out of favor and x86 architecture became the norm, VMware overcame considerable challenges to bring virtualization to the x86 architecture.

Today, virtualization has become a standard feature in almost every computer. Even regular run-of-the-mill desktops/laptops can support virtualization. As we will see in the upcoming sections, virtualization forms a fundamental building block of cloud computing. *Figure 3.1* gives a pictorial view of how VMs share the host machine's time:

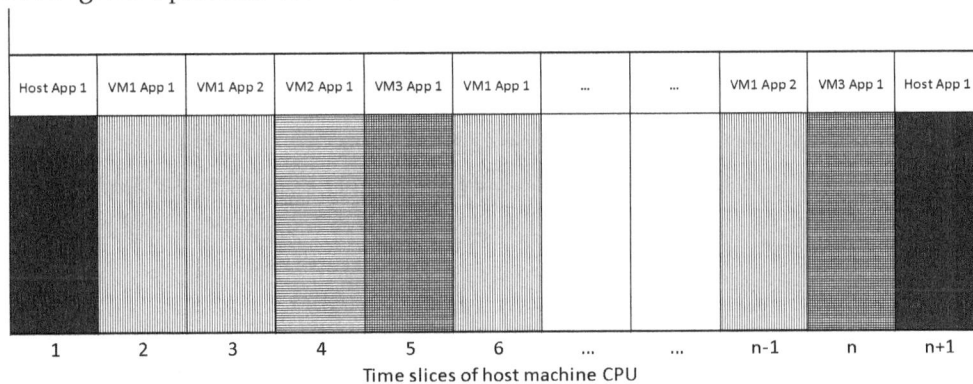

Host App 1	VM1 App 1	VM1 App 2	VM2 App 1	VM3 App 1	VM1 App 1	...	...	VM1 App 2	VM3 App 1	Host App 1
1	2	3	4	5	6	...	...	n-1	n	n+1

Time slices of host machine CPU

Figure 3.1: *VMs benefiting from time-sharing*

Learning tidbits:

- Before virtualization for x86 became widely available, multiple approaches were attempted to solve the problem with limited success. Some familiar examples for developers can be **Wine** (**Windows Emulator**) software and Cygwin. However, note that these are only emulators and are not true virtualizers.

- If you like experimenting with VMs, you can start by downloading Oracle VM Virtual Box software. It is a feature-rich, high-performance, open-source product for customers and is available free of cost. As an enterprise-grade product, it provides all the facilities expected from virtualizer software and can give you an enormous understanding of the beauty of VMs.

Benefits of virtualization

Virtualization offers multiple benefits to organizations. It is essential to understand the benefits so that the various features of VMs can be put into perspective:

- **Reduced capital and operating costs**: In the traditional data centre approach, each application had a dedicated machine. As a result, the capital investment increased significantly. Virtualization allows the simulation of multiple virtual machines on a single physical device. VMs do not cost anything except for guest operating system licensing costs. This greatly reduces physical infrastructure costs and translates into significant cost savings for organizations.

- **Minimized or eliminated downtime**: Physical machines have physical failures, like electrical and network failures. Maintaining these for multiple devices is a challenge for IT administrators. With VMs, this problem is minimized. IT administrators need to worry about only a handful of host machines, and all VMs can run without issues. Even if one physical machine goes down, the virtual disks can be moved to a different host machine, and all VMs are available without any problems. With proper configuration, application downtime can be reduced to near zero.

- **Increased IT agility**: IT administrators no longer have to get budget approval, place an order for hardware, wait for its delivery, and plug it into the data centre. With virtualization, it is now only a matter of configuring a VM. This is a minimal activity, and the machines are provisioned within no time. Moreover, the underlying host hardware can be modified as per the needs of administrators, and end users are oblivious to it. This dramatically increases IT agility.

- **Simplified data centre management**: Above all facilities, the data centre is not the terrifying monster it used to be. Instead of managing mind-boggling hardware and configurations, data centres are streamlined, and the complexity is shifted to the software side. Software complexity being considerably easier to maintain, data centre management is now a much more simplified activity.

Does this mean virtualization is one-size-fits-all? Of course not. There are scenarios wherein it is not beneficial. If you have an application that has a steady demand of compute power throughout its lifetime and runs on hardware optimised for it, then such hardware is unlikely to have much idle time. In this scenario, adding virtual machines to this host can be counterproductive. However, such systems are few and far between. CPUs and RAMs with idle time are much more common. Even when such scenarios are encountered, a case can be made to move all such physical machines to VMs on a high-power computer to gain economies of scale.

Exam topics

Let us now delve into the topics related to VM as relevant for the examination. We specifically omit the discussion on the feature comparison of individual VM software. CVO-003 exam is vendor-neutral, and so is the rest of the section. ·

Hypervisor

In the *Overview of Virtual Machines* section, we referred to application software that simulates the hardware. Hypervisor is the technically correct name for this application software or virtualizer. A hypervisor is responsible for simulating and maintaining the resources, such as CPUs, RAM, storage disks, network interfaces, and the like, which are needed for the guest OS.

Hypervisor types

There are two types of hypervisors. Some hypervisors run as applications on top of the host OS, as described earlier. Other hypervisors, however, do not need a host OS. They are launched along with the bootup of the host machine and operate directly on the bare metal infrastructure of the host machine.

Type 1

Hypervisors run directly on the host machine's hardware. They do not require a host operating system and interact with the underlying infrastructure directly, eliminating the overhead of running a host OS. With the absence of a host OS comes the additional security of guest OSs being unable to contaminate each other's data. This makes Type 1 hypervisors the most secure and efficient; using them is the preferred approach for enterprise-grade applications. However, IT admins will have to use additional software to handle specific management tasks typically performed by the host OS.

Type 2

It is the scenario described in the *Overview of Virtual Machines* section. The hypervisor runs as a software application on top of the host OS. Unless the host OS is up and running, a Type 2 hypervisor cannot be launched. Subsequently, the host OS becomes one of the single points of failure for a Type 2 hypervisor. If the host OS fails, then all VMs on that host will be impacted too.

Types of virtualisation

Certain parts of x86 architecture do not lend themselves to virtualization. VMWare has innovated multiple approaches to address this problem, from modifying the guest OS kernel to translating the non-virtualizable binary code into equivalent virtualizable binary code. Let us look at them in brief:

- **Full virtualization** using binary translation refers to the technique of non-virtualizable kernel code being translated into instructions that the hypervisor can understand. Full virtualization offers the highest level of isolation and security for virtual machines. However, achieving full virtualization is challenging for hypervisors.

- **Para virtualization or OS-assisted virtualization** is a technique in which the guest OS kernel is modified to replace non-virtualizable instructions with hyper-calls that communicate directly with the hypervisor. This requires modifying the guest OS; not all OS can be run as VMs in this approach.

- **Hardware-assisted virtualization** is using a computer's hardware to support the creation of virtual machines. The host machine's CPU has additional support, like extended paging tables, which hypervisors can use to provide better virtualization than full or paravirtualization.

Virtual machine software

When choosing a hypervisor for an enterprise, it is essential to compare the benefits and disadvantages of each one. In this section, we will only look at the names of a few popular hypervisors. A vis-a-vis comparison of the hypervisors is out of scope for the CVO-003 certification. The latest open-source hypervisors are almost as feature-rich as commercial hypervisors. They struggle with the same problems that plague open-source software, that is, a lack of support. The arguments supporting both open-source and licensed hypervisors are lengthy and passionate. *Table 3.1* lists some virtualization software and the licenses under which they are offered:

Name	Creator	License
DOSBox	Peter Veenstra, Sjoerd with community	GPL
KVM, Virtual Machine Manager	Qumranet, now Red Hat	GPL version 2
VirtualBox	Oracle Corporation	GPL version 2
Hyper-V	Microsoft	Proprietary
VM Server	Oracle Corporation	Proprietary
PowerVM	IBM	Proprietary
ESX Server	VMware	Proprietary

Table 3.1: Hypervisor software and licensing

Virtualization on a host machine

So, let us understand how virtualization works. As discussed earlier, it consists of three components: the host machine, the hypervisor, and the guest machines. We already discussed the hypervisor; we will discuss the host machine in this section.

Basic Input/Output System and firmware

Basic Input/Output System (**BIOS**) is software that comes pre-installed on a chip and is provided by a desktop/laptop/server manufacturer. This software offers certain minimum facilities like interacting with keyboards, mice, hard disks, and CD drives. The capability to host VMs needs BIOS-level firmware support. So, older machines cannot support virtualization, but almost all modern computers have built-in support for virtualization. BIOS system was conceived in the olden days when machines were still 16-bit. BIOS standard is now replaced with **Unified Extensible Firmware Interface** (**UEFI**), which has better support for 32-bit and 64-bit computers. UEFI also supports the Secure Boot facility, which is needed to ensure operating system integrity and reduce the security vulnerability named **Rootkits**.

Central Processing Unit

The **Central Processing Unit** (**CPU**) is the hardware unit of a computer where the logic and mathematical processing happen. CPUs need special features to support the latest virtualization requirements. Fortunately, both major chip makers, that is, Intel and AMD, support virtualization. The most important aspects of a CPU that are relevant to virtualization are listed here:

- **Cores**: A core is simply the processing unit on a microprocessor. The number of cores is the number of processing units executed from a single physical integrated circuit. A dual-core processor has a single integrated circuit, but two different processing units can run instructions simultaneously. On a quad-core processor, four sets of instructions can run simultaneously.

- **Clock speed**: The performance of the CPU has a significant impact on the speed of the programs. Clock speed (also called clock rate or frequency) is the number of cycles the CPU operates in a second. Different CPU instructions (like addition and multiplication) consume different cycles. So, the higher the number of CPU cycles, the higher the total number of operations that can be performed in a single second. Clock speed is measured in Hz. Almost all modern processors can perform at a frequency of GHz.

- **Simultaneous multi-threading**: Multi-threading is the ability of a processor to execute multiple programming instruction sequences concurrently. While multi-threading is commonly heard in higher-level programming languages like Java, C++, and the like, the support is natively available from the processor. When discussing processor-level capability, the term simultaneous multi-threading is used. SMT offers crucial advantages to virtualization.

- **Oversubscription of CPUs**: When creating VMs, the sum of the VM's CPU capabilities does not need to be less than or equal to the host CPU capabilities. We can have the total virtual CPU capabilities exceed the host machine's capabilities; this is called over-subscribing. The oversubscription approach assumes that all VMs will not simultaneously demand the full CPU they have been assigned.

For example, if you have a host with a 2.2 GHz processor, you can run three VMs with a 1 GHz processor each. As long as any one application is idle, the total CPU usage does not breach the 2.2 GHz limit, and users will not observe any difference. However, this requires careful planning because the three applications do not simultaneously demand their share of the CPU.

If all the applications simultaneously demand their CPUs, it is called over-commitment. This results in a loss of performance for all applications.

Random Access Memory

Random Access Memory (**RAM**) is where the OS stores all information related to an application. This is a short-term memory; data is lost when the power supply is turned off. Typically, better RAM gives better performance to a machine. The same is true of virtualization as well.

Hypervisors use techniques like virtual allocation tables, nested page tables, and shadow pages to map physical memory to VMs. Some hypervisors allow for min and max memory usage limits to be defined, and the VMs are allocated higher and lower memory based on actual usage. The maximum amount of memory usable by a VM is called **burst memory**.

It is possible to oversubscribe memory. Overcommitment is a challenge here as well. When memory over-commitment happens, the host machine resorts to paging to handle it. Frequent paging leads to thrashing and will impact performance.

Multiple VMs may have the same OS or application running on them. It is prudent to recognize duplicate pages and reuse them in such a case. This technique is called transparent page sharing. The hypervisor has to take sufficient care to ensure that memory pages are duplicates and that VMs are not contaminating each other's data.

As a rule of thumb, memory can be oversubscribed at a ratio of 1.5:1 for VMs and physical machines, but this is only a guideline. IT admins should thoroughly consider the application and guest OS memory usage before deciding on VM creation policies.

Network interface card

Network interface cards (**NICs**) are how computers talk to each other. There exists a wide variety of network interfaces to address multiple communication needs. While choosing a host machine, it is crucial to consider the physical networking aspects of the host machine network. For example, it is not meaningful to configure VMs with 100 Gbps when the host machine is connected to a 10 Gbps network.

As with CPU and RAM, oversubscription is possible with NICs as well. The oversubscription ratio is significantly moderate here; a ratio of 10:1 is not a bad starting point.

Virtualization on virtual machine/guest machine

In this section, we shall consider the various aspects that need to be planned when configuring virtual machines. As mentioned earlier, creating a VM from a **template** is common. Templates enable super quick provisioning and standardize best practice implementations. Sometimes, there may be requirements to modify the template for the purposes specific to a team or an application. An IT admin needs to be familiar with the different aspects of a VM in such situations.

Virtual disks

Just as a physical computer needs storage disks to install the OS and applications and store files, a virtual machine also needs disks. Hypervisors create these disks in two different approaches. In the fixed disk or thick disk approach, the disk size of the VM is predetermined, and space is locked on the host machine for the VM's use. In the variable disk or thin disk approach, VMs are allocated small disk space initially, and the space grows as needed. Overprovisioning is not possible in the fixed disk approach.

The disk created for the VM can be configured to have the same protocols as a physical disk. Irrespective of the host machine's storage setup, the VM can be configured to have a **Small Computer System Interface (SCSI)**, **Hard Disk Drive (HDD)**, or **Solid State Drive (SSD)** device. This helps low-level applications run seamlessly on VMs. Hypervisors utilize either full or paravirtualization approaches to provide this seamless experience.

The VM's configuration, operating system, applications, and user files are all stored in a single file (extension vdi, vmdk, vhd, vhdx and the like). This file contains everything related to the VM. Even the memory contents can be stored in this file. The advantage of this approach is that the virtual storage file can be moved to a different host machine, and the hypervisor can load the VM machine as-is.

Virtual network interfaces

Planning for a virtual NIC is crucial while creating a VM. A **virtual NIC (vNIC)** is associated with a physical NIC on the host machine and allows the VM to communicate with the network. A vNIC is a software component emulating a physical NIC. A vNIC has the same properties as a physical NIC, i.e., MAC address, VLAN ID, and network connections. When VMs are installed, the host machine acts as a software router. All the VMs on a host connect to the virtual router, that is, the host machine network, and network communication happens as if all the VMs are connected via a LAN. This provides a high degree of flexibility for configuring and controlling the vNICs and for applications running on the VM. For example, the VMs can host web servers that receive traffic on different virtual ports. Alternatively, the VM could be running an internal enterprise app and is not permitted to communicate with the internet. Configuring the VM with a different number of vNICs compared to the host's NICs is possible. This is done to simulate network redundancy.

Virtual network components

Once the NIC is virtualized, it is only logical that the different components in the intranet are also virtualized. The important one among these is a switch. A virtual switch can connect multiple VMs with external networks, like a physical switch. A virtual switch supports many security policies supported by a physical switch, like network isolation and traffic shaping. However, unlike physical switches, virtual switches cannot be connected.

Virtual RAM

Compared to physical machines, VMs have greater flexibility regarding RAMs. Increasing memory for a physical machine requires switching off the device, opening it, and adding RAM modules, but VMs do not have such hassles. We can simply modify the configuration file and relaunch the virtual machine for additional memory. Also, VMs grow in their memory usage. Whenever a VM's actual memory usage is less than the maximum limit, VMs relinquish the memory and give it back to the host. The host can allocate that memory to other VMs. Consequently, oversubscription is very common in VMs. Dynamically increasing the RAM allocated to a VM is called the dynamic memory approach (intelligent name, is it not), and allocating a fixed memory limit is called the static memory approach.

Earlier, we discussed how over-commitment results in the thrashing problem on the host machine. One way to intelligently tackle thrashing is called **memory ballooning**. In this approach, the hypervisor informs the OS about the lack of memory. VMs can choose which of their processes can relinquish memory and swap them out. This reduces overall memory needs and optimizes usage, but it requires the guest OS to receive memory free-up requests.

One thing we need to remember is that a VM cannot ask for more memory than the host machine has. If the host machine cannot allocate the memory needed by a VM, the VM will not be booted at all. This is typically not a problem with Type 1 hypervisors, but should be considered for Type 2 hypervisors.

Tools

All hypervisors provide software add-ons called **guest tools**, which are useful software components installed on guest OS, that is, on the VM. These tools provide significantly high flexibility in working with and managing VMs. From handy tricks like maintaining a shared clipboard between the host and the guest OS to sharing each other's file systems and accessing networks, guest tools considerably ease the job of maintaining the VMs. It should be noted, however, that the tools provided by hypervisors are not standardized across companies. Each hypervisor provides its own set of tools along with benefits and drawbacks specific to it.

Virtual storage

Note that virtual storage is different from virtual disks. Virtual disks are disks attached to a VM, as explained earlier. On the other hand, virtual storage refers to the physical location where these virtual disks are stored and how they are made accessible to VMs. Storage approaches in modern computing are myriad and complex. As with everything, this complexity results from the application and user requirements. We shall deal with this in detail in the next chapter. No matter the storage architecture, virtual storage presents the storage to VMs as locally available. The physical disk storing data need not be attached to the host machine, and it need not be in the same data centre as the host machine. Virtual storage abstracts all that complexity and makes the VM believe that the storage is available locally.

Virtualization as the building block of cloud computing

So far, we have discussed approaches for creating virtual resources used in virtual machines. So, *why is this relevant for cloud computing?* Simply put, virtualization is one of the fundamental building blocks of cloud computing. If the concept of virtualization is eliminated, cloud computing would not be half as viable as it currently is. Let us look at a few examples. The currency used in these examples is **Indian Rupees** (**INR**).

Scenario 1: Consider a high-performance computer that costs ₹10,00,000. A startup needs this machine to run its software on Windows Server 2022 OS every Sunday. For one day of the week, the device is used 90%, and on the other days, its usage shall be ~1%. The same startup needs to run another software every alternate working day on a Redhat server, costing another ₹500,000. The startup has to spend ₹15,00,000 for its primary operations, but never utilizes 100% of its investment. This is a lot of capital locked up for a startup.

How can virtualization help here? The answer is evident if you have understood the theory discussed so far. The startup can purchase a single computer costing 10,00,000 and virtualize it. One VM will run a Windows server, and the other VM will run a Redhat server. The oversubscription approach is employed, and it is not a problem due to their workload schedules. The startup easily saved ₹500,000. This is the benefit of virtualization in a private cloud.

Scenario 2: If we analyze the preceding scenario, there is still some idle time for the computer. Assuming VM containing RHEL runs every Monday, Wednesday, and Friday, the system has idle time every Tuesday, Thursday, and Saturday. If the startup cannot find an application that runs only on these days, there are no further gains from private computing.

However, consider this: A third-party cloud service provider procures the machine and rents it out to customers for creating VMs. With a projected shelf life of 5 years for the hardware, the CSP charges ₹600/day for running VMs.

The startup subscribes to this cloud and configures the VMs to run on Sunday, Monday, Wednesday, and Friday. This easily saves the entire ₹15,00,000 investment for the startup. During the lifetime of the hardware, the startup pays only for the days it uses the VMs, which is roughly 1040 days and translates to ₹6,24,000. This is a considerable amount of savings for the startup. The cloud service provider can allow different organizations to run their VMs on idle days. This gives significant cost savings to the startup and profit for the CSPs, and it decreases the wastage of resources for everyone, a win-win situation. *Figure 3.2* shows these cost benefits as a graph.

Truth be told, the mentioned scenario is greatly simplified. Organizations must worry about scenarios like business continuity, disaster recovery, and fail-safe, and have multiple hardware installations to address them. This results in a multi-fold increase in costs. Cloud helps organizations manage these situations without having to empty their coffers.

Therefore, cloud computing has become a mainstay (if not a go-to approach) of enterprise application development. Without virtualization, capabilities like fault tolerance and disaster recovery would have been the hallmark of only organizations with deep pockets. Virtualization and the cloud have democratized this and made enterprise-grade application development accessible to any developer building the next great internet revolution in their garage. Refer to the following figure:

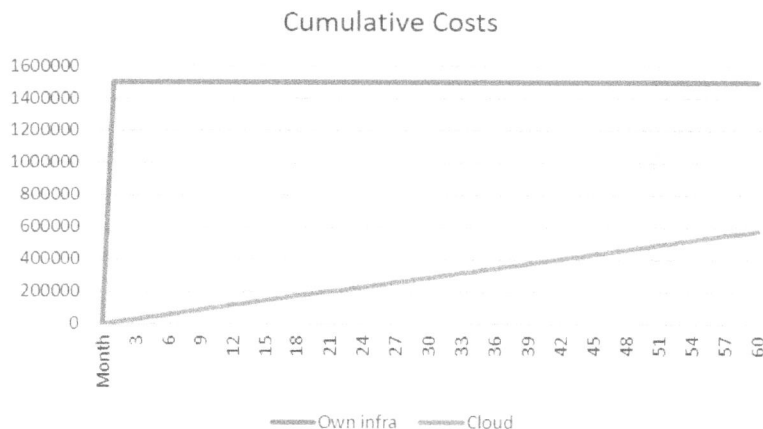

Figure 3.2: Organizations benefiting from cloud

Conclusion

In this chapter, we learned about VMs, the difference between host and guest machines, various hardware and software approaches to virtualization, the complexities of such approaches, when virtualization is/is not helpful, and how virtualization has come to be the mainstay of modern computer architecture. The next chapter will get into the details of how persistent storage is managed in virtual environments.

Glossary

- **BIOS:** The first program used by a computer's microprocessor after power is turned on.

- **Clock speed:** A measure of the number of CPU cycles for each second; it is measured in Giga Hertz.

- **CPU Core**: A small CPU built into a larger CPU device; each core can execute instructions independently.

- **Emulator:** A hardware or software unit that allows one computer system to imitate the functions of another.

- **Firmware:** Software instructions offering low-level control of the device's hardware; firmware is generally built into and shipped along with the device hardware.

- **Full Virtualization:** A virtualization technique in which non-virtualizable kernel code is entirely translated into instructions understandable by the hypervisor.

- **Guest Machine:** The virtual computers created on a host machine.

- **Hardware-assisted virtualization:** A virtualization technique in which the host machine hardware has additional functionalities targeted to support virtualization.

- **Host Machine:** The physical machine that executes the virtual machine software.

- **Hypervisor:** A software or hardware that creates and runs virtual machines.

- **Mainframe:** A large and powerful computer with high levels of reliability, availability, and serviceability capable of performing mission critical applications needing heavy computing resources; it is less powerful than a supercomputer.

- **NIC:** A hardware component used by computers to communicate with other computers over a network.

- **Oversubscription:** A technique in which the sum of resources requested by guest virtual machines exceeds the resources physically available with the host machine

- **Para virtualization:** A virtualization technique in which non-virtualizable kernel code is modified to suit the needs of the hypervisor.

- **Static and dynamic memory allocation:** Techniques of allocating RAM to virtual machines.

- **Virtual machine:** An instance of computer created using virtualization technique.

- **Virtualization**: A software or hardware technique for creating virtual computers with hardware or software configurations different from that of the machine on which they are running.

Practice questions

S. No	Question	Correct Answer
1	**Which of the following is virtualization software?**	D
	A) Wine	B) Cygwin	
	C) Crossover Linux	D) Virtual Box	
2	**A system administrator is choosing a hypervisor. Their virtual machines run enterprise software and require the highest possible security and efficiency. What type of hypervisor should they choose?**	A
	A) Type I	B) Type II	
	C) Hardware-assisted virtualization	D) Para virtualization	
3	**Which of the following is not an advantage of Type II hypervisor**	D
	A) Simplified management	B) Suitability of personal/small deployments	
	C) Convenience	D) Security	
4	**Which of the following types of virtualizations requires modification to guest OS code?**	B
	A) Full virtualization	B) Para virtualization	
	C) Hardware-assisted virtualization	D) Type II	
5	**Which of the following types of virtualization isolates guest OS from hardware and virtualization layers?**	A
	A) Full virtualization	B) Para virtualization	
	C) Hardware-assisted virtualization	D) Type II	
6	**How many instruction sets can be run simultaneously on an octa-core processor?**	D
	A) 2	B) 4	
	C) 6	D) 8	

S. No	Question		Correct Answer
7	_____ multithreading refers to multithreading support provided by hardware.		C
	A) Full	B) Hardware-assisted	
	C) Simultaneous	D) Both A and B	
8	What is the unit for measuring a CPU's clock speed?		A
	A) Hz	B) Seconds	
	C) A dimensionless number	D) None of the above	
9	A systems administrator has created three virtual machines of 6 GB RAM each on a machine with 8 GB RAM. What approach have they used?		A
	A) Over-subscription	B) Over-committing	
	C) Over-allocation	D) Overuse	
10	All the virtual machines are demanding the full extent of memory allocated to them. This situation is called _____.		B
	A) Over-subscription	B) Over-committing	
	C) Over-allocation	D) Overuse	
11	What does it mean to configure burst memory?		A
	A) Specifying the maximum amount of memory that a VM can use	B) Reserving memory on the host machine, which can be consumed when VMs are over-committed and thrashing	
	C) Both A and B	D) None of the above	
12	A host machine has 12 GB RAM. Which of the following can be considered a reasonable oversubscription of RAM?		C
	A) 12 GB	B) 6 GB	
	C) 18 GB	D) 48 GB	
13	What should be the care taken when configuring VMs on a host machine with 10 Gbps NIC?		A
	A) Oversubscription should be around 100 Gbps	B) Guest machines should not exceed 10 Gbps NICs	
	C) Guest machines should not exceed 100 Gbps NICs	D) Oversubscription should not exceed 1 Gbps	
14	Which of the following is not supported by virtual switches compared to physical switches?		C
	A) Network isolation	B) Traffic shaping	
	C) Connecting to other switches	D) All the above	

S. No	Question		Correct Answer
15	**What information belonging to a Guest OS can be stored in the virtual disk file:** i. Application Software and Data ii. Network information like AP address and so on iii. Information in VM's RAM iv. Host machine information		C
	A) i only	B) i and ii only	
	C) i, ii and iii only	D) i, ii, iii and iv	
16	**Which of the following features is a building block of cloud computing?**		A
	A) Virtualization	B) Internetworking	
	C) Software licensing	D) Security	
17	**Which of the following is not a benefit of virtualization?**		C
	A) Reduced Capex and Opex costs	B) Improved availability	
	C) Improved vendor complexity in the supply chain	D) Improved agility	
18	**Hypervisor is responsible for which of the following items:** i. Simulating CPU configurations needed for guest machines ii. Managing RAM needed for guest machines iii. Maintaining the hardware on host machines iv. Maintaining the software on host machines		A
	A) i and ii only	B) iii and iv only	
	C) i and iii only	D) i, ii and iv	
19	**BIOS standard is replaced with _____ on 32-bit and 64-bit computers.**		C
	A) SCSI	B) UNC	
	C) UEFI	D) Secure Boot	
20	**Which of the following is not a technique used by Hypervisors for mapping physical memory to VMs?**		B
	A) Virtual Allocation Table	B) Transparent page sharing	
	C) Nested page tables	D) Shadow pages	
21	**Which of the following techniques is used by hypervisors to reuse shared memory across VMs?**		B
	A) Virtual Allocation Table	B) Transparent Page Sharing	
	C) Nested Page Tables	D) Shadow Pages	

S. No	Question		Correct Answer
22	**Which disk allocation approach allows for over-provisioning of disk space?**		C
	A) Thick disk	B) Fixed disk	
	C) Thin disk	D) All of the above	
23	**What is memory ballooning?**		A
	A) It is a technique by which hypervisors request VMs to relinquish unused memory back to the host machine.	B) It is a problem caused by improper configuration of VMs	
	C) It is a problem that occurs when VMs run applications with memory leakage issues.	D) All of the above	
24	**Which of the following is a facility provided by guest tools on a VM?**		D
	A) Clipboard sharing	B) Accessing each other's filesystems	
	C) Sharing resources	D) All of the above	
25	**What is cloud sprawl?**		B
	A) It is a situation where the physical machines hosting the VMs are spread across a large area.	B) It is a situation where the number of VMs in an organization grows in an uncontrolled manner.	
	C) It is a situation where the VMs of an organization overlap private and third-party machines.	D) None of the above	
26	**What are the general causes of cloud sprawl?**		D
	A) Bugs in hypervisor	B) Improper configuration of VMs	
	C) Malicious virus attack	D) Improper control over the virtual machine creation process	

Join our Discord space

Join our Discord workspace for latest updates, offers, tech happenings around the world, new releases, and sessions with the authors:

https://discord.bpbonline.com

CHAPTER 4
Managing Storage

Introduction

This chapter deals with the traditional way of storage for applications and how it is implemented in the cloud. We will deal with the standard and popular technologies available for storage. All the different technologies will be discussed and explained, from tapes and cassettes to the latest Solid State Drives and flash drives. The common challenges in the storage domain will be discussed, and industry-standard solutions will be explored.

The second half of the chapter will discuss how the same challenges are present in cloud computing and how they have been addressed in the cloud computing world. The incremental and game-changing innovations in the cloud storage domain shall be explained here.

Structure

We will cover the following topics in this chapter:

- History of computer storage
- Traditional storage technologies
- Networked storage

Objectives

This chapter aims to discuss the evolution of storage and the relevance of the latest technologies from a cloud computing perspective. CVO-003 focuses on how storage is provisioned in the cloud and how cloud administrators and developers can maximize its value and use it for their needs.

History of computer storage

It is common for modern computers to have storage in the range of Terabytes. Data storage techniques deal with storing digital data in a physical medium so that it can be retrieved later. Data stored in RAM is lost the moment the power supply is off, but data in storage stays there even after the power supply is cut off. The terminology we presently use points to the long and thrilling inventions that have aided technology to mature to its current state. For example, the word **disk** is synonymous with the storage device. This is because some of the earliest storage devices were spinning disks. Once computers started learning to read and write data using punch cards, the demand for storing more data drove it through various technologies like punched tape, magnetic drum memory, magnetized hard disks, floppies, laser disks, DVDs, and the current state-of-the-art SSD storage.

All technologies up to SSD storage had moving parts and a spinning magnetic disk. SSD got rid of all moving parts, improving the stability and resistance to damage, and improving the speed of reading and writing data. For some, old habits die hard, so it is not uncommon to come across a few IT admins and users using the term **flash disk** for general humor.

In this section, we will look at the different storage systems and the specific capabilities and drawbacks of those individual systems.

Traditional storage technologies

We will now discuss computer storage as it was used in the traditional way. Computers have come a long way, from the earliest magnetic storage media like cassette tapes to the latest SSDs. We will discuss their evolution in detail here.

Direct Attached Storage

Traditionally, storage devices were always physically attached to the computer. This approach is still followed in all desktops, laptops, and mobile devices. Any extra storage like **Gdrive**, **OneDrive**, and the like are secondary and complement the primary storage. This approach of having the storage attached directly to the computer is called **Direct Attached Storage** (**DAS**). With DAS, it is not possible to connect a storage device to multiple computers, but one computer can have multiple DAS devices.

Storage medium

So, let us understand how information is stored. Unlike RAM, where information is lost upon power loss, storage mediums are designed to store data and even be carried away from power sources. We will discuss their history and details here.

Hard disks, tapes, floppies, CDs

IBM designed the first **Hard Disk Drive** (**HDD**) in 1956 with a capacity of 5 MB. The first hard drive with more than 1 GB capacity was released in 1980. It weighed 250 kg and cost nearly 1 lakh USD. Since then, hard disks have become an inalienable feature of computers. Floppies decreased in size from 8 inches to 3 ½ inches and gave way to CDs. Both hard disks and floppies have the same basic approach. Memory was stored on revolving disks, which could store digital data in magnetic format. Tape storage also stores data using a magnetic format, but does not have a rotating disk. These gradually gave way to optical storage media like CDs and DVDs.

Solid State Drive

Solid State Drive (**SSD**) is a high-performance storage device. It is a very different way of storing memory. SSDs use integrated circuits, NOR and NAND gates, to store memory electrically. They do not have any moving parts, that is, the spinning disks that are central to an HDD. This provides significant advantages to SSDs compared to HDDs. A summary of the comparison is mentioned in the following table. SSDs generally include their own processing units for storage management. This enables SSDs to support a remarkably high data transfer speed. Look at *Table 4.1* for a list of the differences between the behaviors of SSDs and HDDs:

Characteristic	SSD	HDD
Electricity usage	Lower; typically, less than ½ of HDD	High because of mechanical spinning disks
Shock resistance	Very high	Low because of moving parts; special mounting is required to absorb shocks
Mounting requirements	Direction, location, and orientation are not issues	Mounting should be done keeping in mind the spinning disk orientation
Noise generation	Practically none	Spinning noise sometimes be distractingly high
Heat generation	Very low	Special cooling is required for large disks
Data transfer speed	Consistent irrespective of the location in memory	Varies significantly due to seeking required for data stored in areas far away from the spindle head
Maintenance	Not much of a problem; fragmentation issue is eliminated	Regular defragmentation is necessary for maintaining the read/write speeds
Cost/GB	High	Low compared to SDD

Table 4.1: Differences between SSD and HDD

SSDs store data using flash memory cells. Each cell holds a certain amount of information: a single-level cell stores 1 bit, a multi-level cell stores 2 bits, a triple-level cell stores 3 bits, and a quad-level cell stores 4 bits. The number of times a cell's value can be changed before it is damaged is counted as **Program Erase** (**PE**) cycles.

Miscellaneous information regarding storage can be seen as follows:

- It is very common to use the word **USB drive** when referring to SSD storage. This is common in colloquial usage but is technically incorrect. Not everyone is aware that SSD is a storage technology and USB is a standard for connecting and communicating with a computer.

- **Write Once Read Many** (**WORM**) is another storage medium. Using this medium, data is written to the device once and is marked read-only forever. This behavior is often seen in CD-Rs and DVD-Rs. Data is stored in these devices using a process called **burning**. Once burnt, the data cannot be overwritten. In the old days, this facility was provided on floppy disks using a physical lock.

Storage interface types

HDDs are attached to the computer motherboard using a data cable. Depending on the requirement, the hard disks communicate data using various means called **interfaces**. If the computer cannot understand the interface, it cannot communicate with the HDD. Refer to the BIOS section of *Chapter 3, Managing Virtual Machines*. BIOS contains the knowledge of one or more interfaces. SSDs can plug into the motherboard without requiring a separate cable:

- **Advanced Technology Attachment** (**ATA**): An interface that connects hard drives, CD-ROM drives, and other drives to a computer. The earlier ATA interface is called **Parallel ATA** (**PATA**).

- **Integrated Drive Electronics** (**IDE**): Another interface that connects hard drives, CD-ROM drives, and other drives to a computer. The innovation in this technology is that it combines a storage controller and storage drive into a single device.

- **Serial Advanced Technology Attachment** (**Serial ATA or SATA**): The successor of PATA and offers several improvements. Most notably, it supports hot swapping, is more efficient in data transfer, has faster throughput, and has smaller cable sizes.

- **Small Computer System Interface** (**SCSI**): Standard defines commands, protocols, and electrical and logical interfaces for connecting drives to computers. SCSI is faster than SATA for data transfer and is more flexible. Multiple SCSI devices with unique IDs can connect over a bus interface.

- **Serial Attached SCSI** (**SAS**): A successor to SCSI. It is backward compatible with SATA devices.

- **Non-Volatile Memory express** (**NVMe**): A storage access and transport protocol for SSDs. NVMe delivers the highest throughput and fastest response times, and it is well-suited for enterprise workloads.

It is to be noted here that SATA3 and NVMe are considered to be superior interfaces for working with SSDs. PATA is mentioned only for historical completeness.

Data storage architectures

Now, let us discuss a few ways in which enterprises use the storage technologies that were discussed earlier. Organizations have well-defined expectations from storage technologies. These can be expressed as low latency of read/write operations, redundancy, fault tolerance, and compatibility with existing hardware. The latency of read/write operations is specific to the device used. **Input/output Operations Per Second** (**IOPS**) is the measurement for it. Compatibility is a feature that manufacturers strive for. A storage system that cannot work with existing infrastructure is a poor one to rely upon. The topics of interest for an IT admin are redundancy and fault tolerance. Here is what each one refers to:

- **Redundancy**: It refers to having multiple components performing the same functionality. By doing this, in the event of a partial failure, the system functioning shall not fail.

- **Fault tolerance**: It refers to a system design approach where a backup component will be available to prevent total loss of service in the event of a partial failure. Humans have two kidneys. Even if one fails, the other kidney can do the job. This is a perfect example of fault tolerance.

Organizations can be paranoid regarding redundancy and fault tolerance, and have good reasons to do so. Imagine a bank restricting salary withdrawals due to a crashed database. If the bank states that all information regarding deposits into your account for the previous week is lost, the damaging impact is unimaginable. We will look at a few fault tolerance and redundancy architectures in the upcoming sections. These architectures are employed with both HDDs and SSDs.

Redundant Array of Independent Disks

Despite its verbose name, the concept behind a **Redundant Array of Independent Disks** (**RAID**) is quite simple. When writing data to a disk, a RAID architecture writes it to multiple disks instead of a single disk. This leads to redundancy of data. If one disk fails, the data is available on another and can be retrieved without any loss. Redundancy is achieved by maintaining multiple disks, and fault tolerance is achieved by replicating the same data. Applications are oblivious to the number of RAID disks and other details. The RAID architecture is visible to the applications as a single storage device. RAID devices are responsible for duplicating data across disks and synchronizing the disks. This architecture has the following primary levels:

- **RAID 0**: In this approach, the data to be written is divided into several blocks, and the blocks are distributed across disks. This approach has low latency but does not offer fault tolerance or parity. If a single disk is lost, then the entire data is lost. This approach suits applications that do not contain important data and require fast read/write speeds. The technique of distributing data across disks is called **striping**.

- **RAID 1**: The data is mirrored across the disks in this approach. Loss of one disk will not result in total data loss. However, the data write speeds are lower than RAID 0 because of the additional overhead of mirroring data. This approach is suitable when applications cannot tolerate data loss but can compromise the speed of data access.

- **RAID 4**: In this level, the system stripes data across disks and maintains a dedicated parity disk. This offers a high read speed but a lower write speed than RAID 0.

- **RAID 5**: At this level, the parity information is not stored in a dedicated disk but is distributed across disks. If a single drive fails, the data is recreated using the parity block.

- **RAID 6**: Parity information is duplicated on two disks in this level. By this, loss of disk containing parity block shall not cause loss of entire data.

- RAID 2 and RAID 3 have fallen out of favor and are not used much anymore.

Nested RAID levels are combinations of the mentioned primary levels. Examples are RAID 10 (RAID 1 + RAID 0), RAID 03 (RAID 0 + RAID 3), RAID 50 (RAID5 + RAID 0). Some of the common RAID architectures are listed in *Table 4.2*:

Level	Description	Minimum number of drives	Fault tolerance
RAID 0	Block-level striping without parity or mirroring	2	None
RAID 1	Mirroring without parity or striping	2	$n - 1$ drive failures
RAID 2	Bit-level striping with Hamming code for error correction	3	One drive failure
RAID 3	Byte-level striping with dedicated parity	3	One drive failure
RAID 4	Block-level striping with dedicated parity	3	One drive failure
RAID 5	Block-level striping with distributed parity	3	One drive failure
RAID 6	Block-level striping with double distributed parity	4	Two drive failures
RAID 10	Stripes data across two RAID 1 (spans)	4	One drive for a span; maximum two drives in all spans
RAID 50	Combines block-level striping of RAID 0 with parity of RAID 5	6	One drive from each of the RAID 5 sets could fail

Table 4.2: RAID levels and behavior

Storage tiers

The storage media we discussed earlier cater to various data access, storage, and retrieval requirements. Each of them has benefits and costs associated with it. Depending on the access requirements, the storage is divided into four tiers. A description and comparison of storage tiers can be seen in *Table 4.3*:

Storage systems	Data access requirements	Example data	Cost considerations	Storage medium
Tier 1	High availability, frequent and near-instantaneous access, no scope for fault	Mission critical data in any system; sensor data in a nuclear power plant	Extremely high; RAID with parity should be considered	Flash memory
Tier 2	Application data is regularly used, but latency requirements are not as harsh as Tier 1	Sensex data, current quarter's banking transactions, emails and so on	A balance between Tier 1 and Tier 2	Less expensive flash memory
Tier 3	Data having occasional access requirements	One-year old archived emails, old family photos	Low	Hard disks can be considered
Tier 4	Data that is never or rarely used	Five-year old banking transactions are maintained only for legal/regulatory purposes	Very low	Tape drives

Table 4.3: *Storage tiers and their characteristics*

Depending on the application and data access needs, admins must provision storage in the appropriate tier.

File systems

Now that we have understood how storage works physically, let us look at the logical level of storage. If you are using a Windows machine, the disk is accessible as `C:\`. On macOS or Linux, the disk is accessible as root folder "/". It has specific implications and relevance to data storage.

No matter which application or operating system we use, the data used by the apps and users is not a single monolithic goop. Data is distributed across files and organized across directories. Storage systems do not bother with this structure. They only write and read data from sectors or flash memory cells. The file system is how the operating system and users interact with storage systems. File systems store, organize, and index the data on a storage device. They also maintain metadata and, in some cases, access to the data.

There are various types of file systems. Major PC manufacturers like **Microsoft** and **Apple** have built their flavors of file systems. Open-source community contributions have also enriched this area considerably. A list of popular file systems is provided as follows. **File Allocation Table (FAT)** is a format introduced by Microsoft for its MS-DOS systems. It is a simple and reliable file system with capabilities aimed at personal computers. With Microsoft releasing further versions like Windows 95, XP, 7, and the latest Windows 11, FAT has also changed. It evolved from FAT16 to FAT32. *Figure 4.1* provides a comparison of the properties of file systems. It is simple and efficient, but does not have the performance of more robust file systems:

- **New Technology File System (NTFS)**: It is another File System introduced by **Microsoft** for their NT operating system. It provided improved file system security and journaling support. MS has added file-level encryption to NTFS in Windows 2000 and sometimes refers to it as **Encrypting File System (EFS)**.

- **Resilient File Systems (ReFS)**: They are another type. In Windows Server 2012, MS upgraded NTFS to add facilities to preserve data and proactively correct corrupted data.

- **Unix File System (UFS)**: It is used in Unix, Linux, and many other variants of Unix. This file system considers all physical drives as a single logical drive and organizes all the data as a tree structure.

Figure 4.1 provides a tabular listing of some popular file systems and their characteristics. There are several other filesystems used in the industry:

File system	Creator	Operating system	Max path length	Max file size	Max volume	Hard links	Symbolic links	Block journaling	Case-sensitive	File Change Log	Stores file owner	Access control lists	Extended attributes
APFS	Apple	macOS	Unlimited	8 EB									
Btrfs	Oracle	Linux	Unlimited	16 EB	16 EB	Yes	Yes	Yes	Yes		Yes	Yes	Yes
exFAT	Microsoft	Windows CE	32760	16 EB	64 ZB	No	No	No	No	No	No	No	No
F2FS	Samsung	Linux	Unlimited	3.94 TB	16 TB	Yes	Yes	Yes	Yes	No	Yes	Yes	Yes
FAT32, FAT32X	Microsoft	Windows 95	Unlimited	4 GB	16 TB	No	No	No	No	No	No	No	No
NTFS	Microsoft	Windows NT 3.1	Unlimited	16TB	16TB	Yes	Yes	No	Yes	Yes	Yes	Yes	Yes
ReiserFS	Namesys	Linux	Unlimited	8 TB	16 TB	Yes	Yes	Yes	Yes	No	Yes	Yes	Yes
ZFS	Sun	Solaris	Unlimited	16 EB	256 ZB	Yes	Yes	Yes	Yes	No	Yes	Yes	Yes

Figure 4.1: *Comparison of file systems*

Data security

Encryption is the technique of modifying the data with a secret passphrase called **key**. The key is required for the data to be modified from its original form. It is impractical to recover the original data without the key. All modern OS and disks provide native encryption for storage. The disk-level encryption is called **Full Disk Encryption (FDE)**.

Backups refer to making a copy of the data in the primary storage into another secondary storage device. Taking data backups at regular intervals is generally a data best practice. Assume that you take backups of data every Friday. If the primary storage fails on Monday, the only data lost is from the previous Friday till date; older data will still be intact. Multiple strategies are in vogue for data backups, and the important ones among them are full backup, mirror backup, differential backup, incremental backup, 3-2-1 backup, and **grandfather-father-son** (**GFS**) backup. Automation of backup strategy is important for effectiveness.

Performance measurement

We have been referring to admins having to understand the application's performance requirements to provide optimum storage devices and tiers. These tools should be measured for their performance. The expectations and requirements from storage are different for enterprises as compared to home users.

Five key factors are commonly considered for the performance measurement of storage devices. They are discussed further.

Storage capacity metrics

Capacity is measured in terms of the number of bytes of information that can be stored. The higher the storage capacity of a single device, the more information it can store. Storage capacity is expressed as the number of bytes. Standard measurements are Terabytes, Petabytes, and Exabytes. For consumer devices, Gigabytes might suffice.

Byte vs. Bibyte

A byte is different from a bibyte, which stands for a big byte. It is important to know the difference between the two. According to the SI system, Kilo, Mega, Giga, and so on are powers of 10; 1 KG is 1000 grams, and 1 mega gram is 1000 Kg. This is a base-10 system. In contrast, computers use a binary or base-2 system. So, in a binary system, Kilo is 2 raised to the power of 10, that is, $2^{10} = 1024$, which is different from 1000. So, a binary Kilo is denoted using **Kibibyte** (**KiB**). Note the subtle change in the spelling.

So, let us understand the actual difference in terms of storage. Different measurements are used based on the purpose, and administrators and engineers need to be aware of the differences between them and the notations for these. *Table 4.4* provides this information:

Binary system			Decimal system		
Kibibyte	KiB	$2^{10}=1024$	Kilobyte	KB	$10^3=1000$
Mebibyte	MiB	$2^{20}=1048576$	Megabyte	MB	$10^6=1000000$
Gibibyte	GiB	2^{30}	Gigabyte	GB	10^9

Table 4.4: Binary and decimal storage notations and values

When referring to raw storage capacity, it is common for manufacturers to use the decimal system. RAM and OS manufacturers generally use the binary system. This is why the number we see on a hard disk's advertising is different from what is reported by the operating system. It is essential to pay attention to the presence/absence of "i" between the M and B.

Throughput and read/write storage metrics

Throughput is the number of bits read or written per second. The read throughput value does not need to be the same as the write throughput value. For example, it takes significantly longer for SSDs to write than it takes for them to read. There can also be differences in throughput when reading/writing sequential data instead of random data. It is essential to understand which metrics are being reported by manufacturers to ensure real-world operations perform as per expectations.

IOPS and latency

IOPS is a metric for measuring performance, and the higher it is, the better. It is a measure of the number of read/write operations in non-contiguous locations performed in a second. IOPS measurements depend on the amount of data being read/written.

Latency is a measure of the time taken by the device to start data transfer after receiving the instructions to do so. It is sometimes considered to be the most critical metric for storage systems. Using a single measurement for calculating latency is misleading in the case of HDDs. This is because the retrieval speed also depends on the distance the magnetic head travels to start reading/writing data. So, it is more accurate to take a sample of measurements and calculate the average.

Reliability metrics

Every device will inevitably fail at some point. A storage device's failure during times of critical need can be catastrophic. Measuring the reliability of storage devices is necessary when working on enterprise applications. Let us look at a few metrics for measuring the reliability of devices:

- **Longevity** is the number of days/years a device can be expected to operate before total failure.

- **Mean Time Between Failures** (**MTBF**) is a commonly used metric to determine the reliability of storage devices. It refers to the average number of hours a device can be used before failure. Note that it is subtly different from longevity. Imagine the refrigerator in your home. It may come with a lifespan of 25 years. However, as the machine ages, it should be repaired every few months. Clearly, this is an annoyance. Users might prefer a refrigerator that works for only 15 years but never fails. MTBF is days in the former case and 15 years in the latter case. A more detailed discussion of the mathematical differences between MTBF and lifespan is out of the scope of this book.

- **Drive Writes Per Day** (**DWPD**) is a metric used for the reliability of SSDs. It is the number of times the entire drive can be rewritten over its lifetime.

- **Tera Bytes Written** (**TBW**) is another metric used for measuring the reliability of SSDs. It indicates the total amount of data that can be written into the SSD over its lifetime.

The metrics of DWPD and TBW are relevant to SSDs because of the nature of their flash memory. Generally, SLC SSDs were more reliable than MLCs, TLCs, and QLCs. Recent advances have improved the reliability of MLC, TLC, and QLC SSDs to a considerable extent. Manufacturers provide these metrics in their hardware warranties.

Networked storage

So far, we have discussed storage devices that are physically attached to a computer, but complexities in business requirements have necessitated a complex data center. The most critical improvement to address the complexities is storage networking. In simple terms, this is all about breaking the requirement of physically connecting storage devices to computers without compromising on functionalities and requirements.

The defining characteristic of DAS is that it can only be connected to one computer at a time. Networked storage differs in this aspect. Networked storage devices can connect to multiple devices simultaneously.

Storage types

As the name implies, networked storage devices connect to computers over a network. The choice of a network depends on the functionality, speed, and cost of building it. Let us discuss the various types of networked storage devices and their advantages and disadvantages in the upcoming sections.

Storage Area Networking

A **Storage Area Network** (**SAN**) is high-speed connectivity over a network dedicated to storage devices. A SANs is typically made up of computer hosts, network switches, and storage devices interconnected using various technology protocols in multiple topologies. The advantage of SAN is that a storage device and a computer connecting to it need not be in the same physical location. The SAN network shall present the same interface to the computer as the storage device. As a result, the computer will **feel** that the device is locally connected. The disks in a SAN can be subdivided, and a unique **Logical Unit Number** (**LUN**) can be assigned to them. These LUNs appear to the computer as disk drives. If you are using a Windows machine, it might appear to you as C:\ in Windows explorer. SANs offer high-performance and can be built in complex configurations to suit application requirements.

Computers needing access to SAN should be equipped with a special SAN adapter card. A SAN network is called **fabric** and comprises ethernet, fiber optic, and special-purpose

SCSI cables. Communication protocols like Fiber Channel Protocol, Fiber Channel over Ethernet, and iSCSI are used for transmitting data. See *Figure 4.2* for a typical SAN layout.

On the flip side, SANs are very expensive. Also, SAN solutions are vendor-specific. This makes their administration a very niche skill and traps organizations into a **vendor lock-in**.

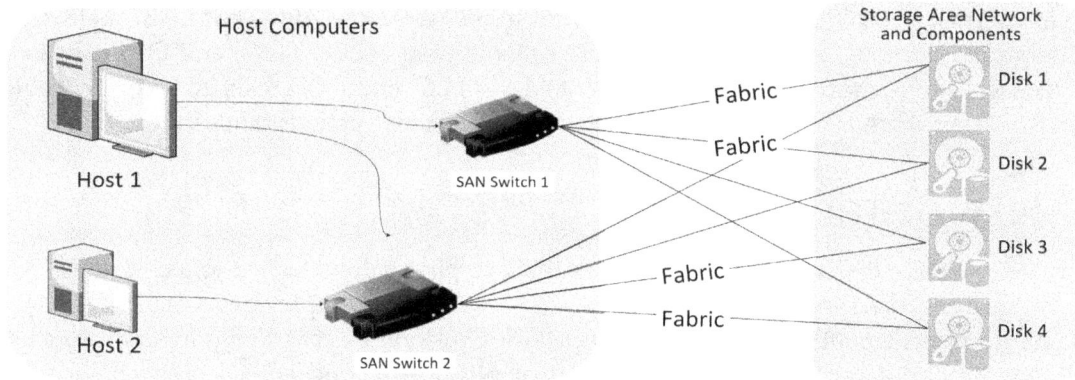

Figure 4.2: SAN

Network Attached Storage

Network Attached Storage (**NAS**) is an alternative to SAN and offers connectivity over TCP/IP traffic. It eliminates the need to build an expensive SAN network and compromises certain facilities. For example, unlike SAN, computers do not "feel" that NAS disks are physically connected. Computers see the storage as a file system on a separate computer. A good example is SMB servers. Computers do not access server "C:\xxx". We must use the UNC or IP path, for example, "\\192.168.1.100\Xxx" or smb:\\192.168.1.100\Xxx. If the BIOS has IP communication capability, NAS storage devices can be used even for booting up the operating system. This is called **Netboot** or **boot from LAN**.

By sharing the networking infrastructure, a NAS significantly reduces cost compared to a SAN. Networking skills are more common than SAN. So, administrators need not worry about a learning curve when working with NAS. Data transfer speeds of NAS are less than those of SAN. The latest advances in fiber optics are making NAS a serious alternative to SAN.

From a user perspective, NAS integrates very well with cloud storage and can provide great flexibility to users.

Object storage

SAN and NAS are great options for storing transactional data. However, often, organizations find that transactional data is only a small fraction of their overall data. Most of the data is unstructured, and once written, it is rarely modified. As an example, compare the storage requirements for software code versus customer invoices. Software code files are modified simultaneously by multiple users. In contrast, numerous users might read customer invoices, but they will rarely (if ever) be overwritten by anyone. Maintaining a SAN or NAS for this data might be overkill. In such cases, it is more convenient to use object storage.

Object storage manages data as objects. Every object contains the data to be stored, its metadata, and a unique identifier. Metadata can be application-specific or user-specific. There will not be a directory hierarchy that is common to file systems. Object storage offers several advantages compared to other types of storage. Lacking a folder hierarchy, the amount of data that can be stored is, theoretically, unlimited. All that is needed is to add more storage devices in scale-out mode, and storage capacity is increased. This allows for greater economies of scale and significantly reduces costs. Metadata does not have many restrictions and, consequently, provides significant flexibility in access and retrieval. Almost all cloud storage providers provide object storage for enterprise usage.

Some cloud providers provide a phantom folder structure. This is not a true folder hierarchy. It is provided purely at a metadata level without losing the familiar feel of the folder hierarchy. **Google Drive**, **Microsoft's OneDrive**, and **Dropbox** are all examples of this approach.

Access protocols

Now, let us try to understand the different protocols available for data transfer. The data in storage must travel across a medium to reach the computer. The earliest such medium was copper wire. The latest is fiber optic cables.

Understanding the difference between the communication medium and the communication protocol is essential. The communication medium is the material used to carry data from one point to another. A copper wire carries electricity; This electric signal should carry the binary 1s and 0s. Some convention is required for this. Both the sender and the receiver should agree and abide by the conventions. Such rules are called **protocols**. It is the descriptions of digital message formats and practices to interpret them. We shall delve into further detail regarding protocols and communication channels in *Chapter 5, Networking Fundamentals*.

Fiber Channel Protocol

Fiber Channel Protocol (**FCP**) is the transmission medium used by enterprises for communicating data at very high speeds, up to 128 Gbps. FCP is the set of rules for carrying SCSI commands on top of fiber channels.

FCP is typically used in SANs. As mentioned earlier, SAN devices and computers connect chiefly in one of three topologies. The topologies are called **point-to-point**, **switched fabric topology**, and **arbitrary loop topology**.

As explained earlier, SAN can be used to connect remote disks to a computer. This means transmitting DAS commands, that is, SCSI commands. FCP transmits SCSI commands and data over fiber. Instead of using a CPU to interpret the messages, FCP devices come with dedicated hardware to interpret FCP. This saves CPU cycles and allows for high-speed data transfer.

Ethernet

Ethernet is the most common technology for connecting devices in a network. It enables devices to communicate with each other via Ethernet protocols. Ethernet is slower than the fiber channel, and the current higher limit is 10 Gbps. However, it is significantly cheaper. The same network can be used for data communication between two computers. As a result, Ethernet has become the go-to approach for communications in enterprises. We shall extensively discuss Ethernet in *Chapter 5, Networking Fundamentals*.

Tunnelling approaches

As described earlier, NAS is cheaper than SAN and does not offer certain benefits. This does not mean we have to compromise when using NAS. The best of both would mean SAN speed and functionality at the cost of NAS. If we are willing to compromise on speed, we can get SAN functionality on NAS, that is, transmitting SCSI commands, the appearance of DAS disks, and so on. This is possible by encapsulating FCP packets in internet protocol packets. This approach is called **tunnelling**.

- Fiber channel over the internet is a tunnelling protocol that connects **fiber channel (FC)** switches over an IP network. This allows remote locations to be connected over an affordable infrastructure.

- iSCSI stands for Internet SCSI. It works on top of TCP, which, in turn, works on top of IP. It is important to remember that iSCSI data is not tunnelled over by TCP. TCP only carries SCSI commands or data in TCP packets.

- **NVMe over Fabric (NVMe-oF)** is an extension of the NVMe network protocol to communicate over ethernet and fiber channels. It is extremely fast and can be compared to DAS SSD latency.

Network storage security

Security threats need not only be from hackers; inadvertent, non-malicious security incidents can and do occur. An unusual concentration of disk access demands to a single disk can negatively impact latency and performance. There are multiple approaches sys admins can take to address these scenarios:

- Zoning is for controlling access to other network devices for every single device. A straightforward example is limiting fiber channel usage for communication between computers and storage devices. Communication between computers can be done via less-expensive means like ethernet. Zoning is configured on network switches.

- LUN masking ensures that only authorized servers communicate with a given storage device. LUN masking is done on storage devices. Each LUN is assigned a set of hosts authorized to access it. The storage device does not respond to requests from any other host.

High availability

After investing so much in SANs, it is natural to expect the storage devices to always be available. However, unforeseen situations might result in loss of access to storage devices. Special planning is needed to handle these situations. An easily understandable example is the data center's loss of electricity. Administrators install an uninterrupted power supply system to handle power outages. Such approaches help the data center run almost without lapse. Uptime is measured as % of time available per year. A data center with an uptime of 99% will not be available for a maximum of 3.6525 days in a year. Depending on the business criticality, this could have disastrous business consequences. A data center with an uptime of 99.999% will be unavailable for a maximum of 5.25 minutes a year. Achieving such high availability is a challenge to any IT team. Various techniques are applied to data centers to achieve such high availability. We will discuss disaster recovery and high availability in detail in *Chapter 12, Disaster Recovery and High Availability Systems*.

Fault tolerance

Redundancy is one way of achieving fault tolerance. Multiple connectivity routes are maintained between storage disks and servers so that even if a single route becomes unavailable, another route shall be available to pick up the responsibility. Redundancy is created at multiple levels. The redundancy of storage transmission medium between various devices within the data center is called **multi-pathing**. A Failover zone is the redundancy of the entire data center by maintaining a mirror image in a different geographical area.

Replication

When maintaining redundant data storage, an often-encountered question is how to ensure that the secondary device is a mirror image of the primary. There are two approaches to doing this. In the synchronous replication approach, data write commands from the application are immediately implemented on all the storage devices. The application is kept waiting until the replication is complete. Data is written to the primary storage in asynchronous replication, and the application continues with further commands. Replication on secondary storage is a continuous **catch-up** process. Applications must make the trade-off between cost and accuracy while deciding on the appropriate replication approach. Conceptually, replication in the cloud is similar to RAIDs in DAS. The difference is the scale and complexity of the data.

In a private cloud, it is the IT team's job to build and maintain the backup, fault tolerance, replication, and recovery approaches. In a public cloud, CSPs take up this burden.

Conclusion

In this chapter, we saw how storage has evolved from punch cards and tape cassettes to flash disks. The access mechanisms originated as direct access devices and evolved into SAN and NAS. We also discussed functionalities expected from a reliable data center and how they are implemented. In the next chapter, we shall start with the basics of networking and cover the topics fundamental to it.

Glossary

- **ATA, PATA, SATA:** Advanced Technology Attachment, Parallel Advanced Technology Attachment, Serial Advanced Technology Attachment are interface standards to connect storage medium to a computer in DAS

- **Bits and Bytes:** Lowest levels of data storage; a bit can store a 1 or 0, and a byte is 8 bits

- **Byte and Bibyte:** Different measures of storage; byte uses a base-10 system, and Bibyte uses a base-2 system

- **CD:** Compact Disk

- **DAS:** Direct Attached Storage

- **DVD:** Digital Versatile Disk

- **Fabric:** A network of SAN devices comprising ethernet, SCSI cables, and fiber optics

- **Fault tolerance:** A storage architecture in which every component has a backup; the backup component performs the jobs in case of the primary component's failure; this allows for unhampered operations in case of partial system failure

- **File systems:** A logical representation of storage, accessing, and indexing data on a storage medium

- **Full Disk Encryption:** A data encryption technique enforced at the storage device level

- **Gate:** An electronic device implemented using transistors or diodes; it takes one or more inputs, implement a mathematical function on them, and produce a single output

- **HDD:** Hard Disk Drive

- **IDE, SCSI:** Integrated Drive Electronics, Small Computer System Interface are interface standards to connect storage medium to a computer in DAS, and are an improvement over ATA, PATA, and SATA

- **Latency:** The most critical metric for measuring a storage device's performance

- **Longevity:** A metric for measuring the reliability of a storage device that measures how long a storage device can operate before total failure

- **LUN Masking:** An approach used by system administrators on storage devices to control access to storage devices

- **MTBF:** Mean Time Between Failures is a reliability metric for storage devices and indicates the average number of hours before the next failure

- **NAS:** Network Attached Storage

- **NVMe: Non-Volatile Memory express (NVMe)** is an interface standard to connect SSDs to a computer in DAS and is capable of very high-speed data transfers

- **Parity:** A technique to determine whether the data is lost during the process; generally used when data moves between storage locations or is transmitted over network

- **RAID:** Redundant Array of Inexpensive Disks is a data storage architecture that has built-in redundancy

- **Redundancy:** A storage architecture in which multiple components perform the same functionality, which allows unhampered access to data in case of partial system failure

- **SAN:** Storage Area Networking

- **SSD:** Solid State Drive

- **Storage tier:** A categorization of storage devices; categorization is done based on data access requirements and cost considerations

- **Throughput:** A metric of storage device performance that measures the number of bits read or written per second

- **Tunnelling:** The technique of encapsulating data of one protocol within another

- **USB:** Universal Serial Bus; an industry-standard protocol for cables and connectors to interface between computers and devices

- **Write Once Read Many (WORM) Storage:** A family of storage devices; data is written to this medium exactly once using a process called burning and can be read multiple times

- **Zoning:** An approach used by system administrators on network switches to control access to storage devices

Practice questions

S. No	Question		Correct Answer
1	**Which of the following is not a storage device?**		B
	A) Floppy	B) USB	
	C) Magnetic Tape	D) SSD	
2	**Which storage technology does not involve moving parts?**		D
	A) Floppy	B) Optical drives	
	C) Magnetic tape	D) SSD	
3	**What is meant by burning a CD or DVD?**		A
	A) It is the activity of writing information to the disk	B) It is the activity of engraving copyright information on the disk	
	C) It is the activity of destroying the disk	D) None of the above	
4	**Which interface supports hot swapping of storage devices?**		B
	A) ATA	B) SATA	
	C) PATA	D) IDE	
5	**Which RAID level does not support fault tolerance?**		A
	A) RAID 0	B) RAID 2	
	C) RAID 10	D) RAID 5	
6	**A storage administrator needs to archive transaction logs older than 6 months. They will be retrieved only if any legal complications arise. Which data storage tier would be ideal for them?**		D
	A) Tier 1	B) Tier 2	
	C) Tier 3	D) Tier 4	
7	**A storage administrator needs to choose a storage tier for their organization. The data is mission critical and has heavy usage. Which architecture will you suggest for them?**		D
	A) Tier 2	B) Tier 3	
	C) Tier 1 with IDE drives	D) Tier 1 with SSD storage	
8	**Which of the following filesystems was designed for personal computers?**		C
	A) NTFS	B) ReFS	
	C) FAT	D) ZFS	
9	**A hard disk manufacturer claims their storage is 1 GiB. What will its capacity be in GB?**		B
	A) 1 GB	B) 1.0734 GB	
	C) 1024 GB	D) 1000 GB	

S. No	Question		Correct Answer
10	**A hard disk manufacturer claims their storage is 1 GB. What will its capacity be in GiB?**		B
	A) 1 GiB	B) 0.931 GiB	
	C) 1024 GiB	D) 1000 GiB	
11	**1 GB = ___ MB**		A
	A) 1000	B) 931	
	C) 1024	D) None of the above	
12	**1 GiB = ___ MiB**		C
	A) 1000	B) 931	
	C) 1024	D) None of the above	
13	**GB stands for**		A
	A) Giga Bytes	B) Giga bits	
	C) Giga Bibytes	D) Giga Bibits	
14	**Gb stands for**		B
	A) Giga Bytes	B) Giga bits	
	C) Giga Bibytes	D) Giga Bibits	
15	**Gib stands for**		D
	A) Giga Bytes	B) Giga bits	
	C) Giga Bibytes	D) Giga Bibits	
16	**A storage administrator configured archival strategy as follows:** 1) **Data is backed up daily** 2) **All data is backed up every 1st** 3) **Only the data modified during previous day is backed up on remaining days** **What strategy are they using?**		B
	A) Full backup	B) Incremental backup	
	C) Differential backup	D) Mirror backup	
17	**A storage administrator configured archival strategy as follows:** 1) **Data is backed up daily** 2) **All data is backed up every 1st** 3) **Only the data modified from the 1st of the previous month till date is backed up on remaining days** **What strategy are they using?**		C
	A) Full backup	B) Incremental backup	
	C) Differential backup	D) Mirror backup	

S. No	Question		Correct Answer
18	An organisation decided to use the following strategy for their data security 3: Create one primary backup and two copies of your data. 2: Save your backups to two different types of media. 1: Keep at least one backup file offsite. What strategy is this?		D
	A) Full backup	B) Mirror backup	
	C) Grandfather-father-Son backup	D) 321 backup	
19	After servicing a storage device failure, the storage administrator has this to say: "On an average, the next failure can happen in 30 days". What metric are they referring to?		A
	A) MTBF	B) Both	
	C) Longevity	D) None	
20	After replacing a failed storage device, the storage administrator has this to say: "The new device should work for 5 years". What metric are they referring to?		C
	A) MTBF	B) Both	
	C) Longevity	D) None	
21	Which of the following metrics is specific to SSDs?1. Longevity 2. MTBF 3. Drive Writes Per Day 4. Terabytes Written		B
	A) 1 and 2 only	B) 3 and 4 only	
	C) All of them	D) None of them	
22	Which of the following metrics are applicable to all storage devices? 1. Longevity 2. MTBF 3. Drive Writes Per Day 4. Terabytes Written		A
	A) 1 and 2 only	B) 3 and 4 only	
	C) All of them	D) None of them	
23	An organization has invested in shared storage for its devices. This storage is accessible as local storage by its devices. What might be the storage architecture used by the organisation?		A
	A) Storage Area Networking	B) Direct Attached Storage	
	C) Network Attached Storage	D) None of the above	
24	An organization has invested in shared storage for its devices. This storage is accessible via UNC paths. What might be the storage architecture used by the organisation?		C
	A) Storage Area Networking	B) Direct Attached Storage	
	C) Network Attached Storage	D) None of the above	

S. No	Question		Correct Answer
25	A network administrator is configuring a switch. They are specifying rules to ensure that only SAN devices can connect and use the SAN fabric. What is this technique called?		A
	A) Zoning	B) LUN masking	
	C) Network shaping	D) None	
26	An administrator is configuring a storage device. They are specifying which computers are permitted to connect to the storage device. What is this technique called?		B
	A) Zoning	B) LUN masking	
	C) Network shaping	D) None	
27	A storage administrator analyzed their datacenter for threats and suggested that the devices should have more than 1 route to each other for fault tolerance. Which approach are they suggesting?		C
	A) Zoning	B) High availability	
	C) Multi-pathing	D) Parity	
28	Which of the following is not an approach to provide high availability?		C
	A) Redundancy	B) Fault tolerance	
	C) Parity	D) None	
29	How do macOS and Windows differ in expressing storage capacity?		A
	A) MacOS uses decimal system; Windows uses Binary system	B) MacOS uses binary system; Windows uses decimal system	
	C) They are the same	D) None of the above	
30	What do USB 1.0, 2.0 and 3.0 refer to?		A
	A) They are generations of USB technology; latest generations support higher data transfer rates	B) They are connector types and indicate how the device can be plugged into a computer	
	C) Both	D) None	
31	What do USB A, B and C refer to?		B
	A) They are generations of USB technology; latest generations support higher data transfer rates	B) They are connector types and indicate how the device can be plugged into a computer	
	C) Both	D) None	

Join our Discord space

Join our Discord workspace for latest updates, offers, tech happenings around the world, new releases, and sessions with the authors:

https://discord.bpbonline.com

CHAPTER 5
Networking Fundamentals

Introduction

This chapter deals with the basics of networking from traditional on-premise networking to the advanced topics of managing cloud networks. The standard topics for networking are discussed in thorough detail. Topics like how data is transmitted over a copper wire, network topologies, routing and switching, network performance management, and such will be covered in detail.

Structure

We will go through the following topics in this chapter:

- Origins of networking
- Network protocols
- Networking topologies
- Network types
- Performance management
- Network components

Objectives

This chapter aims to provide the background needed to understand the advanced concepts related to networking. The advanced concepts of networking discussed in the later chapters build on the concepts introduced in this chapter. Also, understanding these concepts is necessary for the CVO-003 exam. These topics are often used by developers, network administrators, and architects when designing enterprise applications.

Origins of networking

Today, it is essential for computers to communicate with each other. A computer that cannot interact with other machines loses its value significantly. It is crucial to understand how computers began exchanging data, especially considering their binary language of 1s and 0s. The history of computer networks is filled with notable milestones, which we will explore in this section.

First of all, binary data is transmitted on a copper wire using electricity. Scientists and engineers mastered the transmission of information over copper wires long before the invention of computers. Technologies such as radio, telephone, and telegraph were already in use before computers were even considered. They achieved this by leveraging the characteristics of electricity, specifically amperage and voltage. By using voltage to communicate data, a series of 1s and 0s could be exchanged. When an electric signal of voltage v1 is sent for a fixed duration, it represents a 1, while a different voltage level, v2, represents a 0. This convention, agreed upon by both sender and receiver, enabled the exchange of data between computers.

Let us take a simple example. In the explanation we just provided, let us say a voltage of 13V stands for 0, -13V stands for 1, and -5V stands for an idle line. If the time duration of the voltage signal is 1 second, then the line can communicate 60 bits per minute. That is roughly seven characters a minute. Lo and behold, computers are exchanging data. It might interest you to know that we just described the serial communication approach. It was called RS232 communication and was common among the earliest computers. The number of bits transmitted per second is called the **baud rate**. By using advanced transmitters and receivers, baud rates of 76800 were possible. This is a speed of 76.8 kbps. Pay attention to the lowercase 'b'. It has a specific meaning, more on that in the later sections.

Transmission modes like simplex, half-duplex, and full-duplex have evolved to improve data transmission.

Tidbits:

- Telegraphs use a voltage range of 100 to 160 volts and an amperage of about 50 milliamps. Alphabets are transmitted using Morse code, a series of dots and dashes.

- In Simplex mode, the direction of data transfer was always in a single direction. One computer acts as a transmitter, and another as a receiver. A perfect analogy is our TVs. We can only receive satellite signals from our TV, but we cannot send a message to the satellite from our TV.

- In half-duplex mode, communication is bi-directional, but at any given time, one computer is a transmitter, and the other is a receiver. A transmitter should indicate that they finished transmitting, and then the receiver can assume the role of the transmitter. The *walkie-talkie* you might have seen in the hands of police personnel is a half-duplex transmission.

- In full-duplex mode, communication is truly bidirectional. Devices can transmit and receive data simultaneously.

Serial communication was a breakthrough, but it came with multiple limitations. For one thing, every computer had to be connected to every other computer using a dedicated cable to ensure communications, which was expensive and impractical.

So, the US Department of **Defense's Advanced Research Projects Agency (DARPA)** got to work to solve this problem. They came up with the internet in 1969. They used a novel *packet switching* approach for communications and designed the **Transmission Control Protocol/Internet Protoco**l **(TCP/IP)** protocol. Every computer is assigned a unique address, and data is sent on the network cable with source and destination addresses. Every device receiving the packet shall check the destination address. If the address is different from its own, then it sends the packet to all devices that are connected to it. All the other devices also do the same. This way, the packet moves from one network to another until it reaches the destination machine, upon which it sends an acknowledgement to the sender. This approach eliminated the need for machines to be directly connected to each other. An indirect connection is sufficient for it to receive data. Such indirect connections can be extended to span an office room or the entire globe.

Thus was born the internet, a network of networks. Simultaneous improvements like frequency switching, parallel transmission technologies, the invention of ethernet protocols, and the recent fiber optics have made packet switching the *go-to* approach for computer networking.

We will understand more about the internet in this chapter. We will understand how it has evolved, and we will also look at the different types and topologies, that is, the different approaches for indirect communication. We will discuss the concepts of network protocols, ports, and components that make up the interconnections.

Understanding computer networking concepts is crucial for architecting an effective cloud solution. While the cloud offers certain features like software-defined networking, the skills needed for networking in a cloud are not radically different from traditional networking skills. We can expect a sizeable number of questions regarding networking in the CVO-003 exam.

Network protocols

We made a passing mention of TCP/IP in the introduction. We shall discuss the theoretical background of network protocols and the different protocols used, and we shall learn about the current reigning protocol TCP/IP in considerable detail.

After DARPA came up with their TCP/IP and the earliest networking design, many companies tried to enter this space with their own networking solutions. Novell's IPX/SPX, NetBEUI, and AppleTalk were more prominent and were chief contenders to TCP/IP.

Over time, all these technologies faded into the background. AppleTalk and NetBEUI could not scale to large networks. Novell had significant success with its proprietary IPX/SPX protocol. Its machines came together with its NetWare operating system, networking, and Office software, but it could not keep up with the open standard TCP/IP. IPX/SPX is now a defunct protocol, and TCP/IP is the uncrowned king of network communications.

Our discussion is limited to TCP/IP stack for the rest of the chapter. The name TCP/IP is commonly used, but other protocols like UDP run on top of IP. We shall see more of this further.

OSI 7-layer architecture

In the 1980s, with competition raging fiercely for network dominance, **International Standards Organization (ISO)** sought to bring some standardization to the networking protocols. They designed an architecture that every networking protocol should adhere to. It is important to note that ISO's efforts were not about framing rules for intercommunication or interoperability. They strove to build a conceptual architecture that would guide network developers, application developers, and computer makers. So, ISO developed the **Open Systems Interconnection** model (**OSI**). OSI contains seven layers, with each layer having a specific purpose. The OSI layer names, numbers, and details can be seen in *Table 5.1*:

Layer			Protocol Data Unit	Purpose
Host layers	7	Application	Data Translating data between networking service and an application; perform big-endian/little-endian character encoding, data compression and encryption Managing continuous exchange of information transmissions between two nodes	High-level protocols; for example, HTTP for remote file access
	4	Transport	Segment, Datagram	Transmitting data between nodes, along with segmentation and multiplexing, in a connection-oriented manner

Layer			Protocol Data Unit	Purpose
Media Layers	3	Network	Packet	Managing network traffic, including addressing and routing
	2	Data link	Frame	Transmitting data frames between two nodes connected by a physical layer
	1	Physical	Bit, Symbol	Transmitting raw bit streams over a physical medium

Table 5.1: OSI 7-layer architecture

OSI was an industry initiative, and much effort went into standardizing the architecture. At one point, the computing industry was bitterly divided into OSI supporters and TCP/IP supporters; this became known colloquially as Protocol Wars. As the saying goes, a camel is a horse designed by a committee. OSI did not gain the acceptance levels it hoped for and gradually fell out of favor. Today, it is used mainly in academic and theoretical scenarios. TCP/IP proved to be more efficient, reliable, and robust.

Transmission Control Protocol/Internet Protocol

So, what is it that TCP/IP did that OSI could not? For one thing, TCP/IP is far more concise: it has only four layers. Unlike OSI, it took a practical approach. It developed protocols first and later fit them into a model. OSI was stringent in differences between layers, while TCP/IP focused more on making things work rather than adhering to a theory. TCP compromised on certain functionalities and delivered working solutions rather than looking for theoretical purity. The resultant openness of TCP/IP made it a darling of network communication enthusiasts. Let us see what the TCP/IP model is made of and what the functionalities of each layer are. *Table 5.2* lists the layers of TCP/IP's 4-layer architecture:

Layer number	Layer name	Example protocols	Purpose of the layer
4	Application Layer	HTTP, FTP, SMTP, DHCP and so on.	Protocols used by user applications to exchange application data; application layer data is packaged into transport layer protocol packets.
3	Transport Layer	TCP, UDP, SCTP	Basic data channel for application-specific data exchange is established in this layer.
2	Internet Layer	IPv4, IPv6	This layer is responsible for sending packets across multiple networks. It is the functionality that makes internetworking of different IP networks possible.
1	Link Layer	ARP, RARP, NDP	Here, the data is sent on a physical medium, like a copper or fiber optic cable.

Table 5.2: TCP/IP 4-layer architecture

Figure 5.1 shows how the layers work to exchange information on two machines:

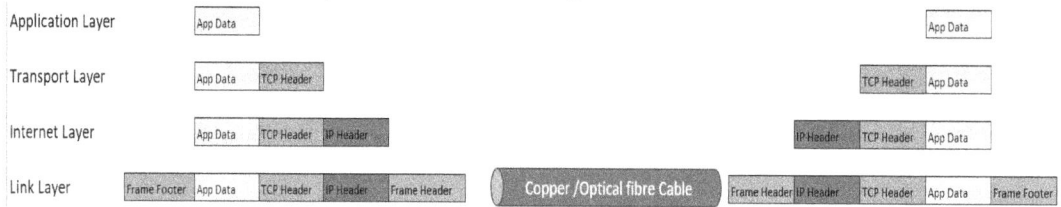

Figure 5.1: *Data communication on TCP/IP*

Link layer

This layer is responsible for moving the packets to different internet hosts on the same link. It understands how to send the packet of the physical medium, whether it is fiber optic cable, copper cable, or Wi-Fi. If the host is beyond the local LAN, the link layer shall send the packets to a central hub/switch/router to move the packets onto the next hop. This is the lowest layer in the TCP/IP architecture. The higher layer (IP layer) is oblivious to the workings at the link layer. Typically, the link layer consists of cables, network interface cards, modems, and the like. Hardware chipsets and software device drivers usually take responsibility for the link layer and send data onto the copper wire from the IP layer.

Internet layer

The ability to send data across multiple connected networks is internetworking's most significant advantage. This process is called routing, and it is achieved by assigning a unique address called **IP address** to every network device. IP addresses are arranged hierarchically to help intermediate devices decide the next hop to which they must route the packets. The internet layer sends the packets across multiple networks. It makes the internetworking of different IP networks possible and establishes the internet.

Take the example of a post office. Letters from all post boxes are collected at the local post office. Using the PIN code on the addresses, postmasters sort the letters as being sent to different geographies. All PIN codes starting with 11 are routed to the Delhi postal zone, and those beginning with 78 are routed to Assam. The postmaster at New Delhi's main post office shall sort the letters based on the 3rd digit, which denotes the sorting district. The fourth digit represents the service routes within the sorting district. The last two digits are for the specific delivery office. So, 110001 refers to a particular post office in *Central Delhi*. Any postal center between your local post office shall look at the relevant number and keep routing the letter until it reaches the destination.

This is the exact purpose served by IP addresses. Each machine on the network has a unique IP address. Based on the information provided by the transport layer, the internet layer looks up and adds the destination IP address to the data packet handed over by the transport layer. All intermediate network devices route the packet to further hops until it reaches its destination. The IP addresses are 32-bit numbers in IPv4 and 128-bit in IPv6. We will discuss this in detail in a later section.

The internet layer is the heart of the internet we use today. The various devices, protocols, and solutions at this layer are fascinating studies in themselves. Understanding the IP layer's different aspects and capabilities is crucial from an examination perspective.

As mentioned earlier, the IP layer is oblivious to the workings of the link layer. It provides minimal instructions to the IP layer for some network translation and assumes that the link layer does the job as needed. Cloud computing capitalizes on this behavior to provide essential features like VPCs and **software-defined networking** (**SDN**) to cloud users. We shall discuss these in detail in the next chapter.

Transport layer

The transport layer is responsible for end-to-end communication and error-free data delivery between applications running on the hosts. Applications are shielded from the complexities of data communication by this layer. The IP layer does not provide reliable data transmission. In other words, it is responsible for sending the data, but does not guarantee that the destination host receives it. This limitation is addressed at the transport layer. Two protocols are popular at the transport layer:

- TCP provides reliable communication between computers. It takes the responsibility of breaking down the application data into sizeable chunks that the IP layer can handle. When receiving data, it takes the responsibility of sequencing the chunks and presenting the data to the recipient application in the way the sender transmitted it. It also demands that recipients acknowledge data receipt. This makes TCP a very reliable protocol. However, it also adds many overheads to communication.

- **User Datagram Protocol** (**UDP**) provides significantly fewer features than TCP. If the applications do not require reliable communication, then UDP is the protocol to use.

- In recent times, major CDNs are increasingly using UDP-based QUIC (HTTP/3), which combines transport and security.

Think of choosing between the protocols as deciding whether a letter needs to be sent via a registered post, speed post, or standard mail delivery.

Application layer

This is the topmost layer of the TCP/IP stack. It is the closest to the end user, and operations like web browsing, chatting, video streaming, and file transfer happen at this layer using appropriate application protocols. The protocols at this layer include HTTP, HTTPS, FTP, TFTP, SSH, SMTP, and NTP. Thinking in terms of regular postal services, this layer is akin to using the post to send legal messages or greeting cards.

Figure 5.2 shows how OSI and TCP/IP layers correspond to each other and the protocols operating at each layer:

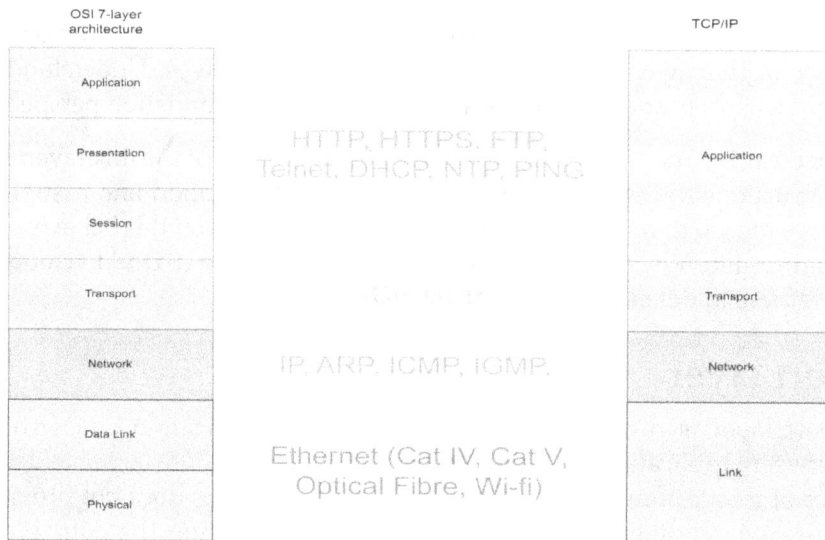

Figure 5.2: *A comparison of OSI and TCP/IP layers*

IPv4, IPv6

As mentioned in the section on the internet layer, every device on the internetworking has a unique address, which is called an IP address. IP addresses differentiate between computers, routers, hubs, and switches and form an inalienable internet component. An IP address is a sequence of numbers separated by period (.). In the early days, IP addresses used 32 bits of memory. This allowed for a maximum of 2^{32} = 4,294,967,296 (roughly 4 billion) devices to be connected. It was called the **IPv4 protocol**. With the explosion of the internet in the 90s, this address space was insufficient, and it was expanded to 128 bits in IPv6. IPv6 can potentially support 2^{128} = 3.4×10^{38} devices. That is roughly the number of molecules on Earth. It is easy to remember IPv4 addresses for limited-size LANs or large enterprises. IPv4 and IPv6 co-exist on the internet, and IPv4 is rapidly approaching extinction.

Example address is 192.168.1.0 or 2401:4900:1f25:1a35:208e:d1d9:c60f:85c. IP addresses are allocated by the **Internet Assigned Numbers Authority** (**IANA**). We shall discuss the conventions and rules for assigning these in the next chapter.

Software and hardware ports

A hardware port is where the physical communication medium connects to the computer. It serves as an interface between the computer and the physical medium. Examples can be an RJ45 port, Wi-Fi adapter, and USB port.

The software port, on the other hand, is conceptual. It is an imaginary point for originating and terminating network connections. It is a number assigned by the operating system, is associated with a specific process, and allows the streaming of the traffic to and from appropriate processes. Hardware ports operate at the link layer, and software ports operate at the transport layer. Some ports are pre-assigned to specific purposes. FTP communication happens on 20, and HTTP communication happens on 80.

Networking topologies

Previously, we examined how packet-switching networks are interconnected indirectly. Let us understand what these indirect connections entail. There are several standardized methods for achieving this; let us explore them. It is important to note that these topologies pertain to the maintenance of link layer connections:

- **Mesh topology**: Every device in the network is connected to every other device in a mesh topology. This approach has built-in redundancy and fault tolerance. Failure of any one cable will not impact the network communications. However, cabling is expensive, and as devices are added to the network, this topology becomes impractical and unwieldy. It is used where cabling is not needed, like in the case of wireless networks.

- **Star topology**: Every device is connected to a central node called a hub in a star topology. Managing the network can be done on a single central node. Adding and removing devices or failure in the connection only has a local impact. However, the central node becomes a single point of failure.

- **Bus topology**: The bus is a simple topology in which all computers and network devices are connected to a single central cable called a **bus**. A signal from the source device reaches all devices connected to the bus, but only the intended recipient will receive it. Bus topology can be very effective for small networks. More devices can be added by increasing the cable length, which is not too expensive. However, adding or removing a device will need downtime of the network. Failure of the bus will result in a complete network failure.

- **Ring topology**: It is a variation of bus topology in that the bus forms a loop or a ring. It places additional constraints on communication, like data always traveling in a single direction. Every device gets a **token** for communication. However, it is better than a bus topology when network traffic is heavy.

- **Tree topology**: This is a variation of star topology and can be thought of as a star-like connection of star networks. Compared to the star, the tree has an increased cable length or **hops** between two computers, but also offers better management.

The different network topologies explained above can be seen in *Figure 5.3:*

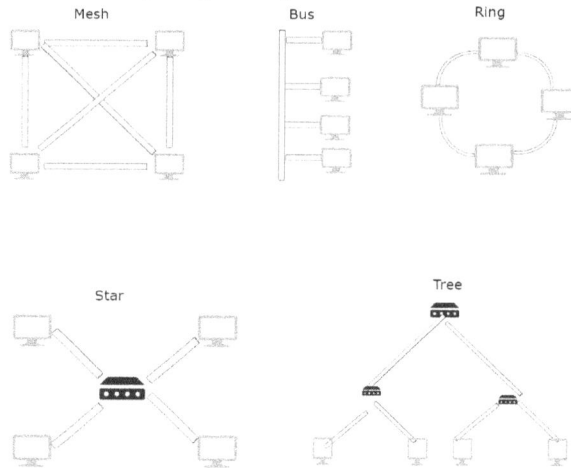

Figure 5.3: *Network topologies*

Network types

As computer networking evolved, business requirements drove its adoption. Terminologies evolved to describe the situations in which businesses adopted the internet; we shall look at the standard terminology. Note that network types deal with the internet layer and are differentiated based on the number and type of devices in the network.

Intranet

Intranet refers to the network of computers and devices strictly internal to the organization. These devices have neither direct nor indirect connections to any other network outside the organization. In the earliest days of computer networking, an organization's computers were typically located in a single building. Such computers were interconnected in one of the topologies discussed earlier, but had no external contact. The intranet can have rich support for various applications and protocols, or even an internal web server. Such a server caters strictly to the organization's internal needs and cannot be reached by external computers. The intranet initially referred to computer networking in a limited area, but today's intranets span continents with technological advances.

Extranet

As organizations matured, they saw a need to permit users to access their intranet from external environments. For this, they employed extranets. The extranet is an extension of the intranet in that select users are allowed to access the company's intranet. This access mechanism can be via a website, file server, or other means. The difference between intranet and extranet is the strictly controlled external user access in the case of extranets.

Internet

Modern life is almost inconceivable without internet usage in one form or another. We use the word internet freely in our day-to-day life, to refer to activities like reading the news, booking movie tickets, searching for information, and the like. All these activities are possible because of the internet but is that all the internet is? Truth be said, it is not. The missing piece here is the **World Wide Web** (**WWW**). WWW is an information system that enables users to access resources over the internet with the help of a web browser. It works on top of the internet and is not the internet by itself. *Tim-Berners Lee* invented it at CERN in 1991. By utilizing the indirect communication capabilities of the internet, the WWW enables sending and receiving information between any two computers in the world.

If you are confused by this, looking at the years of invention of these technologies is recommended. Internet predates WWW by nearly 2 decades. One does not need a web browser to access the internet. Protocols like FTP, UDP, SMB, Telnet, and the like, can be used for internet communications but a browser is needed for WWW. It is technically incorrect to use the term internet for web browsing, but the concepts are so tightly interwoven that they are used interchangeably in daily life. WWW is not in scope for the examination.

Local area networking

A **local area network** (**LAN**) is a group of devices in a physical location connected to one another. A LAN can vary from a home network with one device to an enterprise network with thousands of devices. Various technologies were used for LANs. Novell's IPX/SPX was once a dominant technology protocol. Ethernet and TCP/IP have taken over networking and have become the de-facto standards now.

Ethernet cables connect laptops/desktops to network switches and routers, and they should conform to specific standards. Previously, Category 3 cables (Cat 3) were used to achieve speeds up to 10 Gbps. Modern networks use Cat5 or Cat6 cables to reach speeds up to 100 Gbps. They are plugged into the ethernet port, also called the RJ45 port, and colloquially called the LAN port.

Cat5 and Cat6 cables were previously used to connect routers, hubs, and switches. They are now being replaced with fiber optics for higher speeds.

MAN

A **metropolitan area network** (**MAN**) connects computers within a metropolitan area or any large area with multiple buildings. MAN covers a larger area than a LAN.

WAN

WAN is the same as MAN, except it covers an even larger area and is not tied to a single location. The internet is considered the biggest WAN there is.

If you are wondering what the differences between LAN, MAN, and WAN are, the answer lies in the scale. The data quantity and speeds needed for LAN differ considerably from a WAN. Different technologies are required at the cabling level. These technologies hide the complexities from an end user or even a regular application developer. They form the backbone of a city or a country's networking infrastructure. Putting it in perspective, every time you access a website server outside your LAN, you are utilizing the MANs and WAN of your country and the server's country. However, for a casual glance, WAN and MAN are all but invisible.

Wireless fidelity (Wi-Fi)

LANs were a fixture of only large or medium organizations and would have remained so if not for Wi-Fi, which is a family of wireless network protocols allowing data exchange by radio waves between digital devices close to each other. Wi-Fi allows for the mobility of computing devices, if only in a limited area. This greatly appealed to the consumers who demanded more of this technology. Wi-Fi networks were marginally slower than their physical counterpart, and recent advances made this a non-issue. Wi-Fi networks do not require cabling and make for easy implementation of mesh topology.

Performance management

Managing internet performance is the primary requirement for a network administrator. For this, any administrator should thoroughly understand concepts like measuring bandwidth, load balancing, and network tiers.

Bandwidth

Bandwidth is the maximum amount of data a network can send or receive in one second. It is generally measured in the form of **bits per second** (**bps**) or, rarely, in the form of **bytes per second** (**Bps**). Bandwidth depends on the capacity of the network cable (or Wi-Fi radio waves) and the network the computer connects to. For example, if a network device uses an 802.11b network adapter, it can send or receive data at a maximum speed of 11 Mbps. It also depends on your network. A computer might be plugged into a 100 Gbps cable. However, if the other end of the cable is connected to a 1 Mbps router, then the entire network's bandwidth is limited to 1 Mbps. After all, a network's bandwidth is only as high as its lowest link.

Dialups, DSL, broadband, and optical fiber

In the olden days, computers connected to the internet using dial-up telephone lines. The dial-up connection tones made by a modem were like music to internet users in the 80s, 90s, and early 2000s. Computers used dedicated hardware called **Modulator-Demodulator** (**modem**) to convert the digital signals to analog format and fit for transmission over telephone connections. These modems dialed in and connected to an **Internet Service Provider** (**ISP**). Telephone lines have a hard upper limit of 56Kbps. Other technologies like **Digital Subscriber Line** (**DSL**) and Broadband have since come into the picture to overcome this limitation. They eliminated the need for dialing into a server and provided a net connection that was always available. DSLs had bandwidths up to 100 Mbps. Broadband has integrated all the different pieces, like the modem and DSL, into a seamless networking option. Broadband runs on copper cables and has certain innate limitations due to properties like electrical resistance of the copper medium. Fiber optics have eliminated many of these problems and can have a bandwidth of 50Tbps.

Tidbits:

- **Bps vs bps**: As in the discussion on Kib and Kb in *Chapter 4, Managing Storage*, there is a misleading representation of network bandwidth. The capital B stands for Bytes, and the lower b stands for bits. The convention is to use bits when measuring bandwidth. Administrators should pay keen attention to unconventional expressions of speed when procuring networking devices.

- **Bandwidth is different from internet speed**: Internet speed is the time taken to send or receive a fixed amount of data. They are slightly different but are used interchangeably in day-to-day parlance. Internet speed depends on the bandwidth and the distance the data travels between the source and destination. If the source machine is only a few meters away, the speed will naturally be very high.

Caching

The word cache means to store in hiding or for future use. This is precisely what networks do to improve performance. If frequently accessed information is stored on a remote server, it would immensely improve internet speed if a copy of the information is stored locally. Instead of travelling to the server, the information can be retrieved from the local cache. Cached information can be anything like database query results, API requests/responses, and web artefacts like HTML, JavaScript, and images. Network speeds can be significantly improved by properly keeping the information copy synchronized with the original. The time to keep the information locally before refreshing it with updated information is called **Time to Live** (**TTL**). Administrators should fine-tune this parameter to balance network costs with up-to-date information availability. Caching has a place in multiple areas, from calculation-intensive computing to data access via **Content Delivery Networks** (**CDN**).

Load balancing

Modern websites serve thousands of concurrent user requests and quickly return appropriate data to them. Having a single server handle all incoming requests is not practical. Scaling up the server offers diminishing returns after a certain point, so the better solution is to scale-out, add more servers, and build a server farm. Load balancing is the efficient distribution of incoming network traffic across servers. This process is invisible to the end-user when they contact the website. The load balancer shall route the request to the available server so that the workload is equally distributed across all servers. This ensures low latency for information requests. Building and maintaining load balancers is crucial for network administrators and application developers. Improper designing of load balancers can cripple applications. A well-designed load balancer offers scalability, redundancy, and low latency for the network:

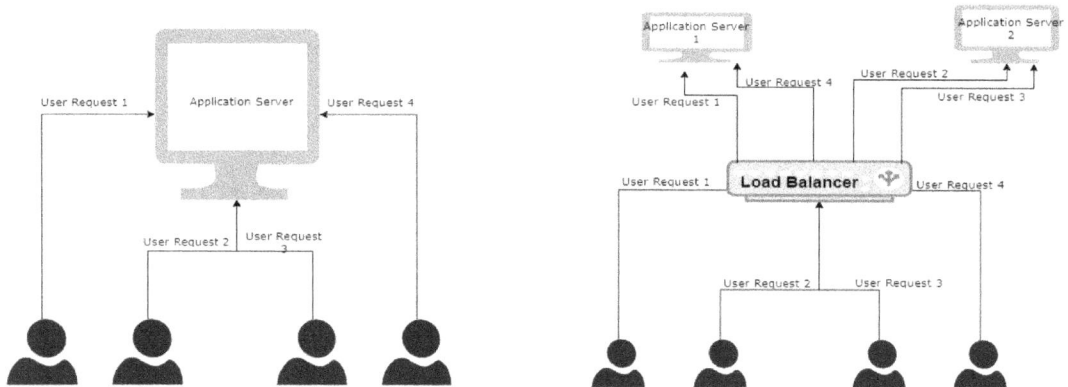

Figure 5.4: *Servers with and without a load balancer*

There are multiple algorithms to distribute traffic across the servers. They are Round Robin, least connections, least time, hash, ip hash, and the like. Among these, least time is exclusively used by Nginx Plus load balancer. A proper understanding of these algorithms is needed to choose the best algorithm for a given application.

Network components

Let us now understand the various components that make up the internet. The internet is more than just a web of computers; it contains various other elements that support the internet span continents. They are needed to address the limitations of copper wire communications mentioned earlier. We shall briefly discuss the different network components and their purpose. These components are available as both hardware devices and software-only implementations. We will keep referring to the example of the post office discussed in the internet layer section when discussing the components.

- Repeater is an electronic device that retransmits a signal it received. As mentioned earlier, an electric signal in a copper wire deteriorates after a certain cable length. Repeaters are placed such that the signal can cover longer distances. For copper cables, repeaters are needed for every thousand feet or so. They are like petrol bunks to refuel the postal van.

- Routers forward data packets between computer networks. They are like the intermediate post offices between source and destination. They direct traffic on the internet. They look at the IP address of the packet and route it to the appropriate network. They rely on "routing algorithms" to detect the shortest path to the destination. Networks connected to a router should have similar characteristics for routing algorithms, topologies, DNS and the like.

- A network switch is a device that connects multiple other devices in the network to establish node-to-node communication. It differs from a router in that a switch is only for sending data packets within a network, while routers send information between different networks.

- A hub is a hardware device for connecting multiple devices. A hub is where data from different devices get placed on a single cable. Sometimes, hubs also perform the job of repeaters.

- Network bridge creates a single, aggregated network from multiple communication networks. Switches are for connecting various devices on a LAN, and bridges are for connecting multiple LANs. Bridges are different from routers. Bridges operate at the link layer, whereas routers operate at the internet layer.

- Firewall is a rules-based network security system that monitors network traffic. A firewall is typically established between a trusted network, like an intranet, and an untrusted network, like the internet. Firewalls perform the duty of customs officers at the port of entry, and they act at the IP and transport layers.

- Gateways are used to connect dissimilar networks. They translate network technologies so that networks can communicate with each other. Gateways are routers with additional network translation functionality.

- A proxy server is not a network component. It is an intermediary that acts between two separate computers and hides the requestor's identity. Organizations typically use it to protect their data from attackers. Every proxy server has an IP address. All hosts in the organization connect to a proxy server when communicating on the internet. The proxy server intercepts the outgoing traffic, replaces the source IP address with its own, and sends the data packet to the destination. It does the same with the response. Consequently, the destination sees only the IP address of the proxy and not the original sender. This greatly improves the network security of organizations.

Note: **At first glance, a switch and router might appear to be the same, but there is an important difference between the two. Switches are used only to connect devices together as a network. Routers connect multiple networks together and are essential for connecting to the internet. A router is sometimes called a poor man's firewall because it provides a limited subset of a firewall's functionalities. Routers and firewalls play a significant role in tackling IP address exhaustion. We will look at IP address exhaustion in detail in the next chapter.**

Refer to the *Network Address Translation* section in the next chapter to understand the router functionality.

Conclusion

We learnt about the various fundamentals of networking in this chapter. From the humble origins of serial communications to the latest optical fiber, we understand how communication has evolved and how TCP/IP has become the backbone of modern communication. We also learnt about the TCP/IP protocol stack and understood how each layer uses various network components to provide the internet experience. We then discussed measuring and maintaining network performance.

In the next chapter, we will learn about managing computer networks.

Glossary

- **AppleTalk:** A protocol used for exchanging information between computers by Apple operating systems

- **ARP:** Address Resolution Protocol

- **Bandwidth:** Maximum amount of data a network can send or receive in one second

- **Baud Rate:** Number of bits of information transmitted per second

- **FTP:** File Transfer Protocol

- **Full-duplex transmission:** A mode of transmission where two devices can communicate, with both devices sending and receiving information simultaneously

- **Half-duplex transmission:** A mode of transmission where two devices can communicate; one device is the sender and the other is the receiver at any given time

- **HTTPS:** Hyper Text Transfer Protocol Secure

- **Internet:** A giant global network of computers connected indirectly to one another, facilitating information exchange

- **IP:** Internet Protocol

- **IPX/SPX:** Internetwork Packet Exchange/Sequenced Packet Exchange, a now defunct protocol used for exchanging information between computers by Novell Netware operating systems

- **LAN, MAN, and WAN:** Local area networking, metropolitan area networking, and wide area networking

- **Load Balancer:** A dedicated machine that distributes incoming requests among the machines in the server farm

- **NDP:** Neighbor Discovery Protocol

- **OSI:** Open Systems Interconnection; an industry initiative taken up to standardize the network communication between systems

- **Packet switching:** A method of transmitting information to a network by breaking it into small variable length pieces called Packets; at the destination, the packets are reassembled to obtain the original information

- **Port:** A physical location on a computer where the computer interacts with network medium

- **Protocol or Network protocol:** A set of rules on how to format, transmit, and receive data over a network

- **RARP:** Reverse Address Resolution Protocol

- **Simplex transmission:** A mode of transmission where two devices can communicate with one device is always a sender, and the other device is always receiver

- **TCP:** Transmission Control Protocol

- **UDP:** User Datagram Protocol

- **Wi-Fi:** Wireless fidelity, referring to conformance to 'IEEE 802.11b Direct Sequence' standard

Practice questions

S. No	Question		Correct Answer
1	**Which of the following approaches is used for TCP/IP networking?**		A
	A) Packet switching	B) Data switching	
	C) Circuit switching	D) Medium switching	
2	**Which of the following mediums is not used for network communications on a laptop?**		D
	A) RS232	B) Ethernet	
	C) Wi-Fi	D) Optical fiber	
3	**Which of the following statements about packet switching is wrong?**		C
	A) Packet switching is less reliable than circuit switching	B) Packet switching is a store-and-forward technique	
	C) Data transmission is done only by the source	D) Packet switching is suitable for bilateral traffic	
4	**Which of the following protocols does not run on top of the IP layer?**		B
	A) TCP	B) IGMP	
	C) UDP	D) Ping	

S. No	Question		Correct Answer
5	**Which protocol is suitable for transmitting data where reliability is not critical?**		C
	A) TCP	B) FTP	
	C) UDP	D) Telnet	
6	**Which of the following statements is true?**		D
	A) TCP is a connection-oriented protocol, UDP is a connectionless protocol	B) TCP is slower than UDP	
	C) TCP uses handshake, UDP does not need handshake	D) All of the above	
7	**Which layer of OSI is meant for data compressions, encryption and so on?**		B
	A) Application	B) Presentation	
	C) Transport	D) Session	
8	**Which of the following layers adds both header and footer to the packet handed over by higher layers?**		A
	A) Link layer	B) Internet layer	
	C) Transport layer	D) All of the above	
9	**What is the memory length allocated to network addresses in IPv4?**		B
	A) 16 bits	B) 32 bits	
	C) 64-bits	D) 128 bits	
10	**What is the memory length allocated to network addresses in IPv6?**		D
	A) 16 bits	B) 32 bits	
	C) 64-bits	D) 128 bits	
11	**A network administrator has connected every device in their network to every other device. What topology did they use?**		B
	A) Star	B) Mesh	
	C) Tree	D) Bus	
12	**A network administrator analyzed their network and identified that a central hub is a single point of failure. What topology leads to this scenario?**		A
	A) Star	B) Mesh	
	C) Tree	D) Bus	

S. No	Question		Correct Answer
13	Ajay logged in to his organization's desktop machine and is able to access all computers in their organization's network but nothing outside it. What is he accessing?		B
	A) Internet	B) Intranet	
	C) Extranet	D) All the above	
14	Ajay logged in to his laptop at home. He needs to be able to access all computers in his organization's network. What is required for this?		C
	A) Internet	B) Intranet	
	C) Extranet	D) All the above	
15	What does a modem stand for?		B
	A) Modern Emitter	B) Modulator Demodulator	
	C) Modulation Emission Manager	D) Modulus Emphasizer	
16	What is the difference between switches and routers?		D
	A) Switches are older technology than routers	B) Routers are older technology than switches	
	C) Switches can connect multiple networks together	D) Switches connect multiple devices into a single network	
17	What is the purpose of a hub?		A
	A) Hub is used for connecting several devices to a single cable	B) Hub has one port for incoming data and another for outgoing	
	C) Hub is used for connecting multiple networks together	D) All of the above	
18	Which of the following statements about Hub and Bridge are true? 1. Hub connects multiple devices into a LAN. 2. Bridge connects multiple LANs that are using the same protocol. 3. Hub operates on the physical layer of OSI model. 4. Bridge operates on the data link layer of OSI model.		D
	A) 1 and 2 only	B) 1,2 and 3 only	
	C) 2 and 3 only	D) All the above	
19	Which of the following is not a load balancing algorithm?		C
	A) Round Robin	B) Least Connections	
	C) First come, first served	D) IP hash	
20	Which of the following devices is called a poor man's firewall?		B
	A) Proxy	B) Router	
	C) Hub	D) Gateway	

Join our Discord space

Join our Discord workspace for latest updates, offers, tech happenings around the world, new releases, and sessions with the authors:

https://discord.bpbonline.com

CHAPTER 6

Managing Networks

Introduction

This chapter deals with the advances in networking and how they are made available over the cloud. Recent advances like software, the e-defined networks, throttling of network speeds, and virtual network interfaces will be covered in detail here. Virtualizing the physical infrastructure for cloud environments and managing them will also be discussed in detail.

We shall dive deep into IP addresses and understand how to read and interpret the various fields in an IP address. We shall also discuss multiple protocols available for the TCP/IP stack. Lastly, we will look into how clouds provide the IP stack to cloud admins to configure the VMs for virtual private computing. It is imperative to understand the workings of the IP address mechanism to appreciate the sophistication of virtual networks. It is impossible to appreciate the beauty and robustness of the networks without a thorough understanding of the IP addressing system. We will start with IPv4 address and then proceed to IPv6.

Structure

We will cover the following topics in this chapter:

- Understanding an IPv4 address
- Understanding an IPv6 address

- Domain Name System
- Dynamic Host Configuration Protocol
- Network Address Translation
- Port Address Translation
- Routing tables
- Networking protocols
- Cloud networks

Objectives

We will start the chapter by understanding the basic entity of the modern internet: the IP address. We will understand how IPv4 and IPv6 addresses should be interpreted. We will then discuss some of the popular internet protocols and move on to look at how the internet is provided on virtual machines and in cloud environments. We will understand how the network functions are virtualized and also discuss software-defined networking, which is one of the main pillars of cloud environments.

Understanding an IPv4 address

IPv4 addresses are expressed in dotted-decimal format, with numbers separated by periods (.). An IPv4 address is a set of 4 numbers separated by a period, for example, 142.250.77.163. *What do these numbers mean? What purpose do they serve?* In the previous chapter, we compared them to postal PIN codes. If that is an accurate analogy, *is there some way to interpret them? What about IPv6? What is the deal with it?* Let us demystify the IP address in this section.

IPv4 addresses are expressed in dotted-decimal format, with numbers separated by periods (.). An IPv4 address consists of 4 numbers separated by periods, for example, 142.250.77.163. These numbers are designated to serve specific purposes and communicate essential information about network locations. This section will thoroughly elucidate the structure and significance of IP addresses, particularly focusing on their interpretation and utilization within network configurations.

Decoding IPv4 address

While configuring a device on the internet, network administrators specify the information shown in *Figure 6.1*:

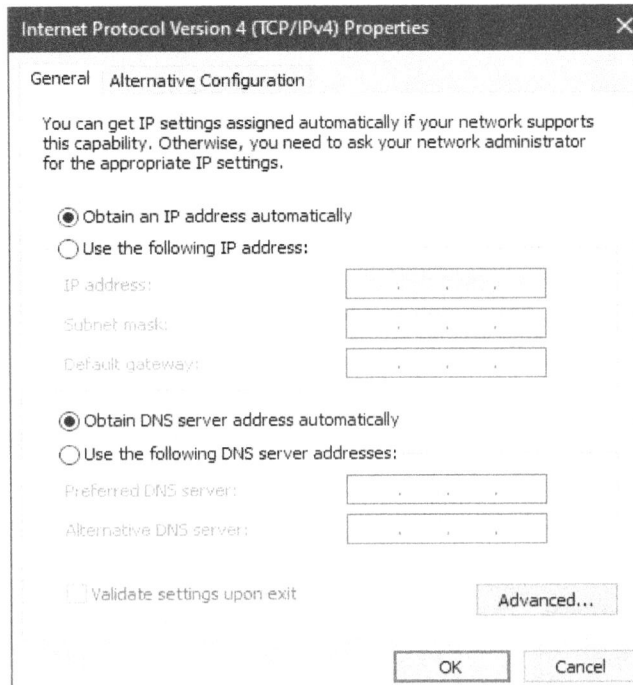

Figure 6.1: IPv4 configuration on Windows 10

IPv4 address is a 32-bit value with four numbers separated by periods, such as 142.250.77.163. This is a human-readable expression of a binary IP address. The binary number of this IP is as follows:

142.	250.	77.	163
11000000	10101000	10101000	10000100

Table 6.1: Components of IPv4 address

Each 8-bit section is called an octet. All 0s or all 1s, that is, 0 and 255, are used for a special purpose in every octet. Every IP address has two components: Network ID and host ID. Together, they uniquely identify each device on the internet. Note that there is no fixed length for breaking down the Network ID and host ID in the IP address. The subnet mask provides this information. We will come to that in a bit.

IPv4 addresses are grouped into five classes: A, B, C, D, and E. Each class has a specific use. Getting the classes wrong will result in significant damage to your organization's network.

- **Class A**: Addresses are for large networks. They use the first octet for the Network ID, and the first bit of the first octet is always zero. This allows 126 networks with IDs ranging from 1 to 127. The 24 remaining bits can be used for 17 million hosts per network. Class A networks use a default subnet mask of 255.0.0.0.

- **Class B**: Addresses are for medium networks. They use the first two octets for its Network ID component, and the first two bits of the first octet are always 10. The remaining 6+8=14 bits allow for 16384 networks ranging from 128.0.x.x to 191.255.x.x. The last 16 bits allow for nearly 65000 hosts per network. Class B networks use a default subnet mask of 255.255.0.0.

- **Class C**: Addresses are for small LANs. They use the first three octets for Network ID, and the first three bits are always 110. The remaining 5+8+8=21 bits allow for 2 million networks. The last 8 bits allow for 254 hosts per network. Class C networks use a default subnet mask of 255.255.255.0.

- **Class D**: Addresses are for multicasting. The first octet ranges from 11100000 to 11101111 (that is, 224 to 239). It is not assigned to any hosts by default and must be explicitly configured.

- **Class E**: Addresses are reserved for research and are not available for general use. The first octet ranges from 11110000 to 11111111 (that is, 240 to 255).

- **Loop-back**: Addresses range from 127.0.0.1 to 127.255.255.255. They are used for testing the network. These are phantom IP addresses and cannot be assigned to a host. Specifically, IP 127.0.0.1 is often used to troubleshoot network connectivity issues and by developers to test their web-based applications locally.

- At first glance, the above information seems to indicate that Class A addresses are limited to 127 organizations in the world and the total number of class B devices, such as laptops, desktops, VMs, servers, printers, router, switches are less than 1 billion. This seemingly contradicts the facts like a billion licenses of Windows 10 alone being sold. The answer to this conundrum lies in the private IP addresses. **Private IP addresses** are designated IP addresses reserved for private/internal use. They are available in every class. They are used in a home or business network for devices like laptops and printers. Internet-facing routers cannot process private IP address packets. Private ranges of each class are listed here:
  - **Class A**: 10.0.0.0 to 10.255.255.255
  - **Class B**: 169.254.0.0 to 169.254.255.255 and 172.16.0.0 to 172.31.255.255
  - **Class C**: 192.168.0.0 to 192.168.255.255

Each organization or home network can assign private IP addresses as they see fit for their internal devices. These devices will not be facing the internet, and their network communications cannot cross the organization's threshold. Internet-facing routers do not know how to process packets from these IP addresses. So, it is perfectly possible to have two devices with the same private IP address to connect to separate organizations' LANs. If you are curious about how such devices browse the internet, you will find the answer in the *Port Address Translation and Network Address Translation sections*.

Subnet masks

It is crucial to focus on separating the Network ID and host ID. When a host sends an IP packet to the router or gateway, the router must determine whether to examine the first octet or the first three octets. This determination is made using subnet masks, which contain 1s in all the octets for the Network ID and 0s for the host ID. For instance, if the IP address is a class B address, the subnet mask will be 255.255.0.0. Refer to *Figure 6.2* for a detailed illustration:

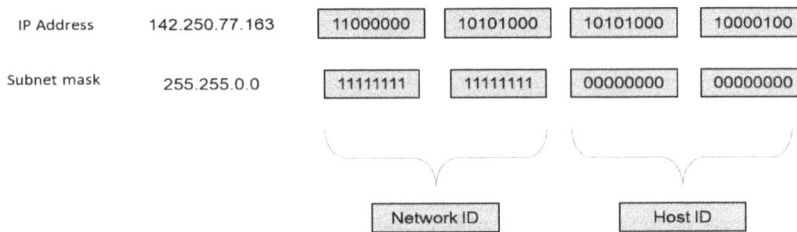

IP Address   142.250.77.163 | 11000000 | 10101000 | 10101000 | 10000100 |

Subnet mask   255.255.0.0 | 11111111 | 11111111 | 00000000 | 00000000 |

Network ID   Host ID

Figure 6.2: Using subnet mask to interpret IPv4 address

All incoming packets contain an IP address. Network admins configure the subnet mask on the router. Using these two pieces of information, the host decides whether the packet should be routed internally or externally.

Default gateway

This is the third piece of information configured by network admins on a device. It is used for streamlining communications. When initiating communication, the host machine checks the destination IP address with its own IP address and subnet mask. The initiator sends the packet to the IP address mentioned in the *Default Gateway* section if the communication is to a remote host on another network. The gateway then routes the packet to the appropriate network.

Subnets and supernets

The subnets mentioned for each IP address class earlier are default values. Sometimes, they do not suit the organization's needs. Consider a case where an organization with a class A or class B address has geographically distributed hosts. In that case, using an entire IP address class in one geography for only a few hosts is impractical. In such cases, admins can divide their networks into smaller networks. This is called **subnetting** and helps tackle the problem of address space depletion. *Figure 6.3* illustrates this:

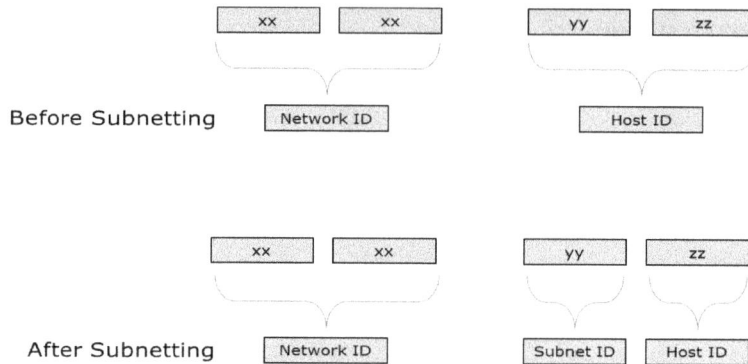

Figure 6.3: Subnetting an IP address

Supernets, on the other hand, combine smaller networks into a single larger network. When creating supernets, the number of bits allocated to the host is increased. The subnet mask in a supernet has fewer 1s on the left side compared to the default subnet mask of that class. It is used for simplifying the routing process.

IPv6

While IPv4 can theoretically support 2^{32} addresses, it became quickly apparent in the early days of adoption that IPv4 address space will be exhausted quickly. Even after a redesign using CIDR, there just were not enough IP addresses available to cater to the explosive growth of internet-enabled devices. Most of the internet registries ran out of IPv4 addresses by 2015.

IPv6 was introduced in 1998 to address this problem. Unlike IPv4, which uses 32 bits for addressing, IPv6 uses 128 bits. This theoretically allows for $2^{128} = 3.4 * 10^{38}$ addresses and also simplifies IP address management. IPv6 is not backward compatible with IPv4. Adopting IPv6 is strongly encouraged; however, IPv4 is expected to co-exist with IPv6 for the foreseeable future.

Understanding an IPv6 address

An IPv6 address uses 128 bits for its address. It is expressed in a hexadecimal format with numbers separated by colons (:). A sample IPv6 address is 2404:6800:4007:0817:0000:0000: 2003:0010. Each 16-bit section is called a **word**.

Decoding an IPv6 address

As can be seen in *Figure 6.4*, the UI for entering an IPv6 configuration looks the same as that of IPv4:

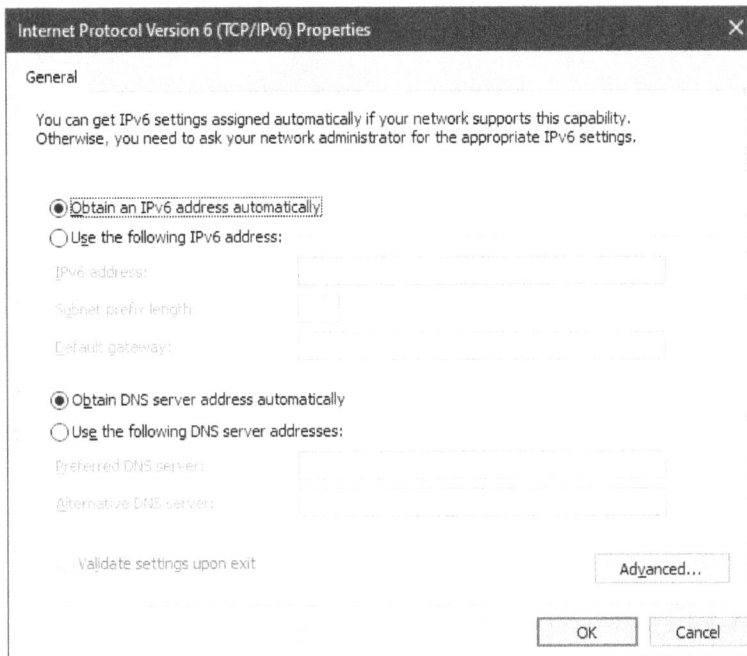

Figure 6.4: *IPv6 configuration on Windows 10*

An IPv6 address contains three components. The first three words (48-bits) are called **Site Prefix**. The next word is a Subnet ID (16 bits), and the last four words (64 bits) represent an Interface ID, also known as a token. *Table 6.2* lists the components of an IPv6 address:

2404:	6800:	4007:	0817:	0000:	0000:	2003:	0010
Prefix			Subnet ID	Interface ID/Token			

Table 6.2: *Components of an IPv6 address*

Modern devices can have multiple interfaces for network communications. So, IPv6 addresses are assigned to an interface rather than the node. It is also possible for an interface to have more than one address.

IPv6 has three types of addresses:

- **Unicast address** is for an interface of a node.

- **Multicast address** identifies a group of interfaces that need not be on the same node. All members in that group receive packets sent to a multicast address group.

- **Anycast address** identifies a group of interfaces generally on different nodes. Packets sent to an anycast address are received by the **physically** closest group member.

- **Loopback address** is ::1

Shortening techniques

The eight words in an IPv6 can sometimes be cumbersome for humans, especially if they have zeros. So, IPv6 uses shortening techniques to make the hexadecimal addresses readable for humans. Some techniques are listed as follows:

- Double colon notation (::) is used to represent contiguous 16-bit fields of zeros.

- A single word of zeros can be represented using a single 0.

- Leading zeros in a word can be omitted.

- To avoid confusion between the colon here and in application port numbers, IPv6 addresses are enclosed by square brackets.

Following these conventions, the IPv6 address mentioned earlier can be shortened as follows:

2404: 6800: 4007: 0817: 0000: 0000: 2003: 0010   becomes [2404:6800:4007:817::2003:10]

Interface IDs

The interface ID deserves a note before we move on. An Interface ID is unique within a subnet and identifies an interface of a node. IPv6 hosts follow the **Neighbor Discovery Protocol** (**NDP**) to generate their own interface IDs using the interface's MAC or EUI-64 address. IPv6 routers and IPv6-enabled servers are configured manually.

Domain Name System

We have seen how IPv4 and IPv6 addresses are assigned to internet-facing hosts. A web server sitting connected to the internet to service requests can be contacted using its IP address. For example, the IPv4 addresses mentioned earlier belong to *Google* India servers. However, an ordinary person cannot be expected to remember the seemingly random sequence of numbers. So, the **Domain Name System** (**DNS**) was designed to make IP addresses accessible to normal users. DNS maintains a 1-to-1 mapping of a website name and the IP address of the web server host. When requested, the DNS server looks up and returns the host's IP address. This allows the users to use website names rather than the cumbersome IPv4 or IPv6 addresses.

Dynamic Host Configuration Protocol

As the number of hosts increases in a network, manually configuring them with IP addresses becomes a challenge. **Dynamic Host Configuration Protocol** (**DHCP**) is designed to overcome this challenge. It allows a host to dynamically request an IP address, subnet mask, router, and DNS addresses. Using the DHCP protocol, a machine can be plugged into the network at an arbitrary moment and expect seamless communication. This facility has become crucial in network admins' daily lives and has contributed to the phenomenal success of Wi-Fi networks in homes and public places. Without this functionality, the mobility of network devices would have been significantly more complicated.

In case a device is unable to obtain an IP address via DHCP, then the device can self-assign an IP address from the class B range of addresses. This is called **Automatic Private IP Addressing (APIPA)**. These addresses range from 169.254.0.1 and 169.254.255.254 and a subnet mask of 255.255.0.0. As explained earlier, this can be displayed as "/16".

Network Address Translation

We discussed private IP addresses earlier. Private IP addresses allow a larger number of devices to connect to the internet without exhausting IP address space. This is achieved by **Network Address Translation (NAT)** and **Port Address Translation (PAT)** on routers and firewalls. A router contains the list of private IP addresses used by the organization and a single public-facing IP address. When intranet devices send an internet access request to the router, the router reads the IP packet. It replaces the outbound request's private IP address with the organization's public IP address and sends it on the internet. When the response is received, it replaces the public IP address in the response with the original IP address and reroutes it to the intranet host. This happens transparently, and neither the host nor the destination knows it. As a result, all hosts in the intranet are **hidden** behind a single public IP address. This process of changing the IP address on outgoing and incoming requests is called NAT. *Figure 6.5* provides a graphical representation of NAT:

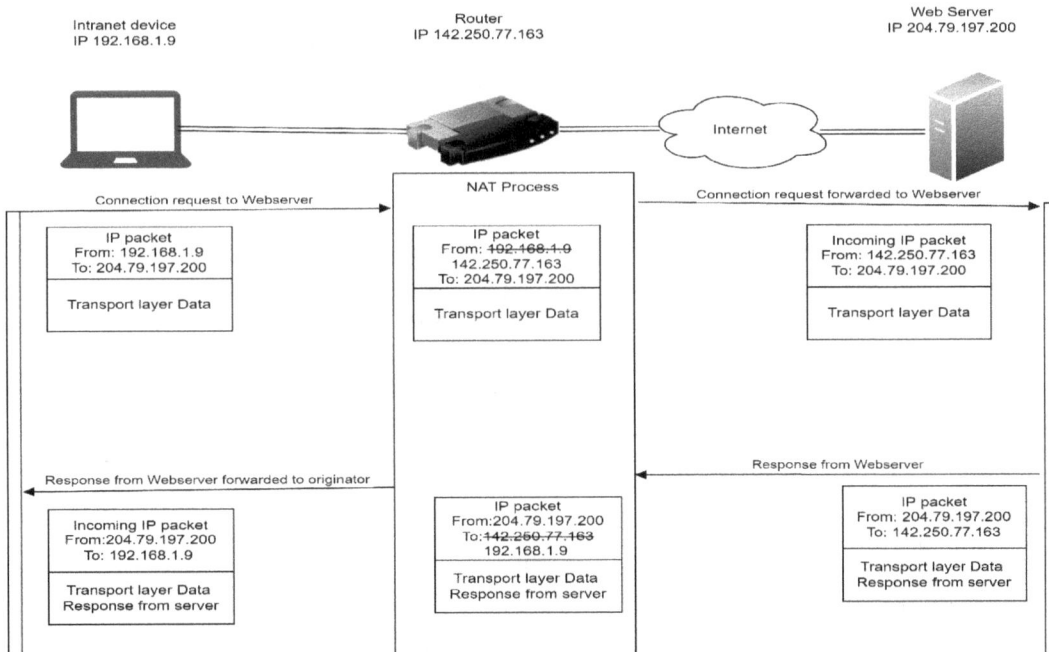

Figure 6.5: NAT in action on a router

This has the added advantage of restricting external network traffic from accessing the internal hosts. The communication has to be originated by internal hosts. Otherwise, an external actor cannot access any internal resources, significantly reducing security threats.

Port Address Translation

PAT serves the same purpose as NAT, allowing multiple hosts to share the same public IP address for internet communication. PAT achieves this by mapping each host's IP address to a software port on the public IP address. You can refer to the *Software and Hardware Ports* section in the previous chapter for more information.

Routing tables

After a router performs NAT, it must send the packet to the intended destination. For this, it must choose the best route traversed by the packet; it uses routing tables for deciding this. A routing table contains information like the networks that are directly/indirectly attached to the router, the route to be taken by the packet for reaching remote networks, and the like. Routers maintain this information statically or dynamically using Border Gateway Protocol, Interior Gateway Routing Protocol, or Routing Information Protocol.

Networking protocols

This section will briefly review some popular networking protocols and their uses. As mentioned in the *Software and Hardware Ports* section of the previous chapter, many networking protocols have port numbers predefined in their RFCs. It is customary but not mandatory to use those port numbers.

The HTTP, HTTPS

Hyper Text Transfer Protocol (HTTP) and **Hyper Text Transfer Protocol Secured (HTTPS)** are used for internet browsing. HTTP defines the rules and standards for transmitting information between browsers and servers on the WWW. HTTP operates on the application layer on port 80. HTTPS is a highly secured version of HTTP and operates at the Transport layer on port 443. HTTPS combines HTTP and SSL/TLS protocols. Refer to *Table 6.3* for a list of differences between HTTP and HTTPS:

HTTP protocol	HTTPS protocol
No built-in security mechanism	Secure the communication using SSL/TLS certificates
Operates at Application Layer	Operates at Transport Layer
Default port is 80	Default port is 443
Transfers data in plain text	Transfers data in cypher/encrypted form

HTTP protocol	HTTPS protocol
Fast compared to HTTPS	Is slow compared to HTTP because of the additional overhead of encryption
Is used strictly when browsing has no risks from security attacks, like a newspaper or blog	Is used for every communication where confidentiality and integrity are needed, like banking websites and emails; it is quickly becoming the default setting on the internet

Table 6.3: Differences between HTTP and HTTPS protocols

The SSH

Secure Shell or **Secure Socket Shell** (**SSH**) provides users with a secure way to access computers over an unsecured network like the internet. SSH provides encrypted data communications between two computers and user authentication using passwords and public keys.

In addition to providing strong encryption, network administrators widely use SSH to manage systems and applications remotely, enabling them to log in to another computer over a network, execute commands, and move files from one computer to another.

The FTP, SFTP, TFTP

File Transfer Protocol (**FTP**) can be used to transfer files between server and client on the internet. It operates on port 21. And SFTP stands for SSH FTP, also called Secure FTP. It is a secured version of FTP and provides encryption of data in transit using SSH. TFTP stands for **Trivial File Transfer Protocol** (**TFTP**) and is a lightweight FTP to transfer files without the overheads of FTP. It is used in SAN and NAS for downloading the bootup operating system image.

The SMTP, POP, and IMAP

In the early days of the internet, email was the lifeline of internet communications. Exchanging emails between users and servers is accomplished using **Simple Message Transfer Protocol** (**SMTP**). SMTP is used to push an email message. Other protocols like **Post Office Protocol** (**POP**) and **Internet Message Access Protocol** (**IMAP**) are used by the receiver to pull emails.

The NTP and NTS

Network Time Protocol (**NTP**) is used to synchronize computer clocks over the internet. Computers can automatically set their clocks and time zones using this protocol. India's official internet time server is maintained by the *National Physical Laboratory* and is available at *time.nplindia.org*.

Network Time Security (NTS) is a secure version of NTP. It allows for client-side authentication to avoid impersonators employing the man-in-the-middle attack.

Cloud networks

So far, we have discussed how networks are built and maintained in private data centers using physical devices. In this section, let us discuss how this works in the cloud and with virtual machines.

As discussed in the chapter *Managing Virtual Machines*, Hypervisors spawn and maintain virtual machines in the cloud. These virtual machines behave almost the same as physical machines. This includes having virtual network interfaces as well. This is easy to understand at the application layer. However, it is crucial to understand the workings of TCP, IP, and MAC layers. The IP address assigned to all VMs on a physical VM must be consistent to ensure seamless VM transitions to different physical machines. This mechanism ensures that multiple VMs on the same machine can possess distinct IPs and operate efficiently.

The answer to all these questions lies in network virtualization.

Network virtualization

Network virtualization is the technique of abstracting the network hardware resources into software. NV is a special-purpose software that can create an overlay on top of the physical network and combine multiple physical networks into a virtual software network. This overlay can create separate virtual networks for use by different VMs.

NV software operates on the IP layer of the underlying communication medium. It can deliver network components like switches, routers, firewalls, load balancers, and VPNs. All IP layer and higher (TCP and application layer protocols) communication from the VMs is tunnelled into an IP packet and is communicated using the physical hardware by the hypervisor. By doing this, the network services are decoupled from the physical hardware. Programmatic creation and management of all network components is possible with this technique. Every VM and application in the cloud has an attached networking and security policy. When the VM moves to another hypervisor, the policies are applied on the new hypervisor, giving the same configuration to the VM/application. This makes the host movement completely transparent to the application. The same applies when scaling the application as well. Take a look at *Figure 6.6* to understand how NV is implemented in the cloud.

It should be mentioned here that sometimes the physical fabric is called underlay, and the tunnel is called overlay for clear differentiation.

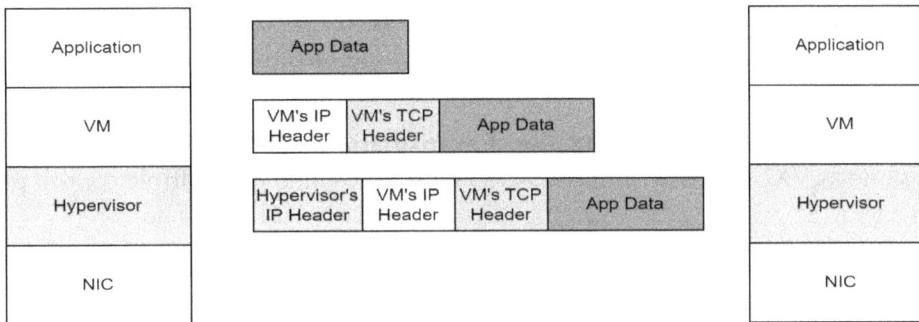

Figure 6.6: Tunnelling of VMs data packets in Hypervisor data packets

Network function virtualization

Network functions virtualisation (**NFV**) replaces network appliance hardware with virtual machines. The processes of routing, switching, and load balancing run on a VM instead of a physical device. Network admins can configure all network components the same way they configure a physical device, except they do so on a virtual machine. A hypervisor or software-defined networking controller executes the configuration in the back end. The following list describes how a virtualized network component differs from its physical counterpart:

- Cloud Firewalls serve the same purpose as physical firewalls. However, unlike a physical firewall device, a cloud-based firewall is dispersed throughout the network. The filtering of incoming/outgoing connections occurs at the cloud level for each application. Some organizations offer firewall-as-a-service for organizations wanting to use IaaS clouds. Next-Generation Firewalls are used for securing VMs offering PaaS and SaaS services.

- Cloud load balancer runs as a software load balancer. It splits the network traffic across multiple machines and is used to ensure scalability. They are particularly useful for taking maximum advantage of the elastic computing properties of the cloud.

- Cloud proxy can integrate with an organization's authentication service (for example, single sign-on) to secure network data. A cloud proxy's behavior closely resembles that of a reverse proxy.

Examples of network virtualization

Network virtualization can be implemented in two ways: Virtual LAN and virtual extensible LAN. Let us look at these:

- **Virtual LAN** (**VLAN**) is a sub-section of a LAN. Using software, it combines network devices into a single group, regardless of their physical location.

- **Virtual extensible local area network** (**VXLAN**) is a framework for overlaying Link layers on top of the Internet layer. It defines an encapsulation mechanism and a control plane.

- **Generic Network Virtualization Encapsulation** (**GENEVE**) is conceptually the same as VXLAN, with additional flexibility provided by multiple control planes.

Virtual Private Clouds

A **Virtual Private Cloud** (**VPC**) is a virtual network closely resembling a traditional network's private data centers from a usage perspective. It secures connections between VMs and cloud resources using **IP Security** (**IPSec**) VPN. It is used to build isolated and highly secure network infrastructure in the cloud for applications. Complicated network topologies can be built for VMs using VPCs. VPCs provide a sophisticated solution to hybrid clouds. Using VPCs, the resources in public clouds can communicate with private data centre resources like DHCP and DNS servers.

Software-Defined Networking

software-defined networking (**SDN**) is an architecture that decouples network control software logic from the network devices. As an example, an SDN separates routing logic from the router device. This architecture allows the software configuration to be modified via programming. As a result, modifying a network infrastructure becomes a programming activity and greatly simplifies infrastructure management.

SDNs have a controller component that overlays the network hardware. The controller separates the network control plane and forwarding plane from the underlying infrastructure. Controllers are controllable via programming, enabling centralized control over the network for the organization. Without SDN, both physical and virtual network components are aware of only the components directly connected to them. SDN architecture allows a centralized view of the entire network. SDN consists of three components that work together using a programmable networking protocol called **OpenFlow**:

- **Software applications**: They communicate with VMs or customer software to process network resource allocation requests.

- **SDN controllers**: They communicate with the mentioned applications to route data packets to the appropriate destinations. Within the context of SDNs, the behavior of a controller can be compared to load balancers.

- **Networking devices**: They receive instructions from the controllers regarding how to route the packets.

Refer to *Figure 6.7* for an architectural block diagram of SDNs:

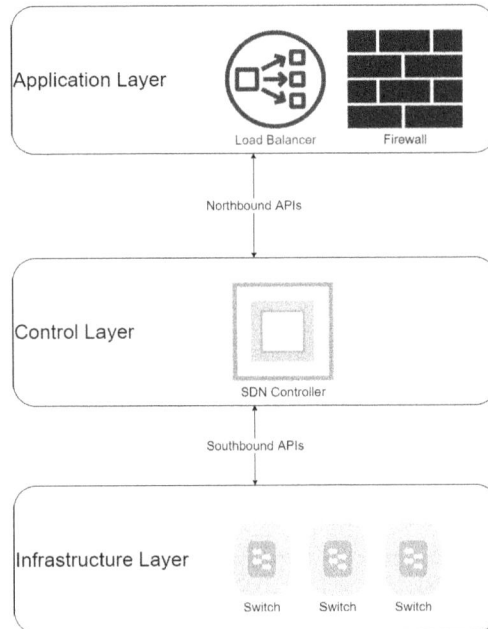

Figure 6.7: Architecture of SDNs

SDN architecture offers several benefits to both cloud service providers and cloud users. Some of the benefits are as follows:

- Ease of network control due to the programmability of network behavior.
- Agility to reshape the network dynamically by managing the traffic flow.
- Increased security by virtue of centralized administration to specify policies and access controls.
- Automation of network resource creation and configuration.
- The need for vendor-specific solutions is avoided by using open controllers.

SDNs can be categorized into four primary types:

- Open SDNs are characterized by their usage of open protocols to control the routing devices.
- API SDNs use application programming interfaces to control the data flow from the device. These APIs are called **southbound APIs**.
- Overlay Model SDNs perform network virtualization to create channels and tunnel data in these channels.
- Hybrid Model SDNs combine SDN and traditional networking. They are an intermediate step between a traditional data center and full-fledged SDN adoption.

The SDN and NV

Combined with network virtualization, SDN allows all components of a network to be virtualizable and controlled individually and programmatically. Combining SDN and NV is one of the key features of cloud environments. It is a misconception that they are the same. A well-designed combination of SDN and NV can yield rich dividends in terms of security and costs for organizations. Cloud service providers can offer highly flexible networks to customers by combining SDN and NV in their offerings.

Conclusion

We started this chapter with an explanation of IP addresses. We then learned how to interpret IPv4 and IPv6 addresses and their classes, and we understood how subnets are used to identify networks and hosts. We also learned how various network components are used to create the Internet as we know it. Further on, we looked at some of the protocols that are used on the internet. Lastly, we saw how these features are available in the cloud.

The next chapter will cover the critical topics related to security. We shall deep dive into different aspects of security, Identity and Access Management, encryption and decryption, security protocols for network communication, and security implementation in cloud. We shall learn about the security of data and APIs, which are the basis of all modern web applications that we use in our everyday lives.

Glossary

- **Binary Octet:** A sequence of 8 bits
- **Binary Word:** A sequence of 2 octets
- **Class A addresses:** A range of IP addresses reserved for large networks
- **Class B addresses:** A range of IP addresses reserved for medium networks
- **Class C addresses:** A range of IP addresses reserved for small LANs
- **Class D addresses:** A range of IP addresses reserved for multicasting
- **Class E addresses:** A range of IP addresses reserved for research purposes
- **DHCP:** Dynamic Host Configuration Protocol
- **DNS:** Domain Name System
- **GENEVE:** Generic Network Virtualization Encapsulation
- **Host ID:** The fragment of an IP address that uniquely identifies the host for a given network
- **IMAP:** Internet Message Access Protocol
- **IPSec:** Internet Protocol Security

- **Loopback address:** A range of IP addresses that allow a device to send and receive its own data packets

- **Multicast address:** An IP address that can be used to communicate with multiple devices on a network in a one-to-many communication style

- **NDP:** Neighbour Discovery Protocol

- **Network Address Translation:** A technique implemented on Routers, Firewalls, and Proxies to allow several devices to connect to the internet without consuming additional IP addresses

- **Network ID:** The fragment of IP address that uniquely identifies the network for a given host

- **Network virtualization:** A technique of abstracting network hardware via software

- **NTP:** Network Time Protocol

- **NTS:** Network Time Security

- **POP:** Post Office Protocol

- **Port Address Translation:** A technique implemented on Routers, Firewalls and Proxies to allow several devices to connect to internet without consuming additional IP addresses

- **Private IP addresses:** A range of IP addresses in every class reserved for internal use

- **Routing Table:** A routing information stored in and used by routers to determine the optimum path to send a data packet

- **SDN:** Software-defined networking

- **SFTP:** Secure File Transfer Protocol

- **SMTP:** Simple Mail Transfer Protocol

- **SSH:** Secure Socket Shell

- **Subnet mask:** A binary number used to indicate the network and host ID fragments of an IP address

- **Subnetting:** Logically partitioning an IP network into multiple, smaller network segments

- **Supernetting:** Logical grouping of multiple networks into a bigger network

- **TFTP:** Trivial File Transfer Protocol

- **Unicast address:** An IP address that represents a unique device on a network

- **VLAN:** Virtual local area network

- **VPC:** Virtual Private Clouds

- **VXLAN:** Virtual extensible local area network

Practice questions

S. No.	Questions		Answers
1	**Which of the following is the default subnet mask for class A IPv4 address?**		A
	A) 255.0.0.0	B) 255.255.0.0	
	C) 255.255.255.0	D) 255.255.255.255	
2	**Which of the following is the default subnet mask for class B IPv4 address?**		B
	A) 255.0.0.0	B) 255.255.0.0	
	C) 255.255.255.0	D) 255.255.255.255	
3	**Which of the following is the default subnet mask for class C IPv4 address?**		C
	A) 255.0.0.0	B) 255.255.0.0	
	C) 255.255.255.0	D) 255.255.255.255	
4	**Which of the following is a multi-cast IPv4 address?**		A
	A) 225.10.124.38	B) 127.0.255.0	
	C) 245.10.124.38	D) 192.168.12.24	
5	**Which of the following is a loop back IPv4 address?**		B
	A) 225.10.124.38	B) 127.0.255.0	
	C) 245.10.124.38	D) 192.168.12.24	
6	**Which of the following IPv4 addresses is reserved for research use?**		C
	A) 225.10.124.38	B) 127.0.255.0	
	C) 245.10.124.38	D) 192.168.12.24	
7	**Which if the following IPv4 addresses is a class C private address?**		D
	A) 225.10.124.38	B) 127.0.255.0	
	C) 245.10.124.38	D) 192.168.12.24	
8	**A network administrator configured a router's IPv4 subnet mask as 255.0.0.0. Which of the following IP addresses should the router consider private addresses?**		A
	A) 10.0.0.0 to 10.255.255.255	B) 169.254.0.0 to 169.254.255.255 and 172.16.0.0.to 172.31.255.255	
	C) 192.168.0.0. to 192.168.255.255	D) None of the above	
9	**A network administrator configured a router's IPv4 subnet mask as 255.255.0.0. Which of the following IP addresses should the router consider private addresses?**		B
	A) 10.0.0.0 to 10.255.255.255	B) 169.254.0.0 to 169.254.255.255 and 172.16.0.0.to 172.31.255.255	
	C) 192.168.0.0. to 192.168.255.255	D) None of the above	

S. No.	Questions		Answers
10	A router receives a network packet with a destination address. How should the router determine whether the packet is destined for its own network?		B
	A) Router should refer to the routing tables	B) Router should identify the Network ID using the subnet mask and compare it with its own	
	C) Both A & B	D) Neither A nor B	
11	A router's IP address is 142.250.77.163 and subnet mask is 255.255.255.0. It received a data packet with the destination address 142.250.77.180. What should the router do?		B
	A) Forward the packet based on routing tables	B) Route the packet to internal network	
	C) Drop the packet	D) None of the above	
12	A router's IP address is 142.250.77.163 and subnet mask is 255.255.255.0. It receives a data packet with destination address as 142.250.132.120. What should the router do?		A
	A) Forward the packet based on routing tables	B) Route the packet to internal network	
	C) Drop the packet	D) None of the above	
13	A router's IP address is 142.250.77.163 and subnet mask is 255.255.255.0. It receives a data packet with destination address as 192.250.132.120. What should the router do?		B
	A) Forward the packet based on routing tables	B) Route the packet to internal network	
	C) Drop the packet	D) None of the above	
14	Which of the following is a loopback address in IPv6?		D
	A) 127.0.0.1	B) 127:0:0:0:0:0:0:1	
	C) 127:::::1	D) ::1	
15	Which of the following is a valid shortening of the IPv6 address 2401:0049:1cb9:0000:0000:7c3d:0000:9eef?		A
	A) [2401:49:1cb9::7c3d:0:9eef]	B) [2401:49:1cb9:0:0:7c3d:0:9eef]	
	C) [2401.0049.1cb9.0000.0000.7c3d.000 0.9eef]	D) [2401.49.1cb9..7c3d.0.9eef]	

S. No.	Questions		Answers
16	**A router receives an outgoing packet from a machine within its network. It performs the following operations on the packet. What is this technique called?**		A
	i. Replace the source IP address of the packet with its own IP address		
	ii. Transmit the packet		
	iii. Receive response from the destination		
	iv. Replace the destination address of the response with the source IP address in step i.		
	A) Network Address Translation	B) Port Address Translation	
	C) Both A & B	D) None of the above	
17	**A router received an outgoing packet from a machine within its network. It performs the following operations on the packet. What is this technique called?**		B
	i. Replace the source IP address of the packet with its own IP address and a software port number dedicated to the source		
	ii. Transmit the packet on that software port		
	iii. Receive response from the destination		
	iv. Replace the destination address of the response with the source IP address in step i.		
	A) Network Address Translation	B) Port Address Translation	
	C) Both A & B	D) None of the above	
18	**A computer is booted up and needs to connect to internet. Which protocol should it follow for obtaining an IP address?**		C
	A) DNS	B) Dynamic IP	
	C) DHCP	D) All of the above	
19	**A computer is configured to use the same IP address every time it is booted. What is this technique known as?**		B
	A) Sticky IP addressing	B) Static IP addressing	
	C) DHCP	D) All of the above	
20	**A web server is hosting a blog where no sensitive information is exchanged between the blog visitor and server. What protocol is recommended here?**		D
	A) SSH	B) FTP	
	C) NTP	D) HTTP	
21	**Which of the following is not an advantage of HTTPS over HTTP?**		B
	A) Security	B) Speed	
	C) Both A & B	D) Neither A nor B	

S. No.	Questions		Answers
22	**Which of the following statements about HTTPS is true?** **1. HTTPS operated as Transport layer** **2. Default port is 443** **3. Data transmission is encrypted** **4. Is slower compared to HTTP**		D
	A) 1, 2 only	B) 3, 4 only	
	C) 1, 2 and 3 only	D) All are true	
23	**Which of the following protocols is ideally suited for loading OS image at bootup time?**		A
	A) TFTP	B) HTTPS	
	C) POP	D) All of the above	
24	**Which of the following protocols are used for email communications?**		D
	A) POP	B) IMAP	
	C) SMTP	D) All of the above	
25	**Which of the following addresses is not determinable by the cloud user by default?**		C
	A) Virtual machine's name	B) Virtual machine's IP address	
	C) Virtual machine's MAC address	D) None of the above	
26	**What is the industry name for the approach of programmatically managing a network configuration?**		B
	A) Virtual networking	B) Software-defined networking	
	C) Robotic process automation	D) All of the above	
30	**Which of the following is not an advantage of software-defined networking?**		D
	A) Ease of network control	B) Improved security	
	C) Dynamic reshaping of network traffic	D) Decentralised administration	
31	**An SDN controller communicates with the application layer using which of the following types of APIS?**		C
	A) Eastbound APIs	B) Westbound APIs	
	C) Northbound APIs	D) Southbound APIs	
32	**An SDN controller communicates with infrastructure devices using which of the following types of APIS?**		D
	A) Eastbound APIs	B) Westbound APIs	
	C) Northbound APIs	D) Southbound APIs	

Join our Discord space

Join our Discord workspace for latest updates, offers, tech happenings around the world, new releases, and sessions with the authors:

https://discord.bpbonline.com

CHAPTER 7

Managing Security

Introduction

It is often said that when you connect to the internet, you do not gain access to the internet; instead, the internet gains access to you. Cyberspace is a dangerous place. Hackers, spoofers, scammers, and other unsavory characters prowl the networks looking to steal your data. Constant vigilance is the only recourse from these cyber criminals and their tactics. In the days before computers came into being, all organization assets were physical. Damaging any assets required physical damage. When computers changed the paradigm and digitized assets, the paradigm changed for the anarchists as well. They could cause much more damage with little effort.

Cybersecurity is a relatively new spawned discipline due to this scenario. It was a simple physical lock to prevent the machines from being stolen in the earliest days, and soon evolved into a sophisticated domain. It now contains multiple sub-disciplines and guiding principles to guide its implementation. A new C-level position called Chief Information Security Officer is created to handle cybersecurity.

Cybersecurity plays an even more critical role in the era of cloud computing. Cloud machines are always connected to the internet, with data in the cloud. Ensuring system security requires careful planning by network admins, application architects, developers, and users. Security is like a shield. Any chink in the armor can be exploited to bring down the system like the mighty Achilles was felled by an arrow to his heel.

Structure

We will cover the following topics in this chapter:

- Security
- Encryption
- Network security threats
- Security mechanisms
- Cloud security implementations

Objectives

We will discuss security in this chapter. Security is an extremely important topic. It is often said *there is nothing called too much security*. Security threats and strategies are vast and varied. Security is so vast a topic that CompTIA offers a separate certification program for it. However, for the purpose of the CVO-003 exam, we shall limit our discussion to aspects that are relevant to cloud operation and utilization.

Let us start with clearing some misconceptions. It is often assumed by novices that implementing a cloud solution will automatically take care of all security challenges. This is not the case. Security is a very broad topic, and there are many facets to it. No cloud service provider can provide blanket protection against all security threats. As with everything else, security responsibilities are shared between CSPs and customers. AWS explains this sharing very well by dividing the responsibilities as the security *of the cloud* and *in the cloud*. AWS is responsible for the security of the cloud, and customers are responsible for security in the cloud. Refer to *Figure 7.1* from the AWS website explaining this. The AWS cloud responsibility model can be read at **https://aws.amazon.com/compliance/shared-responsibility-model/**.

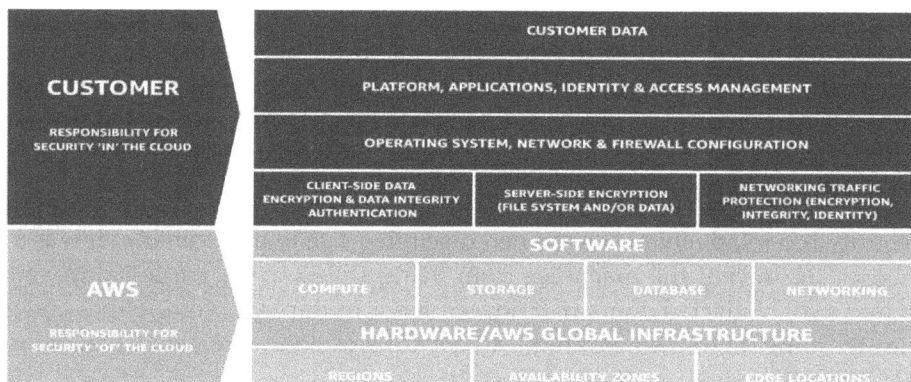

Figure 7.1: Shared responsibility model for security

Figure 7.1 is a general indication of responsibility distribution; the specifics vary depending on whether the CSP provider is offering IaaS, PaaS, or SaaS. Refer to *Table 7.1* for a clearer explanation of responsibility distribution:

Aspect	IaaS	PaaS	SaaS
Servers and Storage	CSP	CSP	CSP
Runtime Environments	User	CSP	CSP
Networks	User	CSP	CSP
Operating Systems	User	CSP	CSP
Data	User	CSP	CSP
Middleware	User	User	CSP
Applications	User	User	CSP
Authentication (passwords and so on)	User	User	User

Table 7.1: Security responsibility sharing in cloud models

Considering the mentioned models, it is imperative for cloud engineers, administrators, and project managers to be familiar with various aspects of security. As organizations' cloud landscapes increase in complexity, a thorough understanding of various facets of security is unavoidable. In this chapter, we shall discuss both aspects of cloud security, that is, *of the cloud* and *in the cloud*.

The interesting aspect of security is that the building blocks of security are the same wherever they are used. The algorithms and techniques vary depending on the situation, but the concepts remain the same. Irrespective of the layer where security is needed, that is, either security of servers, networks, or applications, the security requirements remain the same. The algorithms can vary from simple symmetric encryption to complex public key infrastructure-based encryption.

We will start by defining the expectations on security using the CIA triad and Parkerian Hexad. Then, we shall proceed to discuss the models available to evaluate them and look at the various algorithms available to achieve each of these aspects. When discussing security, we must consider security for both data and systems. Data security threats differ from system security threats, and different techniques and solutions are needed to address them. We shall discuss them here in detail.

We shall restrict the discussion in this chapter to security in the cloud. Generally speaking, security of the cloud deals with physical security requirements for the cloud infrastructure and is out of scope for the CVO-003 exam.

Security

There is a joke in the airline industry: the best and most secure way to avoid airplane hijacking is to sedate all the passengers for the duration of the flight. While that might be a sound approach for avoiding hijacking, it is impractical for obvious reasons.

Security implementation for any software application is a similar scenario. There are several security solutions available, but only a few suit the needs. You need a sounding board to evaluate the security solutions, and this section discusses the most popular aspects to be considered for security. CIA triad and Parkerian Hexad are two such sounding boards.

CIA triad

Systems and data security aspects are generally described using the CIA triad. CIA stands for Confidentiality, Integrity, and Availability. It covers both data security and systems security. Throughout the rest of the section, the word *assets* shall refer to data and systems. Refer to *Figure 7.2* for the CIA triad:

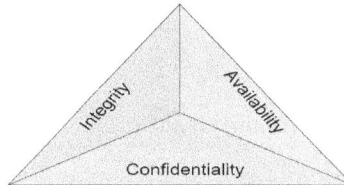

Figure 7.2: CIA triad

The following list explains these terms:

- **Confidentiality** refers to assets being accessible only by the people authorized to access them.

- **Integrity** refers to data being received as it was sent. The words **sent** and **received** are not limited to transmission time.

- **Availability** refers to assets being available when they are needed. The inability to access assets at a time of need is considered an availability failure.

Parkerian Hexad

While the CIA triad is the most popular model for discussing cybersecurity, other models like Parkerian Hexad are also used. *Figure 7.3* illustrates the Parkerian Hexad model. It is a matter of debate whether Parkerian Hexad is superior to the CIA triad.

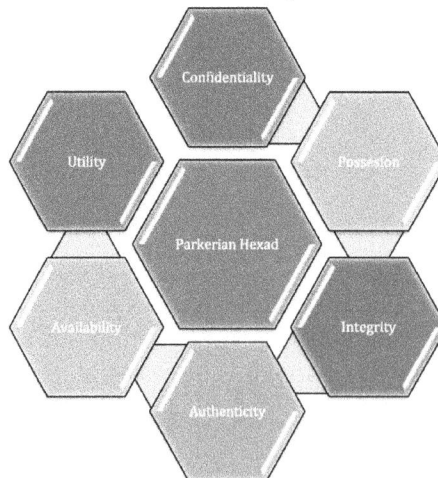

Figure 7.3: Parkerian Hexad

Following is the explanation of terms introduced by *Parkerian Hexad*. The CIA terms have been discussed previously:

- Possession refers to assets being in the control of the rightful owner.

- Authenticity refers to the genuineness, verifiability, and trustworthiness of data.

- Utility refers to the usefulness of the data to the possessor. This is the only aspect of Parkerian Hexad to take non-binary values. This is because data can have multiple levels of usefulness to the possessor.

Here is an example for discussing possession, authenticity, and utility. Let us say an organization collects credit card data from its users and stores them in encrypted form. If the database is not hacked, then the organization is in possession of the data. If a hacker gets access to the database, then they are also in possession of it. Encryption ensures that their utility with the data is zero.

For the rest of this chapter, we will discuss security with reference to the CIA triad. This is owing both due its simplicity and popularity in the industry. Professionals interested in security certifications will need to learn the nuances between these models. A detailed comparison of these and other models is out of scope for CVO-003.

Confidentiality

Confidentiality refers to assets being accessible only by the people authorized to access them. People or processes unauthorized to access a given asset should not be able to do so. An excellent example of this is a country's defence and military information. The defence capabilities of any country are a top-level secret known only to a few individuals. On the other hand, the government leader's name, its exact borders, and the like are openly accessible to anyone worldwide. Both of these are pieces of government information. While the former is a national security secret and requires the highest level of clearance, the latter is a matter of public record and is freely accessible to all.

The confidentiality of any system is maintained using a combination of identity and access control mechanisms and classification levels. IAM and classification levels complement each other to offer a high level of confidentiality.

Identity and Access Management

As mentioned earlier, confidentiality levels are for assets but tagging of assets means little if they cannot be enforced. Classifying an asset as **top secret** offers little value if we cannot judge whether the requestor is eligible for that access level. It would be like a random human walking into an army office and trying to read the *top-secret* files. That is not acceptable. **Identity and Access Management (IAM)** is the solution for this scenario. It has two facets. One is confirming the requester's identity, and the other is verifying that the requester is cleared to access the asset. Non-repudiation is an integral part of identity confirmation. IAM is an interesting topic and deserves a thorough discussion. We shall discuss it in detail in the next chapter.

Classification levels

Let us expand on the government data example mentioned earlier. Governments regularly produce data ranging from census details and voter lists to espionage information. Spy agencies meticulously follow the **need to know** maxim to share data. This need to know forms the basis for classification levels. Assets are grouped into specific categories: highly sensitive or restricted access, and so on. Then, based on the user's role and their need to know, access is provided for the assets. Only authorized users can access the assets after proving their identity. For example, the *Government of India* has declared these levels for government assets: "top secret", "secret", "confidential", "restricted", and "unclassified"[1]. The levels are explained as shown in *Figure 7.4*:

7. Information classification guidelines

7.1.   Information classification

All information available with organizations should be classified into one of the following categories (based on existing classification of Manual on paper records issued by Ministry of Home Affairs, 1994):

7.1.1.Top Secret: Information, unauthorized disclosure of which could be expected to cause exceptionally grave damage to the national security or national interest. This category is reserved for nation's closest secrets and is to be used with great reserve

7.1.2.Secret: Information, unauthorized disclosure of which could be expected to cause serious damage to the national security or national interest or cause serious embarrassment in its functioning. This classification should be used for highly important information and is the highest classification normally used

7.1.3.Confidential: Information, unauthorized disclosure of which could be expected to cause damage to the security of the organization or could be prejudicial to the interest of the organization, or could affect the organization in its functioning. Most information, on proper analysis, will be classified no higher than confidential

7.1.4.Restricted: Information, which is essentially meant for official use only and which would not be published or communicated to anyone except for official purpose

7.1.5.Unclassified: Information that requires no protection against disclosure. e.g. Public releases

Figure 7.4: Information classification levels from the Government of India

It is important to remember that these classes have a sequence. As we move up the order, the security sensitivity increases, and fewer people are authorized to know that information. Every asset should be tagged with exactly one level of information. However, sometimes, an asset is classified with two different levels. It is important to have a guiding principle for such tie-break situations when designing security systems. The *official secrets act of India* [2] introduced in colonial times, is an example of such a guiding principle. Generally, the guiding principle is that the *highest level* takes precedence. In other scenarios, the *lowest level* might be acceptable. *Infosys* has achieved a high level of transparency and trust with its *when in doubt, please disclose* principle. Choosing the guiding principle is a matter of high importance and is generally decided at the highest levels of the organization.

In the example of the *Government of India*, the access levels will be ordered as follows:

Top Secret | Secret | Confidential | Restricted | Unclassified

Bell-LaPadula model

Confidentiality implementation in an organisation is generally checked using the Bell-LaPadula model. It has three rules. They define the approaches for allowing requesters to read-write information and assets. The model uses the word **subject** to refer to the requester, and we will follow the same. The idea behind this model is that a subject can **read down**, **write up**. This model has three rules:

- Simple confidentiality or no read-up rule says that subjects can read and write information in classes to which they have clearance, and lower classes, but cannot read higher class data.

- Star confidentiality or no write-down rule says that subjects can write information in classes they have clearance in and in higher classes, but not in lower classes.

- Strong confidentiality or no read/write-up down says that subjects can read and write information only in classes they have clearance, not in higher or lower classes. This is the most restrictive rule among the three.

Table 7.2 provides a tabular representation of the **Bell-LaPadula model**:

Confidentiality rule	Access control	Lower class	Same level class	Higher class
Simple	Mandatory	Can Read	Can Read	Cannot Read
Star	Mandatory	Cannot Write	Can Write	Can Write
Strong	Discretionary	-	Can Read, Can Write	-

Table 7.2: Bell-LaPadula model for confidentiality

Once the IAM system and confidentiality levels are in place, the Bell-LaPadula model can be used to evaluate the effectiveness of confidentiality.

Integrity

Integrity refers to data being received as it was sent. The words **sent** and **received** are not limited to transmission time. In general, data meant for another should reach the recipient the way it was sent. Data integrity will be compromised by third parties tampering with the data without the knowledge of either party. When we post a letter, we would not want the contents of the letter to be modified in transit. All sorts of complications can arise if this condition is not met. Starting from someone intercepting your data to sending misinformation in your name, the possibilities for mischief are endless.

The same problem holds even with computers. Integrity generally refers to data. When data is stored or sent over the network, we do not want anyone to modify it without our knowledge. While confidentiality ensures that only authorised users can read and modify the information, it does not detect malicious modifications to data. Integrity takes care of that.

Note the following conventions for data; we will use these conventions in the rest of the chapter:

- When data is transmitted, it is generally called **data in transit**.

- When data is not being transmitted, that is, in a file or database, it is called **data at rest**.

Data integrity has requirements like data consistency, prevention and detection of unauthorized modification, and non-repudiation of data. It is important to ensure an honest and trustworthy operating environment in the organization.

Biba model

Integrity implementation in an organisation is generally checked using the Biba model. It is almost an inverse of the Bell-LaPadula model. It has three rules as well, which are listed as follows. The idea behind this model is to ensure that a process with a given level of clearance cannot corrupt data at a higher level, referred to as **read up, write down**.

- Simple integrity or no read-down rule says that a subject at a given integrity class cannot read data at a lower class.

- Star integrity or no write-up rule says that a subject at a given integrity class cannot write data to a higher class.

- Invocation property says that a subject at a given integrity class cannot request access to a higher class.

Refer to *Table 7.3* for a representation of the Biba model:

Integrity rule	Access control	Lower class	Same level class	Higher class
Simple	Mandatory	Cannot read	Can read	Cannot read
Star	Mandatory	Can write	Can write	Cannot write
Invocation	Discretionary	Can read and write	Can read and write	Cannot access

Table 7.3: Biba model for integrity

IAM cannot help with data integrity measures. Data integrity is generally achieved either by message digests or by encryption.

Apart from the Bell-LaPadula and Biba models, several other models are used in the industry. Some of the more notable examples are state machine model, take-grant model, access control matrix, Clark-Wilson model, brewer and Nash model (also known as Chinese Wall), and the like.

Let us now look at a few algorithm families that help in achieving data integrity.

Message digests

Message digest is a technique for detecting unauthorised data modification. It is a mathematical function that works on arbitrary data length and generates a fixed-length output. If the original data is modified even by a single bit, the output, called **hash**, will be different. By sending the data and original hash separately, it will be easy to determine whether the data is modified during transit. Popular message digest algorithms are MD5, SHA, and BLAKE, and their versions.

Encryption

Encryption converts the information (called **plain text**) into a different form, called cipher text, using a clearly defined methodology. This is a reversible process; plain text can be achieved if the conversion procedure is known. The encryption and decryption processes need a key, a secret piece of information known only to the sender and receiver. Without knowing the key, recipients cannot understand the data. Encryption has been known to humanity for a long time, with the earliest known attempt named **Caesar's Cipher**. We shall discuss encryption in the upcoming sections. By combining message digest and encryption, organizations can achieve considerable data integrity.

Encryption is a go-to approach in the software industry for achieving data integrity for both data at rest and data in transit, and the cloud is no exception.

Availability

Availability refers to assets being available when they are needed. The inability to access assets at a time of need is considered availability failure. High availability systems should be available nearly 100% of the time. They should plan for **force majeure** contingencies like power outages, floods, and the like. They should also plan for security threats like Denial of Service, ransomware attacks, and the like, which can bring down systems and prevent their availability.

Denial of Service

Denial of Service (DoS) is a brute-force attack on the system. Attackers send an overwhelmingly large number of requests to the system, making it unavailable for other users. DoS is a simple but effective attack on availability. Organizations need to carefully architect their applications to distinguish between genuinely heavy and malicious workloads.

Techniques like blocking selective IP addresses have been implemented to restrict DoS attacks. It is also common for many organisations to block the ICMP port on their internet-facing machines to prevent DoS from using ping requests.

Distributed Denial of Service (DDoS) is a technique employed by hackers to circumvent IP blocking. DoS attacks happen simultaneously from multiple locations, making IP blocking very ineffective.

Generally, cloud providers have sufficient internet and computing bandwidth to prevent outages. With the autoscaling feature, cloud applications can spawn additional VMs to withstand a reasonable volume of DoS attacks. However, organizations risk running up their expenses in such cases. Approaches like quotas and limits can be used to prevent this, but they need careful balancing against making systems unavailable to genuine users.

Malware and ransomware

Malware is software that gets installed on a computer either by mistake or by surreptitious means. Once installed, malware can perform various damages, from showing excessive advertisements to stealing information. Ransomware is a type of malware that renders the system unusable. Attackers generally ask for monetary or other favours to restore access. Malware generally is an attack on the availability of the system.

Encryption

Encryption is a technique for converting information into a different form and hiding its true meaning. The study of encryption and decryption is called **cryptography**. Encryption is fast becoming a ubiquitous approach for all internet communication. Well-designed encryption can make brute-force decryption impractical, if not impossible.

The basic tenet of encryption is easy to understand. Encryption is a mathematical function with two inputs. One input is called plain text, which is the original information. A second input is called a key, which is a secret known only to the sender and receiver. Using these two inputs, the function shall algorithmically encode the information to produce a cipher text output. The cipher text can be input to another function, along with the key, to reverse the encryption and get the plain text. So long as the key is a secret, the information remains secret. The earliest known encryption was Caesar's Cipher, where the algorithm was a simple replacement of each letter in the alphabet with a different one. Since then, the encryption process has improved significantly. The length of the key plays an important role in the security strength of the algorithm. Longer keys are more resistant to brute-force attacks and offer greater security.

Encryption algorithms work in two different ways. The plain text is divided into equal-sized blocks, and the encryption function is run on one block at a time to produce cipher text; this is called **block encryption**. The other way is that algorithms accept data in binary bits and encrypt one bit at a time; this is called **stream encryption**.

Symmetric encryption

Symmetric encryption is where the key used for the encryption algorithm is the same as the one used for decryption. This is like using a lock and key. The same key should be used for locking and unlocking. Examples of symmetric key encryption algorithms are Blowfish, AES, DES, and IDEA.

Asymmetric encryption

For a long time, the key used for encryption and decryption had to be the same. Then came algorithms like RSA, where the encryption key is different from the decryption key; this came to be known as public key encryption. A public key is used to encrypt data, and a private key is used to decrypt it. Every receiver has a pair of keys. The public key is announced openly, and anyone can use it to encrypt the data being sent to the receiver. Only the receiver possesses the private key and can use it to decrypt data, and this greatly improves data security. Communication protocols like TLS and SSL use asymmetric encryption extensively. RSA is the most widely used asymmetric key encryption algorithm. ECC is a relatively recent algorithm developed for this purpose.

Block encryption

As explained earlier, in block encryption, the plain-text data is broken down into blocks and encrypted one block at a time. The encryption key can either be provided to the algorithm or be generated from each encrypted block. Popular block encryption algorithms are RC5, DES, AES, DSA, and RSA.

Stream encryption

Unlike block encryption, stream encryption works on a single bit at a time. Consequently, it can work on arbitrarily long data sizes and is much faster than block encryption. Popular stream encryption algorithms are RC4, FISH, and the like. The Enigma machine used in WWII was one of the first large-scale uses of stream encryption. The plain text should be at least as long as the cipher key here.

Speed and simplicity of operation are the main advantages of stream encryption. However, a stream cipher is less secure as compared to block encryption. The positional alignment of cipher text and plain text makes key deduction easier.

Note: **While symmetric keys are commonly used in stream encryption, they are not mandatory. Theoretically, it is possible to have asymmetric keys for stream encryption.**

Public key infrastructure

When encrypting information intended for another, there is a need for the sender to know the receiver's public key. That information is provided by **public key infrastructure (PKI)**. It is a hierarchy of security certificates and a combination of hardware, software, and processes required to create, manage, and revoke digital certificates and public keys. PKI facilitates the secure transmission of information over the internet for use in e-commerce, secure messaging, and so on. X.509 is the most commonly used standard.

Let us understand what a digital certificate is. It is an electronic document that validates a public key. It is issued by trusted companies called **Certification Authority** (**CA**). All browsers come with a set of CA identities pre-installed, and users can add authorities.

Web of trust scheme

The web of trust scheme is another way to exchange public keys. It is used extensively in PGP, GnuPG, and OpenPGP-compatible systems. There is no central authority or hierarchy for validating keys in this scheme. Users sign each other's keys directly. The decentralization of trust anchors prevents a single point of failure from compromising the CA hierarchy. The challenge with this approach is that new users might find it difficult to get their keys signed by others (who tend to be strangers). The lack of a central authority also means a loss of accountability.

Protocols

Encryption is a mathematical function. It can be implemented at multiple layers in a TCP/IP stack to secure data in transit. Implementation at each level has its advantages and disadvantages. In this section, we will look at various protocols implementing encryption and their internal workings.

When discussing protocols, it is important to understand which protocols employ tunnelling and which ones do not. Refresh tunnelling from the corresponding section in *Chapter 6, Managing Networks*.

SSL/TLS

As mentioned earlier, **Secure Sockets Layer** (**SSL**) and **Transport Layer Security** (**TLS**) use asymmetric key encryption extensively. These protocols are custom-built for applications like secure internet browsing, SMTP, and LDAP. By relying on PKI, these protocols provide authentication and encryption to applications.

IP Security

IP Security (shortened as **IPSec**) secures traffic at the internet layer. It also relies on PKI for authenticating keys. IPSec is more flexible than SSL/TLS because it is not specific to the application. All TCP packets are treated the same and encrypted. All communication between two hosts is secured by IPSec. It carries the additional overhead of encryption and decryption as compared to unsecured IP communications.

Generic Routing Encapsulation

Generic Routing Encapsulation (**GRE**) is a simple, lightweight authentication protocol. A wide variety of IP packets can be tunneled into a GRE packet to provide a private path for two hosts communicating over the public internet. It is used with IPSec to create **Virtual Private Networks** (**VPN**). GRE offers an optional checksum-based authentication mechanism but does not encrypt data, so it is not considered secure.

Point-to-Point Tunnelling Protocol

Using **Point-to-Point Protocol** (**PPTP**) along with GRE gives us PPTP, which is very flexible for encryption and authentication. The PPP and GRE frames can also be compressed to save on network bandwidth. **Compression Control Protocol** (**CCP**) is used to exchange encryption keys between two parties.

Layer 2 Tunnelling Protocol

Layer 2 Tunnelling Protocol (**L2TP**) is an improvement of PPTP. It takes advantage of IPSec for encryption and **Encapsulating Security Payload** (**ESP**) for authentication of data. However, L2TP is CPU-intensive.

Network security threats

In this section, we will read about some common threats to network security. Network security threats are colloquially called cyberattacks. They can be either passive or active attacks. In passive attacks, malicious users only read the data without modifying it. In active attacks, malicious users pose as genuine users and modify the data. Cyberattacks are generally considered to have evolved in complexity and impact over five generations. Refer to *Figure 7.5* to understand how threats have evolved over time:

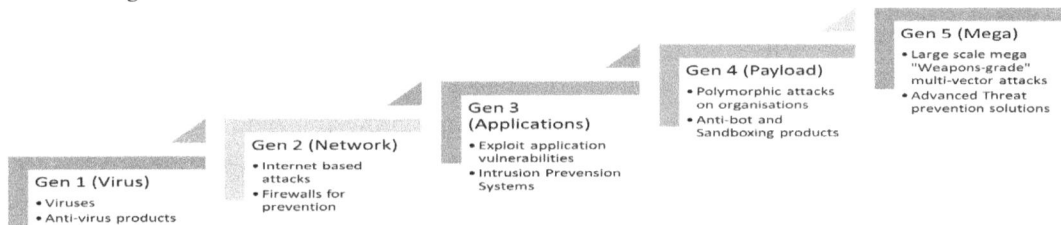

Figure 7.5: Generational evolution of network security threats

IP spoofing

IP spoofing is a technique used by attackers to impersonate a different sender. The source address field in **Internet Protocol** (**IP**) packets is modified to either hide the sender's identity, impersonate another computer system, or both. This technique is often used by attackers when attempting DDoS-style attacks. They can be avoided using HTTPS communications, VPN networks, and endpoint security. Ingress filtering and Egress filtering are common defense techniques against IP spoofing.

Ingress filtering

Ingress filtering is usually implemented on a network edge device like a router or a gateway. It examines incoming IP packets and looks at their source headers. They reject the IP packets whose origin field does not match the packet's source headers.

Egress filtering

Egress filtering is the opposite of ingress filtering. The network edge device examines the IP packets exiting the network, which prevents someone in the network from performing an outbound attack using IP spoofing.

Man-in-the-middle attacks

A **man-in-the-middle** (**MITM**) attack is a serious security threat in which an attacker intercepts the network communication between two parties by impersonating both parties. Thereby, the attacker can steal information from both parties without them being aware. IP spoofing, DNS spoofing, HTTP spoofing, SSL hijacking, and ARP Cache poisoning are some examples of MITM attacks.

Security mechanisms

In this section, we will look at common mechanisms for securing networks.

Segmentation

Segmentation is the technique of isolating network traffic along specific networks or devices. For example, critical organization services are permitted to run via selected networks and are not mixed with regular intranet and browsing requirements. By doing this, impacts on one segment shall not disturb other segments. This is common in SAN zones.

Antivirus

Antivirus is software installed in computers to protect against viruses and malware like spyware, adware, and spamware. It uses techniques like signature detection, behaviour-based protection, and in recent days, machine learning-based detection.

Firewalls

We discussed Firewalls briefly in *Chapter 5, Networking Fundamentals*. Let us understand them a little better here. A firewall is a watchman sitting between a private network and the internet. It keeps malicious traffic out and allows only genuine traffic inside.

Firewalls originated as packet filtering devices but soon evolved with additional features. In addition to packet filtering, modern firewalls perform functions like a proxy, stateful inspection, and application-level inspection of packets. Network-level firewalls inspect only IP-level packets and perform better but miss malicious applications tunnelling data inside genuine-looking traffic.

Application-level firewalls are also called **Next Generation Firewalls**. They inspect traffic at the application layer of the TCP/IP stack and can identify applications running on the machine, that is, they can differentiate between *Slack* and *Facebook messenger* and can enforce security policies. NGFWs provide superior management, robust threat prevention, application-based inspection, identity-based inspection, encrypted traffic inspection and control.

Intrusion Detection and Prevention

An **Intrusion Detection System (IDS)** is a hardware or software security tool that monitors networks for malicious activity. These systems generally run as part of the firewall and inform the network administrators when they detect malicious activity.

An IPS is more advanced than an IDS. IPS systems can be configured to take preventive and corrective actions like reporting and blocking such activities. It typically sits right behind the firewall *in the flow* of the traffic and monitors the communication between the source and destination.

IPS uses multiple techniques for detecting and preventing threats:

- **Signature-based method** compares the network activity to signatures of well-known threats. This method can stop previously identified attacks, but cannot recognise new ones.

- **Anomaly-based method** compares samples of network activity against a baseline and identifies anomalous behaviour. Artificial intelligence is increasingly being used for this purpose.

- **Policy-based method** follows security policies defined by administrators and blocks non-conforming traffic.

There are several types of IPS based on the requirement:

- **Network intrusion prevention system (NIPS)** is installed at select points to monitor traffic and proactively scan for threats.

- **Host intrusion prevention system (HIPS)** is installed on a machine and looks at inbound and outbound traffic of that machine only.

- **Network behavior analysis (NBA)** analyzes and detects unusual traffic flows.

- **Wireless intrusion prevention system (WIPS)** is for scanning and blocking unauthorized devices connected to a Wi-Fi network.

Cloud security implementations

Now that we have seen how network security is managed in private data centers, let us look at how network security works in a cloud. It might be difficult to imagine the need for security when neither machines nor networks are physical in a cloud. As it so happens, the network assets might be virtual, but the threats are real. Data is vulnerable to theft from malicious users, so it is imperative to provide network security and additional security protections specific to cloud environments.

As mentioned at the beginning of the chapter, cloud adoption does not absolve customers of security responsibilities. Depending on the cloud model adopted, the reduction in security responsibilities can be only marginal for the customers. There is also an additional security threat of the data stored on the cloud becoming accessible to inadvertent or malicious attacks. So, certain standardized techniques are adopted to check for the most frequent security lapses. We shall discuss them as we move on.

Systems hardening

Systems hardening is the activity of reducing vulnerability in technology systems and components. The possible threats are minimized by following a set of best practices and techniques. These techniques aim to eliminate the attack vectors and condense the attack surface. Systems hardening consists of several areas, as listed here:

- Endpoint hardening
- Application hardening
- Operating system hardening
- Server hardening
- Database hardening
- Network hardening

We will discuss endpoint hardening in the next section. Application hardening is discussed as a part of API hardening. The remaining areas broadly have the following activities:

- Identifying and removing default and hardcoded passwords
- Identifying passwords and other credentials stored in plain text files
- Identifying unpatched software and firmware vulnerabilities
- Identifying poor configurations to BIOS and network components (like firewalls, ports, routers, and the like)
- Instances of unencrypted data-at-rest or data-in-transit
- Identifying unnecessary accounts and improper access controls

Systems hardening is not a one-time activity. It is a continuous effort taken up by security-conscious organizations. In addition to security improvements, organizations benefit from the enhancements to compliance and auditability of systems that result from hardening.

Endpoint protection

Endpoint protection (**EPP**) secures the entry points of a network from vulnerabilities, that is, devices like desktops, laptops, and mobile devices. These devices generally operate at the boundary of human-machine interactions and are a prime target for malicious actors. **Bring Your Own Device** (**BYOD**) trend has made securing endpoints a complex activity. Classic endpoint security was an antivirus, anti-malware software. Modern systems have evolved into comprehensive suites to protect against zero-day threats. EPP provides a centralised console installed on a network gateway or server to administrators. It allows administrators to control devices remotely. EPPs range from standalone desktop installations to SaaS. It is highly recommended to install EPP on all cloud VMs.

Securing data

Data has a life cycle. It is continuously created, used, stored, and destroyed. Refer to *Figure 7.6* for the data life cycle; the stages shown occur in both cloud and private data centers. However, additional care is necessary in the cloud.

Figure 7.6: *Life cycle of data*

Create

Data can be created either in the cloud or on a remote device and can be uploaded to the cloud. Either way, data should be classified and tagged with appropriate levels and marked with appropriate metadata. Data stored on cloud storage and transmitted on the network must be secured to prevent eavesdropping. Data can be in two different categories, as listed below:

- **Data-at-Rest** is about securing data residing in files, blocks, databases, and BLOBs. It is additional to the disk-level security provided by the storage devices (refer to *Data Security* section in the *Chapter 4, Managing Storage*). Options like ownership of objects, **Access Control Lists** (**ACL**), the granularity of public access, versioning of data, and server-side encryption must be configured.

- **Data-in-Transit** is about securing data when it is moving between hosts. Typically, such movements are done as part of the application and can be encrypted by the applications. CSPs generally provide secure options for transferring large-scale data between cloud and private data centers.

Use

It is generally difficult to predict all the uses of data when it is created. So, administrators should plan access to data carefully. Data access should be restrictive enough to prevent leakage without dissuading genuine users from accessing it. This is a delicate balance to manage. If an organization has a BYOD policy, then such devices should be secured before being permitted to access and download data.

Store

Store generally refers to near-term storage. In this stage, administrators should choose which type of storage is needed for the application and the organization. Block storage, object storage, databases, and other options discussed in *Chapter 4, Managing Storage*, are applicable here.

Share

Sharing data comes with a host of legal implications. Administrators should decide which data is being shared and how. Sharing personally identifiable information requires several legal and administrative restrictions. There may also be political and geographic restrictions on sharing data; for example, export controls might restrict data from being shared with users or entities in certain countries. Security techniques like encryption, segmentation, and the like, which were discussed earlier, should be applied here.

Archive

Archival refers to long-term storage of data. Archived data is typically used less frequently. Data storage techniques involving taped storage discussed in the chapter on storage are applicable at this stage.

Destroy

Destroying data on cloud is very different from destroying data in private data centers. Physically destroying a magnetic tape or storage device shall permanently destroy data, and it is easy to do in a data center. However, this is not possible in public clouds. Erasing the data using crypto shredding techniques is the only option presently available for this.

API security

Application programming interfaces (**APIs**) allow interactions between internet applications. They are fundamental to modern software architecture patterns like microservices, service-oriented architecture, and the like. They are legitimate entry points to organizations' networks and are meant to serve a business purpose. If you are providing cloud-based APIs to your customers or if your APIs are invokable via the internet, you should pay additional attention to securing APIs. APIs are prime targets for attackers and increase the attack surface that hackers can target. If an organization is compared to a fort, APIs can be considered entrance gates. The difference is that while a fort has few well-guarded entrances, the number of APIs can range from a handful to a few thousand. Also, by the very nature of development, APIs are prone to frequent changes. Moreover, the protocols for API communications can be of a wide variety.

The most common security threats to APIs are listed by the **Open Web Application Security Project (OWASP)**. *Table 7.4* shows the top 10 threats they identified in 2019. Content is taken from their website as is at **https://owasp.org/www-project-api-security/**:

S. No.	Title	Explanation
API1:2019	Broken Object Level Authorization	APIs tend to expose endpoints that handle object identifiers, creating a wide attack surface level access control issue. Object level authorization checks should be considered in every function that accesses a data source using an input from the user.
API2:2019	Broken User Authentication	Authentication mechanisms are often implemented incorrectly, allowing attackers to compromise authentication tokens or to exploit implementation flaws to assume other users' identities temporarily or permanently. Compromising a system's ability to identify the client/user, compromises API security overall.
API3:2019	Excessive Data Exposure	Looking forward to generic implementations, developers tend to expose all object properties without considering their individual sensitivity, relying on clients to perform the data filtering before displaying it to the user.
API4:2019	Lack of Resources and Rate Limiting	Quite often, APIs do not impose any restrictions on the size or number of resources that can be requested by the client/user. Not only can this impact the API server performance, leading to **Denial of Service (DoS)**, but it also leaves the door open to authentication flaws like brute force.

S. No.	Title	Explanation
API5:2019	Broken Function Level Authorization	Complex access control policies with different hierarchies, groups, and roles, and an unclear separation between administrative and regular functions, tend to lead to authorization flaws. By exploiting these issues, attackers gain access to other users' resources and/or administrative functions.
API6:2019	Mass Assignment	Binding client provided data (for example, JSON) to data models, without proper properties filtering based on an allowlist usually leads to mass assignment. Guessing objects properties, exploring other API endpoints, reading the documentation, or providing additional object properties in request payloads, allows attackers to modify object properties they are not supposed to.
API7:2019	Security Misconfiguration	Security misconfiguration is commonly a result of unsecure default configurations, incomplete or ad-hoc configurations, open cloud storage, misconfigured HTTP headers, unnecessary HTTP methods, permissive **Cross-Origin resource sharing (CORS)**, and verbose error messages containing sensitive information.
API8:2019	Injection	Injection flaws, such as SQL, NoSQL, and Command Injection, occur when untrusted data is sent to an interpreter as part of a command or query. The attacker's malicious data can trick the interpreter into executing unintended commands or accessing data without proper authorization.
API9:2019	Improper Assets Management	APIs tend to expose more endpoints than traditional web applications, making proper and updated documentation highly important. Proper hosts and deployed API versions inventory also play important roles in mitigating issues like deprecated API versions and exposed debug endpoints.
API10:2019	Insufficient Logging and Monitoring	Insufficient logging and monitoring, coupled with missing or ineffective integration with incident response, allows attackers to further attack systems, maintain persistence, pivot to more systems to tamper with, extract, or destroy data. Most breach studies demonstrate the time to detect a breach is over 200 days, typically detected by external parties rather than internal processes or monitoring.

Table 7.4: Top 10 API security threats listed by OWASP in 2019

It is important to pay attention to API security when developing applications in cloud. We will discuss app development for the cloud in *Chapters 9, Migrating to Cloud,* and *11, Troubleshooting in Cloud.*

Conclusion

We learned how to manage security in this chapter. We learned about the CIA triad, how they can be compromised, and the techniques available to overcome them. We also learned about encryption, the different encryption algorithms, and the protocols for implementing them. Further on, we discussed how security is possible in the cloud and the methods to address some of them.

In the next chapter, we will discuss IAM. We will discuss what a digital identity is, how authentication should be performed, how to authorize usage of assets, and access control of digital assets.

Glossary

- **Asymmetric encryption**: An encryption algorithm that uses different keys for encryption and decryption

- **Authenticity**: The property of an entity being genuine, verifiable, and trustworthy

- **Availability**: An aspect of system security referring to assets being available when needed

- **Block Cipher**: An algorithm that encrypts fixed-length chunks of plain text

- **CA**: Certification Authority

- **CIO**: Chief Information Officer is a C-level executive responsible for Information Technology strategy of an organization

- **Confidentiality**: An aspect of system security referring to assets being accessible only by authorized people

- **Cyber Security**: A domain dealing with the defense of computing systems, networks, and data from malicious attacks

- **Cipher text**: Encrypted data

- **Data classification**: A method for defining and categorizing business information based on its sensitivity

- **Digital Signature**: The signature used for encryption in asymmetric encryption algorithms

- **DoS**: Denial of Service

- **Encryption**: A mathematical algorithm that scrambles the data, rendering it unreadable by unauthorized entities

- **Hardening**: Activity of reducing vulnerability in technology systems and components

- **IAM**: Identity and Access Management

- **IDS**: Intrusion Detection Systems
- **Integrity**: An aspect of system security referring to data being received as it was sent
- **Malware**: A software intentionally designed to cause harm to a computer or data
- **Message Digest**: A fixed-length numeric representation of data
- **PKI**: Public Key Infrastructure
- **Plain text**: Unencrypted Data
- **Possession**: As an aspect of system security, referring to assets being in the control of the rightful owner
- **Private Key**: The key used for decryption in asymmetric encryption algorithms
- **Public Key**: The key used for encryption in asymmetric encryption algorithms
- **RSA**: A popular asymmetric key encryption algorithm
- **Spoofing**: A cyberattack approach in which a malicious entity poses as a genuine entity
- **Streaming Cipher**: An algorithm that encrypts plain text bit by bit
- **Symmetric encryption**: An encryption algorithm that uses the same key for encryption and decryption
- **Utility**: The property of data referring to the usefulness of the data

Practice questions

S. No.	Questions		Answers
1	**Which of these is not part of the CIA triad?**		D
	A) Confidentiality	B) Availability	
	C) Integrity	D) Authenticity	
2	**Which of the following areas is not part of the cybersecurity domain?**		D
	A) Application security	B) Device security	
	C) Data security	D) Personnel security	
3	**Which of the following areas of Parkerian Hexad takes a non-binary value?**		A
	A) Utility	B) Possession	
	C) Authenticity	D) Integrity	

S. No.	Questions		Answers
4	**Which of the following is not part of Parkerian Hexad?**		B
	A) Utility	B) Identity	
	C) Authenticity	D) Integrity	
5	**Which of the following classification levels can be used for information that does not require protection from disclosure?**		C
	A) Restricted	B) Private	
	C) Public	D) None of the above	
6	**What are the aims of Identity and Access Management?**		D
	A) Establishing a digital identity for a user or resource	B) Verifying access clearance	
	C) Non repudiation	D) All of the above	
7	**Which of the following sentences summarizes the Bell-LaPadula model?**		B
	A) Read up, Write Up	B) Read Down, Write Up	
	C) Read Up, Write Down	D) Read Down, Write Down	
8	**Which of the following sentences summarizes the Biba model?**		C
	A) Read up, Write Up	B) Read Down, Write Up	
	C) Read Up, Write Down	D) Read Down, Write Down	
9	**Which of the following algorithms can be used for verifying data integrity?**		C
	A) RSA	B) Blowfish	
	C) MD5	D) None of the above	
10	**Which of the following is not an encryption algorithm?**		D
	A) RSA	B) Blowfish	
	C) Caesars Cipher	D) MD5	
11	**Which of the following algorithms can be used to achieve confidentiality**		A
	A) RSA	B) BLAKE	
	C) MD5	D) SHA	
12	**Which of the following techniques can be used to deny availability?**		C
	A) Denial of Service	B) Malware	
	C) Both	D) None of the above	
13	**Which of these is a symmetric key algorithm?**		B
	A) Diffie-Hellman	B) AES	
	C) ECC	D) El Gamal	

S. No.	Questions		Answers
14	A network administrator has configured a routing device to monitor incoming packets and filter out packets of suspicious origin. What technique are they using?		A
	A) Ingress filtering	B) Egress filtering	
	C) Firewall filtering	D) ARP Cache cleaning	
15	Which of the following is generally not part of hardening?		B
	A) Identifying and removing default and hardcoded passwords	B) Identifying users with weak passwords	
	C) Identifying passwords and other credentials stored in plain text files	D) Identifying unpatched software and firmware vulnerabilities	
16	Which of the following is generally not part of hardening?		C
	A) Identifying poor configurations BIOS and network components	B) Instances of unencrypted data-at-rest or data-in-transit	
	C) Identifying poor coding practices	D) Identifying unnecessary accounts and improper access controls	
17	Which of the following are the functionalities expected from endpoint protection software? 1) Detecting zero-day threats 2) Anti-malware and anti-virus protection 3) Network traffic monitoring 4) Email and web traffic monitoring		C
	A) 1 and 2 only	B) 3 and 4 only	
	C) All of them	D) None of them	
18	Which of the following data life cycle stages differs between cloud and private data centers?		D
	A) Create	B) Share	
	C) Use	D) Destroy	
19	Which of the following activities can reduce the utility of sensitive data to a hacker in case of data breaches? 1. Encrypting data 2. Creating hashes for the data 3. Masking the data 4. Creating multiple backups of the data		A
	A) 1 and 3	B) 2 and 4	
	C) 1 and 2	D) 3 and 4	

S. No.	Questions		Answers
20	**Which of the following is not a benefit of Endpoint Protection Platforms compared to a traditional antivirus software?**		D
	A) Centralised visibility of network components in the enterprise	B) Centralisation of administration responsibilities to IT team	
	C) Protection for zero-day attacks	D) Decentralised flexibility for software patch management	
21	**A PaaS API returns non-PII information like gender and age. A subsequent upgrade of the API added user's phone number to it. What type of security threat is created here?**		C
	A) Broken object-level authorization	B) Broken user authentication	
	C) Excessive data exposure	D) Lack of resources & rate limiting	
22	**A SaaS application allows users to transfer very large files using its service. A malicious user exploited a vulnerability and uploaded multiple Peta bytes of data, jamming the server space and driving up the network costs. What type of security threat is created here?**		A
	A) Lack of resources & rate limiting	B) Broken user authentication	
	C) Injection	D) Security misconfiguration	
23	**An enterprise application running in a public cloud was hacked. Investigators realised that there is no activity trail for the application. What kind of security threat has occurred here?**		D
	A) Security misconfiguration	B) Injection	
	C) Improper assets management	D) Insufficient logging & monitoring	

References

1. https://www.surveyofindia.gov.in/documents/NATIONAL%20 INFORMATION%20SECURITY%20POLICY%20AND%20GUIDELINES.pdf

2. https://www.indiacode.nic.in/bitstream/123456789/2379/1/A1923-19.pdf

Join our Discord space

Join our Discord workspace for latest updates, offers, tech happenings around the world, new releases, and sessions with the authors:

https://discord.bpbonline.com

CHAPTER 8

Identity and Access Management

Introduction

Most of us carry an identity card of some form. Whether provided by the government or by the organization we are associated with, an identity card is a piece of paper that serves as proof that we are who we say we are. ID cards generally mention a name, photograph, address, and the issuer's name. They are used to grant access to locations restricted to the public. The identity issuing authority is an essential aspect of identities. Every system accepts a set of identity issuers. It will not accept identities provided by other issuers. For example, international travel requires a passport, which is a piece of paper issued by the government and is acceptable to other countries' governments. No matter how classy or respectable, a document issued by others, like your school or club, will not be acceptable in that scenario.

This is precisely what a digital identity does as well. It is your digital representative in the system, and all the processes, policies, technologies, and controls use it to fulfill their duties. Every IT system has an acceptable list of identity providers and generally does not accept identity issued by others. In this chapter, we shall discuss how identities are created and managed. We will also understand how IT systems recognize, allow, and prevent users from accessing resources.

Structure

We will go through the following topics in this chapter:

- Identity
- Authentication
- Accountability
- Authorisation
- Access control

Objectives

This chapter covers various aspects of Identity and Access Management. We will discuss identity, authentication, authorization, and access control. We will also discuss how user identities are maintained and managed across organisations. We will understand how a single ID can be used across applications within and across organisations. We will understand the details of how an application can retrieve user information maintained by another application. We will also discuss the relationship between identification and authentication. Finally, we will look at authorization and the approaches available for authorization and access control.

Identity

Access privileges are assigned to identities. Access management shall clarify if the identity has the necessary access privileges to an asset. All user details needed for connecting the identity to a person are collected and associated with the digital ID.

Identity systems can be either on-premise or from third-party providers. It is generally the practice for systems to have their own identity management system in addition to honoring third-party's identity.

The most common form of digital identity is simply a username. It is a unique sequence of alphabets, numbers, and select special characters. Whether an individual is permitted to have multiple user IDs is a business question, and every organization has its approach to doing this. Depending on the scenario, user IDs are generated centrally and assigned to individuals, or individuals are permitted to choose their IDs. The former is generally the case in organisations for their employees, and the latter is usually seen in massive online offerings like email accounts, social media handles, and so on. It is generally the convention that user IDs resemble users' actual names for ease of remembrance and recognition. But this is not a hard-and-fast rule.

Identities can be provided for individuals, groups, organizations, and even governments. An individual is made accountable for maintaining the digital identity of non-human entities.

In the olden days, usernames were made of only ASCII printable characters. However, Unicode support has changed the scenario, and some systems allow Unicode characters in usernames, especially for non-English users. Intermixing Unicode and ASCII characters requires special attention from system admins and developers.

Technically, digital identity refers only to the username. However, every aspect of the user activity is linked and tightly bound to it. This raises concerns regarding privacy and misuse. Security consultants routinely advise against revealing usernames. For example, UIDAI designed pseudo-IDs like VID to mitigate this problem. It is not uncommon to see social media websites taking extra precautions, like masking the email address to prevent it from displaying on their websites.

Authentication

Authentication is different from identification. Authentication is the process by which an individual or process claiming an identity is verified as the owner of that identity. Authentication can be done using a password, multi-factor authentication, time-based One Time Passwords, and biometrics. A combination of these is also employed for improved security.

Consider this: you are applying for a bank account or a mobile SIM card. The bank asks you to present an ID proof and submit your Aadhaar. This is only identification. Authentication is done when you provide your fingerprint or iris scan. Biometrics confirms that you are indeed the person to whom the Aadhaar number belongs. Similarly, when logging in to your email account or social media, your email address or user ID is simply identification. Authentication is when you provide your password.

Multi-factor authentication

Password is the traditional approach used for authentication. Passwords have been used since classical times in history and have the benefit of being simple and easy to remember. However, they are also compromised easily. A leaked password is sufficient to compromise system integrity. While humans are careful not to leak passwords, they are also predictable. A clever social engineering attack is enough to gain passwords, so multi-factor authentication is employed to overcome this.

Multi-factor authentication, as the name indicates, is a multi-step process. In addition to the password (information the user knows), users are asked to provide other information that an attacker is not likely to possess (information the user has). The additional information can either be a static passphrase, a dynamic one-time passcode, or a special device assigned to the user. Refer to the following figure:

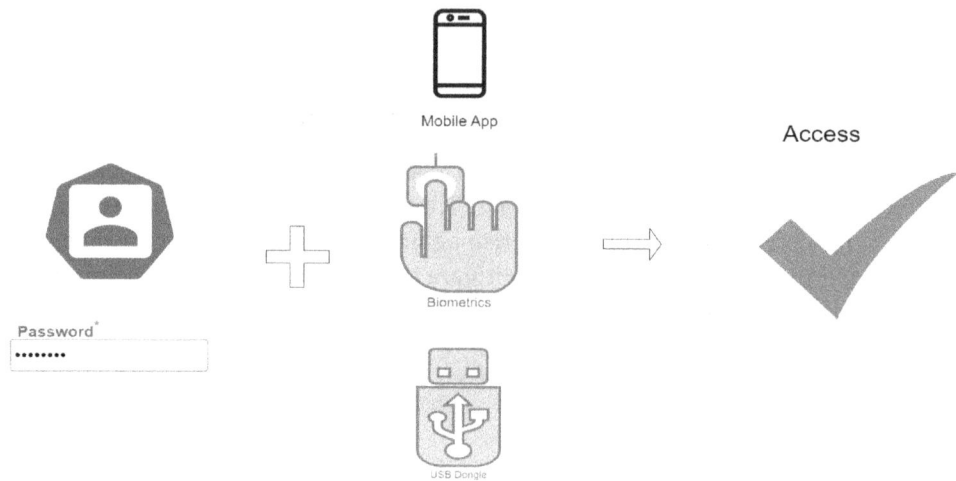

Figure 8.1: Multi-factor authentication

Dynamic one-time passcode is a multi-factor authentication approach to validate the information the user has. This is implemented either by the **HMAC-based One-time Password (HOTP)** algorithm or the **Time-based One-time Password (TOTP)** algorithm. In both HOTP and TOTP, the user is provided with a device or software that generates a new passcode at regular intervals. The authentication system generates the same passcodes. When user-provided password and passcode match the password and the passcode in the system, it provides additional confidence about the user and the identity owner being the same.

Adaptive authentication

Adaptive authentication is a risk-based authentication approach. It is based on the concept that having the same sign-in approach in every scenario is vulnerable to security attacks. Instead, adaptive authentication has different sign-in requirements, depending on a user's intentions for logging in. For this, the login-related information is analyzed by the authentication systems, and the risk profile is analyzed. For low-risk activities, a low login requirement, such as a username and password, might be sufficient. For activities involving higher risks, a more detailed authorisation, like multi-factor authorisation approaches, might be tried.

Consider an example. If a user is trying to log in from home or from the organisation network, then it might be considered a low-risk scenario. However, if a login attempt is detected from a new location, like an internet café or a different geography or device, such an attempt can be classified as high-risk, and users can be asked for further authentication using MFA. *Figure 8.2* shows how this works. In recent times, advanced technologies like machine learning are being used to identify the low risk, medium risk, and high-risk scenarios.

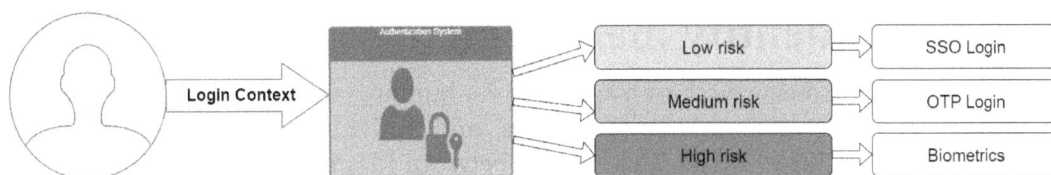

Figure 8.2: *Adaptive Authentication*

It is interesting to note that many Indian banks use the adaptive approach in their net banking transactions. For initial login, they require a normal user ID and password. However, a cash transfer transaction has higher risk, so banks typically require an OTP sent via SMS or email.

Password over a network

With passwords being so crucial to information security, it is only natural that we take all possible steps to prevent them from being leaked. Some of the popular approaches for securing passwords are mentioned here:

- Make brute force or social engineering attacks impractical by maintaining a long password with a combination of lower case, upper case, numbers, and special characters.

- Encrypt the password when sending it over a network to overcome man-in-the-middle attacks. An example is the ssh protocol.

- Never send the password over the network; instead, store a hash of the password on the server. Whenever the user enters the password, it is hashed on the local machine, and the hash is sent to the server. Authentication is successful only if the hashes match. This prevents hackers from stealing the password database. An example is the Kerberos protocol.

LDAP

Light Weight Directory Access Protocol (**LDAP**) is used for retrieving user information from the **Active Directory** (**AD**). It can also be used for authenticating users. One can retrieve information about users, resources, and even organizations using LDAP. For example, it can be employed to know a user's email address using their name.

It is important to remember that LDAP is different from AD. AD is a directory server developed by Microsoft to store information about enterprise users. LDAP is the protocol used to access the AD, which supports authentication, group policy management, access policies, and so on. LDAP can be used to retrieve information from any directory server that supports LDAP and is not restricted to AD.

Federated identity management

Federated identity management is an approach for building access control systems where an identity provider centrally manages users, and individual **service providers** (**SP**) manage access privileges. It is a trust system between **identity providers** (**IdP**) and SP. SP trusts the IdP to authenticate users. After successful authentication, IdP sends the SP an assertion containing the user's sign-in name and other attributes needed for the SP to determine the user's privileges. By employing federation, users can access multiple services using the same username and credentials. **Security Assertion Markup Language** (**SAML**), SSO, Open ID, and OAuth are different standards of federation. The relationship between these standards can best be expressed using *Figure 8.3*:

Federated Identity Management

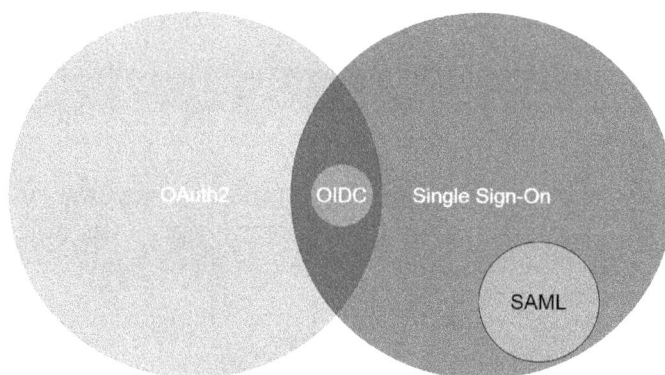

Figure 8.3: Relationship between federated identity management technologies

Single sign-on

Single sign-on (**SSO**) authentication enables users to use the same credentials for multiple applications and websites. A single sign-on facility cannot be done unilaterally by the users. It is possible only by modifying the authentication systems to honor the authentication of another server. For this to work, the authentication system asks the users to sign in with the third-party provider's credentials. The third-party provider authenticates the user and sends a confirmation to the authentication system. At that point, the authentication system shall mark the user as authenticated, just as when using the system's authentication mechanism. Look at the following figure:

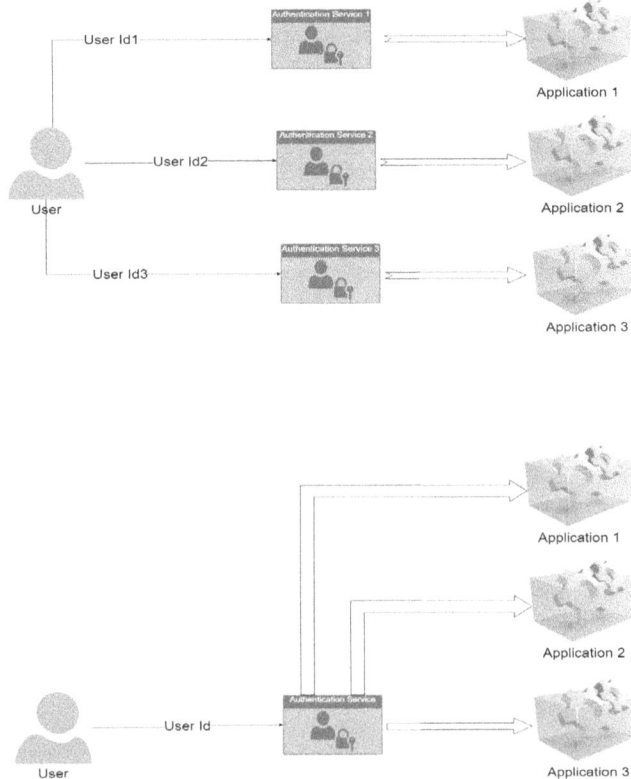

Figure 8.4: User experience with SSO (above) and with SSO (below)

SSO is a part of **federated identity management (FIM)**. The **Open Authorization (OAuth)** framework enables a user to be authenticated using a third-party authentication provider without revealing the user's password. SSO significantly simplifies user management for users and system administrators alike. However, a wide range of information is also compromised if the SSO is compromised. Systems offering SSO authentication become a single point of failure.

There is an important difference between SSO FIM. SSO is used to authenticate a user ID across various systems within one organization, while a FIM system is used to allow accessing systems across various enterprises.

SAML

SAML is used for the transfer of authentication information between identity providers and services. It serves the same purpose as SSO, but unlike SSO, it does not use cookies. This is a crucial benefit of SAML. Cookies are limited to a single domain, so all applications using SSO should belong to the same web domain. However, SAML does not have that limitation. *Figure 8.5* shows how SAML is used for authenticating users:

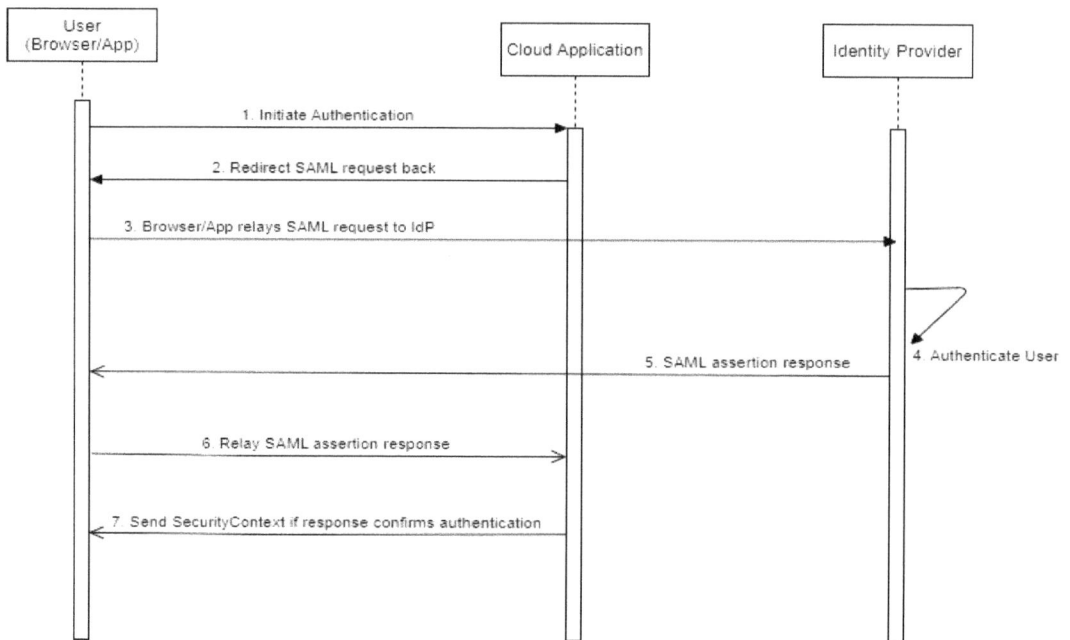

Figure 8.5: SAML used for SSO

OAuth

OAuth stands for **Open Authorization**. It is a widely adopted standard that allows the sharing of information between services without exposing passwords. OAuth is used exclusively for authorisation and not for authentication. OAuth specifications support the following personas:

- Resource owners
- Resource server, that is, OAuth provider, where the resource is hosted
- OAuth consumers who want to access the resource

OAuth 2.0 is the latest version of the OAuth protocol and is the current industry standard. It focuses on simplicity of use for developers. It does not inherently support security features like signatures and encryption, but assumes such support to be available from the underlying transport layer (either TLS or SSL).

OpenID

OpenID is an open and decentralized authentication protocol. It is employed by systems that wish to provide SSO facilities to other systems. It is important to remember that OpenID is different from OAuth. They are used in close conjunction in many systems, but there are substantial differences. OpenID is used to provide login services, while OAuth is used to authorize one system to access user data from another system. Generally, OpenID is used to provide an SSO experience for non-enterprise consumers on the internet.

As an example, Facebook provides OpenID. You can use your Facebook ID to log in to the SlideShare website. However, for SlideShare to retrieve information about you (your full name, email, and so on, which are maintained in *Facebook*), it cannot use OpenID; it should use OAuth.

Figure 8.6 shows the login page of **www.slideshare.com.** Users have the option to use their LinkedIn or Facebook IDs to log in to SlideShare:

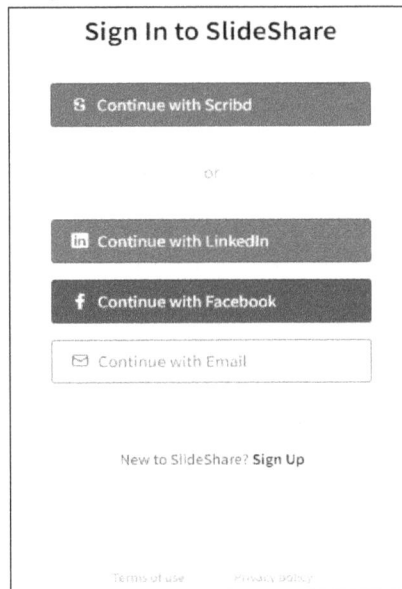

Figure 8.6: *Login page of www.slideshare.com*

Identification and authentication

It is important to note that identification and authentication always occur together as a two-step process. Identity is provided in the first step, and authentication information is provided in the second. Both steps are needed for an entity to gain access to the system or resource. It is common to refer to these two steps as **authentication**. The authentication process output is Boolean, which is either Yes or No. An entity is either who it claims to be or it is not. There is no scope for fuzzy interpretation here.

Accountability

Accountability is another aspect of Identity and Access Management. It refers to the ability to hold users accountable for their actions. It is very important to ascertain that a certain user has performed a given action when troubleshooting issues. The most successful way to do this is to maintain an audit trail. Audit logs maintain the information about which entities have requested access to assets when they accessed or modified them, and so on. If the authentication is done in a reliable manner, audit logs provide for non-repudiation. *Figure 8.7* shows an example of audit log from AWS Cloud Trail. The example's contents will not make sense to anyone except the cloud administrators. Also, they vary from one cloud provider to another. So, we shall not spend time discussing the contents. For the purposes of the CV0-004 exam, it suffices to know that cloud administrators have access to tools that help them hold users accountable for their actions.

```
{
    eventVersion:"1.05",
    userIdentity:{
      type:"IAMUser",
      principalId:"principalId",
      arn:"arn:aws:iam::accountId:user/userName",
      accountId:"111122223333",
      accessKeyId:"accessKeyId",
      userName:"userName",
      sessionContext:{
        sessionIssuer:{
        },
        webIdFederationData:{
        },
        attributes:{
          mfaAuthenticated:"false",
          creationDate:"2020-11-19T07:32:06Z"
        }
      }
    },
    eventTime:"2020-11-19T07:32:36Z",
    eventSource:"auditmanager.amazonaws.com",
    eventName:"CreateAssessment",
    awsRegion:"us-west-2",
    sourceIPAddress:"sourceIPAddress",
    userAgent:"Mozilla/5.0 (Macintosh; Intel Mac OS X 10_15_7) AppleWebKit/537.36 (KHTML, like Gecko) Chrome/87.0.4280.66 Safari/537.36",
    requestParameters:{
      frameworkId:"frameworkId",
      assessmentReportsDestination:{
        destination:"***",
        destinationType:"S3"
      },
      clientToken:"***",
      scope:{
        awsServices:[
          {
            serviceName:"license-manager"
          }
        ],
        awsAccounts:"***"
      },
      roles:"***",
      name:"***",
      description:"***",
      tags:"***"
    },
    responseElements:{
      assessment:"***"
    },
    requestID:"0d950f8c-5211-40db-8c37-2ed38ffcc894",
    eventID:"a782029a-959e-4549-81df-9f6596775cb0",
    readOnly:false,
    eventType:"AwsApiCall",
    recipientAccountId:"recipientAccountId"
}
```

Figure 8.7: Sample audit log from AWS Cloud Trail

Authorisation

Once the user's identity is authenticated, the next step is to check whether the user is permitted to access the resource. This is called authorisation, also known as access control.

In contrast to the Yes/No approach of authentication, authorisation has a wide range of values associated with it. An authenticated user may have permission to read an asset but not modify it, or write to it but not delete it, and so on. Access control was implemented as file-level permissions in Unix systems and has come a long way since.

Access Control Lists (**ACLs**) control which users can access a given resource to which the ACL is attached.

Groups and roles can be used to simplify access management. It is cumbersome for administrators to configure every user's access to every resource. In such cases, it is common for administrators to group the users based on their job persona and define access to the group. This is considerably easier for administrators. However, care should be taken when deciding the group's privileges, and the minimum possible set of accesses should be approved.

The prevalent practice is to declare policies and provide access based on them. Policies offer significant flexibility in fine-tuning access privileges based on various parameters. They are generally expressed in JSON format.

- Identity-based policies define access privileges for identities, roles, or groups. They are defined and implemented for identities. For example, user James Bond has clearance to access **`"Top Secret Documents"`**, **`"Latest Weapons"`**, and **`"Cool Gadgets"`**.
- Resource-based policies define access privileges for resources. Each resource is defined as being accessible by a list of identities. For example, **`"Top Secret Documents"`** are accessible by **`"James Bond"`, `"M"`**. **`"Cool Gadgets"`** are accessible by **`"James Bond"`, `"Q"`**.

The difference between Identity-based and Resource-based access policies can be seen in *Figure 8.8:*

```
{
  "James Bond": [
    "Top Secret Documents",
    "Cool Gadgets",
    "Latest Weapons"
  ],
  "M": [
    "Top Secret Documents",
    "Latest Weapons"
  ],
  "Q": [
    "Cool Gadgets",
    "Latest Weapons"
  ]
}
```

```
{
  "Top Secret Documents": [
    "James Bond",
    "M"
  ],
  "Cool Gadgets": [
    "James Bond",
    "Q"
  ],
  "Latest Weapons": [
    "James Bond",
    "M",
    "Q"
  ]
}
```

Figure 8.8: *Example of Identity-based v/s Resource based access policies*

Access control

So far, we have discussed how authentication and authorisation are done. Let us now discuss the process of access control itself. Controlling access to assets is a crucial aspect of security. Different security systems should work together to provide access control, which is generally required for the following class of assets:

- Information stored in files or databases, or metadata
- Systems
- Devices
- Facilities
- Personnel

Security professionals use the terms **subject** and **object** when discussing access controls. In the context of access control, there are two entities: the active entity trying to retrieve the information, and a passive entity that provides the information to the active entity. The active entity is called subject, and the passive entity is called object. Subjects can be users, programs, processes, devices, or anything else that can access resources. Objects can be files, databases, programs, processes, and devices. It is important to remember that the subject always refers to the active entity, which retrieves the information, and the object is always the passive entity that provides it.

It might be easy and even tempting to use *user* and *data* instead of *subject* and *object*. While such a substitution is technically correct, it is often incomplete. Depending on the requirement, the data retrieval can be performed by entities that are not users. Sometimes, the information retrieval requirement can change between entities. So, subject and object terms are more technically accurate. However, for the rest of the chapter, we will use *user* and *asset* for simplicity.

When a user tries to access a resource or asset, the system should check with the identity provider for authentication and verify that the user is authorized to access the resource. Access to the asset should be granted only if the user is authenticated and authorised to do so. Access control includes the following steps:

1. Identify and authenticate users attempting to access resources
2. Check whether the access is authorized
3. Permit or deny access based on the subject's identity
4. Monitor and record access requests

We discussed identity and authentication in the previous sections. We will discuss the details of authorization in the upcoming sections. There are many types of access control driven by administrative, technical, and legal requirements. The following list introduces the names of access control types. A detailed discussion of access control types is out of scope for the CVO-003 exam.

- Preventive Access Control

- Detection Access Control

- Corrective Access Control

- Deterrent Access Control

- Recovery Access Control

- Directive Access Control

- Compensating Access Control

Access control models

Access control models use many types of authorisation methods to control access to objects. The important access control models relevant to the CVO-003 exam are listed here:

- In mandatory access control, the rules are rigidly defined by the organisation and enforced by a policy. Individual users cannot override the policy.

- In discretionary access control, access control is defined by individual object owners. Each object has its ACL and is controlled by the owners.

- In role-based access control, access control is assigned to a role, and all subjects having that role can access the object. For example, all legal teams might have read access to the system.

- In task-based access control, access control is provided to a task, that is, a system process. Subjects can access data only as part of the process. For example, managers might be permitted to access employees' data only in case of disciplinary complaints and not during other times.

- In rule-based access control, a global rule applicable to all subjects is used to determine access.

- Attribute-based access control is an extension of rule-based access control. Here, rules are defined based on a combination of attributes. This allows for higher flexibility and customizability. Software-defined networks employ attribute-based access extensively.

Whatever the scenario, the authentication and authorisation details should be securely exchanged between the requestor and the service provider. Multiple protocols exist for this purpose. We will discuss the popular approaches here.

Kerberos

Kerberos is the protocol used for user authentication and authorization. It is the default standard used in Windows OS and is very popular. Three entities participate in the authentication and, as such, have a symbolic similarity to the Greek myth of Cerberus, after which it was named. It uses strong encryption and third-party ticket authorization techniques for protection against hackers. It is a very popular protocol employed for robust authentication and authorisation mechanism in systems like AD, NFS, and Samba.

Kerberos protocol follows the given steps for authentication. These steps are entirely transparent to the user. Here, **Client** refers to the system on which the user logs in and requests access. The systems named **Key Distribution Centre** (**KDC**) and **Ticket Granting Service** (**TGS**) participate in the process.

- Client requests an authentication ticket, named **Ticket Granting Ticket** (**TGT**), from KDC.
- KDC verifies the credentials, generates a TGT, encrypts it using TGS, and sends back the encrypted TGT and session key to the client.
- Client stores the TGT for the duration of a session. After its expiry, it will request another TGT.

For authorization, the following steps are performed:

1. Client sends the TGT to TGS with the resource's name to be accessed.
2. KDC verifies TGT and whether the user has permission to access the resource.
3. TGS returns a session key to the client.
4. Client communicates with the resource using the session key.
5. Resource checks with TGS regarding the validity of the session key. If TGS confirms the validity, the resource will permit access.

The mentioned steps have been captured in *Figure 8.9*:

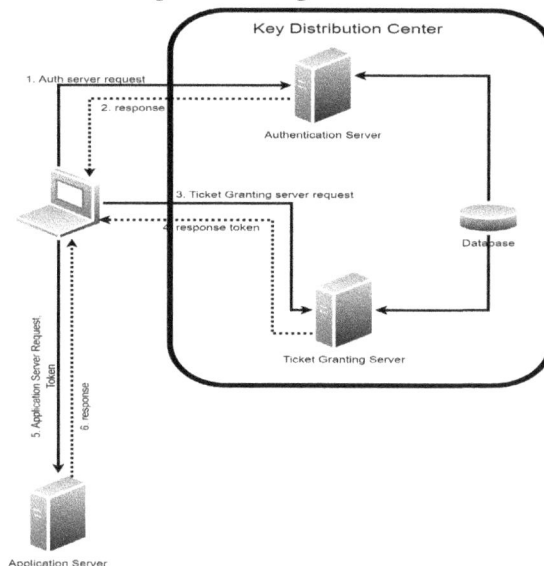

Figure 8.9: *Kerberos authentication sequence*

Conclusion

In this chapter, we learned about Identity and Access Management. We learned about the differences and the relationship between identity, authentication, and authorization, and we looked at the different protocols available for authentication and authorization.

The chapters so far have discussed the fundamental concepts that are necessary to understand the cloud and build a cloud application. In the next chapter, we will put the concepts together and discuss migrating an application to the cloud. We will discuss types of migration, migration strategies, roadmap, and life cycle.

Glossary

- **ACL**: Access Control List
- **Adaptive Authentication**: A risk-based authentication approach where the user is asked for different authentication information based on the risks analyzed for the login scenario
- **Attribute-based access control**: An access control model where access privileges are based on the attributes of the entity requesting access
- **Audit Log**: A record of all activities performed in the system and details related to them
- **Authentication**: The act of verifying the identity of a computer system user
- **Authorization**: The act of giving permission to perform an action
- **Biometrics**: Measurement and statistical analysis of physical and behavioural characteristics of people so as to identify them uniquely
- **Discretionary access control**: An access control model where access control rules are defined by individual users
- **FIM**: Federated identity management
- **HMAC**: Hash-based Message Authentication Code
- **HOTP**: HMAC-based One Time Password
- **Identity**: The fact of being who or what a person or thing is
- **Identity-based policies**: A practice of defining access privileges for objects for each user
- **IdP**: Identity provider
- **JSON**: Java Script Object Notation
- **Kerberos**: An industry standard protocol used for authentication and authorization of users

- **LDAP**: Light Weight Directory Access Protocol
- **Mandatory access control**: An access control model where access control rules are rigidly defined at the organization level and cannot be modified by individual users
- **MFA**: Multi-factor authentication
- **OAuth**: Open Authorization
- **OAuth2**: The current version of the OAuth protocol
- **OIDC**: Open ID Connect
- **OTP**: One Time Password
- **Repudiation**: Act of claiming an activity as invalid; in a security context, it refers to a user or entity performing an action and later claiming not to have done so
- **Resource-based policies**: A practice of defining access privileges for users for each object
- **Role-based access control**: An access control model where access privileges are based on the user's role
- **SAML**: Security Assertion Markup Language
- **SSO**: Single Sign-On
- **Subject and Object**: In the context of access control, subjects are active entities trying to retrieve information, and objects are passive entities that provide information
- **Task-based access control**: An access control model where access privileges are based on the task or process requesting access
- **TOTP**: Time-based OTP

Practice questions

S. No.	Questions		Answers
1	**Which of the following is an example of multi-factor authentication?**		C
	A) User ID, password	B) Secret pass phrase	
	C) SMS-based OTP	D) None of the above	
2	**Which of the following is not an example of multi-factor authentication?**		B
	A) Mobile app-based passcode	B) Captcha	
	C) Iris verification	D) All of the above	

S. No.	Questions		Answers
3	**Which of the following statements about adaptive authentication is/are false?** i. The sign-in experience can change based on login characteristics. ii. Authentication service should support multiple types of login facilities. iii. Risk assessment has to be performed on the login data to tune risk profiles. iv. Risk classification can be fine-tuned using AI.		D
	A) i and ii only	B) ii and iv only	
	C) All of them	D) None of them	
4	**Which of the following is a use case for LDAP protocol?**		D
	A) Perform user authentication	B) Retrieve user information	
	C) Neither A nor B	D) Both A and B	
5	**Which of the following technologies uses SAML?**		A
	A) SSO	B) Oauth	
	C) LDAP	D) OIDC	
6	**Which of the following statements is true?** i. For accessing multiple applications in an organisation with multiple user IDs, SAML should be used. ii. For accessing email servers of multiple organisations with a single user id, SSO should be used. iii. For accessing a user's information stored in another application, OAuth should be used. iv. For allowing a customer to log in to an application using their Gmail credentials, OpenID should be used.		D
	A) i	B) ii	
	C) iii	D) iv	
7	**Which of the following is used to provide SSO experience for enterprise users within a single organisation?**		B
	A) OpenID	B) SAML	
	C) OAuth	D) Federated identity management	
8	**Which of the following is used to provide SSO experience for users on social media?**		A
	A) OpenID	B) SAML	
	C) OAuth	D) Federated identity management	

S. No.	Questions		Answers
9	**Which of the following is used to retrieve the social media information of a user?**		C
	A) OpenID	B) SAML	
	C) OAuth	D) Federated identity management	
10	**Which of the following is used to provide SSO experience to users across multiple organisations?**		D
	A) OpenID	B) SAML	
	C) OAuth	D) Federated identity management	
11	**Which of the following is not a use of LDAP?**		B
	A) Modifying and retrieving user information in the active directory	B) Storing and archiving user information	
	C) Authenticating a user	D) All of the above	
12	**An organisation has declared their access policies as follows:** **Marketing team: Product documentation, legal information** **Technical team: Product documentation, software code** **Legal team: Product documentation, legal background** **What kind of access policy is being employed here?**		A
	A) Identity-based access policy	B) Mandatory access policy	
	C) Resource-based access policy	D) None of the above	
13	**An organisation has declared their access policies as follows:** **Production servers: L1 support team, IT team** **Source code: Engineers** **Production databases: Affiliate users, Legal teams** **What model of access policy is being employed here?**		C
	A) Identity-based access policy	B) Mandatory access policy	
	C) Resource-based access policy	D) None of the above	
14	**A software company designed its product to work as follows:** **Step 1: Application accesses a user's profile details from Facebook** **Step 2: Facebook accesses user activity information from the application** **Which of the following statements is true?**		A
	A) Facebook is the subject in step 1 and the object in step 2.	B) Facebook is the object in step 1 and the subject in step 2.	
	C) Facebook is the subject in both steps.	D) Facebook is the object in both steps.	

S. No.	Questions		Answers
15	**Which step is not part of access control?**		B
	A) Identify and authenticate subjects	B) Check the password security of users	
	C) Permit or deny access	D) Check access authorisation	
16	**An organization has mentioned that access control rules are specified centrally and are non-negotiable. What access control model is this?**		A
	A) Mandatory access control	B) Discretionary access control	
	C) Both	D) None	
17	**Which of the following statements about a subject is true?**		C
	A) A subject is always a user account.	B) The subject is always the entity that receives information about or data from an object.	
	C) The subject is always the entity that provides or hosts the information or data.	D) A single entity can never change roles between being the subject and the object.	
18	**What is the purpose of user's login ID?**		D
	A) Authentication	B) Authorization	
	C) Accountability	D) Identification	
19	**Which of the following supports federated identity management?**		B
	A) Cyphertext	B) SAML	
	C) XML	D) UAML	
20	**What access control model is used in Firewalls?**		B
	A) Mandatory access control	B) Rule-based access control	
	C) Attribute-based access control	D) Detection Access Control	
21	**What access control model is commonly used in software-defined networking?**		C
	A) Directive Access Control	B) Rule-based access control	
	C) Attribute-based access control	D) Role-based access control	

S. No.	Questions		Answers
22	An organisation has allowed open internet access for its managers: only social media sites for its marketing team and only newspapers and tech blogs access to developers. What is this access control model an example of?		D
	A) Directive Access Control	B) Rule-based access control	
	C) Attribute-based access control	D) Role-based access control	
23	What is the primary purpose of Kerberos?		D
	A) Authentication	B) Access control	
	C) Authorization	D) All of the above	

Join our Discord space

Join our Discord workspace for latest updates, offers, tech happenings around the world, new releases, and sessions with the authors:

https://discord.bpbonline.com

CHAPTER 9
Migrating to Cloud

Introduction

So far, we have discussed various fundamentals crucial to computing. We discussed the origins and evolution of computing, memory, storage, networking, and how they are implemented in the cloud. In this chapter, we will put them all together. We will discuss how to build a new cloud application and how to migrate an existing application to the cloud. We will look at how developers, system administrators, and product managers bring in the concepts described earlier to build a cloud application that serves the organization's business goals. Whether you are building an entirely new application or migrating an existing one, all the learnings will be incorporated into the activity.

Structure

We will discuss the following topics in this chapter:

- Types of migration
- Migration strategies
- Migration roadmap
- Migration life cycle

Objectives

With the cloud becoming mainstream, it has become imperative for organizations to include cloud capabilities in their portfolios. Organizations are likely to migrate their existing applications into the cloud in one form or another. This makes familiarity with cloud migrations necessary for system administrators, network administrators, solution architects, developers, and product managers. Consequently, the CVO-003 exam places significant importance on the topic of migration.

This chapter intends to cover migration in detail. We will focus primarily on migrating an application. However, all discussions apply to building applications ground up as well. As we shall discuss shortly, building an application ground-up can be considered a special case of migration.

Types of migration

The word migration means the movement of people from one place to settle in another. In the context of cloud computing, it is four different flavors. The source and destination can be physical or virtual, leading to four combinations.

Physical-to-physical

This refers to moving applications, storage, and network from one physical machine to another. This is common when updating or replacing hardware in a data center. Like any system, computers need upkeep and have a lifespan. Once the lifespan ends, it is neither likely nor desirable for the new systems to be a replica of the existing systems. It is always a good idea to evaluate what is new with hardware and software, understand new features and changes, and incorporate them into the application software. For example, the US Army was forced to upgrade its computers when *Microsoft* announced the end-of-life support for *Windows XP*.

Physical-to-virtual

This is the classic cloud migration and is the rage in the IT industry. In this migration, an existing application is moved from the private data center to a public or private cloud. We shall discuss this scenario extensively in this chapter.

Virtual-to-virtual

This scenario is required when switching between **cloud service providers (CSP)**. It could be switching from a private to a public cloud, like AWS, Azure, Google Cloud, or vice versa. This would require you to analyze the vendor lock-in you have, that is, the dependency of your application on the features specific to the cloud provider. Suppose your new CSP does not have feature parity with the existing provider. In that case, you will have to build some customizations into your application to ensure that your business requirements are not disturbed. All major CSPs have a significant level of feature parity, but they also have considerable differences. It is important to understand these differences to ensure that business processes do not suffer from migration.

Virtual-to-physical

A virtual-to-physical migration happens on a few occasions. It involves moving assets out of the cloud onto a physical machine. This niche scenario might be necessary for legal reasons or if the cloud is offering diminishing returns. There is more to this migration than buying hardware resembling virtual machines and running applications. A cloud's implicit and explicit benefits should be considered carefully to ensure the continuity of business processes and SLAs.

Migration strategies

Irrespective of the migration type, the activities involved can be grouped under certain standard strategies. These are referred to as **Gartner's 5R strategies**. Various organizations have since expanded on this list, and we hear the terms 6R and 7R. Most migration projects fall into one of these strategies. It helps identify the strategy early in the project, to take help from the body of knowledge available in the industry for each strategy. While the following discussion is for a physical-to-virtual migration scenario, the strategies are not limited to P2V.

The first five strategies listed as follows are quoted from the original *Gartner publication*. Their list is neither definitive nor exhaustive. Multiple cloud organizations added the remaining strategies to address different migration scenarios. Google, Microsoft Azure, and AWS routinely use 7R in their official documentation.

Rehost

Rehosting strategy is also called a **lift-and-shift strategy**. This is considered the quickest route to the cloud. In this strategy, CSP is treated as an infrastructure provider, Infrastructure as a Service. Physical hardware is replicated using CSP's virtual machines, software configuration is retained as-is, and the application is hosted on them. The application is hosted on cloud machines effectively; hence, the name is re-hosted. IaaS is often the first step in an organization's cloud journey. Rehosting applications on the cloud can significantly reduce expenses without vendor lock-in. All the capabilities of a cloud are not utilized when rehosting. CSP's responsibility is limited to the upkeep of physical machines for hosting the VMs. All other responsibilities remain with the organization. For example, configuring the VMs, maintaining OS patches, network management, backup management, and so on are the responsibilities of the organization's IT team.

Refactor

Refactoring is the strategy of restructuring application code without modifying the original functionality. This strategy is pursued to take additional advantage of cloud functionalities. For example, the enterprise application might have in-house code written for balancing network traffic. When migrating in a refactoring strategy, the cloud load balancer is configured where applicable instead of using in-house code. This requires modification to the application code without changing the business functionality. This strategy requires a careful analysis of in-house implementations with cloud features and an understanding of the modifications. Compared to rehosting, refactoring takes higher advantage of cloud functionalities.

Revise

Revising strategy involves modifying the existing code to support the updated features and rehosting or refactoring. It generally means that the application needs deeper architectural changes compared to refactoring strategy. This allows organizations to tailor applications to exploit a wide range of features offered by the CSP. This process is time-consuming and requires significant changes to the application code. If they can get this correctly, this approach offers considerable improvement for the organization's agility and reduced expenses.

Rebuild

Rebuilding involves discarding the application code almost entirely. The application code is rewritten from the ground up, with only the business requirements being the same. The architecture is envisioned afresh and is completely changed to become cloud native. As mentioned earlier, building a new cloud application is similar to the rebuild strategy and can be considered a niche case of migration.

Replace

The replacement strategy involves replacing one software component with another. For example, the organization might use an MS Office Exchange in its private data center. When migrating to the cloud, it might be replaced with Office 365 or Google office suite. All the supporting applications and the automation code will have to be replaced. This might look very similar to refactoring, but it is much more extensive than that. The changes required for replacement are not necessarily confined to a piece of code, but they can entirely change the organization's culture. If the replacement is for a SaaS product, the extent of changes is limited to data migration alone. Replacing a PaaS product is a considerable challenge.

Re-platform

Re-platforming strategy is also called a **lift-tinker-and-shift strategy**. This involves greater modifications to the applications compared to rehosting, but not extensively. An example of the changes could be using PostgreSQL instead of a Microsoft SQL server. This requires not-too-extensive changes to the application. The burden of maintaining and managing the database shifts to CSP, and the organization can benefit from the economies of scale offered by the cloud.

Relocate

Relocation is required when the applications and data must be migrated across geographies. Even if the CSP remains the same, relocating applications and data requires an analysis of internal processes like legal and regulatory compliances, disaster recovery mechanisms, and consideration of latency.

Retire

As the name suggests, this is about retiring unnecessary software components. The list of to-do items increases for an organization over time. A commonly seen item is retiring old software components used in only certain cases. It might be easier for organizations to renew licenses and run the business process than to take time to rewrite an application. The Retire strategy is applicable in those scenarios.

Division of responsibilities is the most important point to remember in any migration project. A SaaS cloud puts the onus on the CSP while leaving the organizations with the least flexibility. Conversely, IaaS clouds give maximum flexibility to organizations, but the responsibility remains with them. Refer to *Figure 9.1* to see the distribution of responsibilities between CSP and the organization:

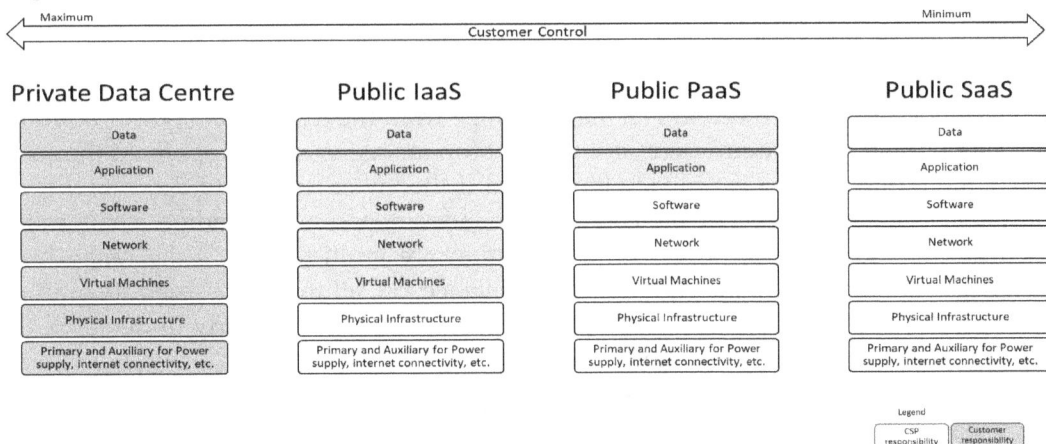

Figure 9.1: CSP-Customer responsibility distribution

Note: *Figure 9.1* **does not speak of ownership. It is only about the responsibility of managing the asset. Ownership is, by and large, the same, with data being the differentiating factor.**

The distribution of ownership is detailed in *Figure 9.2*. Irrespective of the cloud service, the customer organization always owns the data.

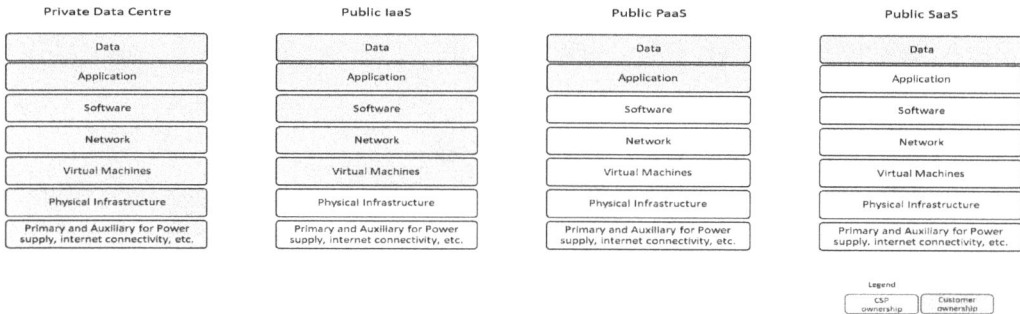

Figure 9.2: CSP-Customer ownership distribution

Migration roadmap

Now that we know the types of migration and strategies, let us discuss how to develop a migration roadmap for the organization. There is no fixed template for the roadmap. CSPs and systems integrators have their proprietary approaches to building a roadmap. Fortunately, all approaches have some similarities, barring finer differences. You shall observe significant similarities if you closely observe the roadmaps suggested by CSPs and systems integrators. So, we will discuss the common aspects of any migration roadmap. We will rely on the roadmap suggested by Gartner's® Rs in the upcoming sections.

Aligning objectives

It is common for organizations to start their cloud migration journey because of management instructions. Cloud is a major change from the traditional style of building applications, and it is seldom successful without top management's support. At the same time, a migration journey is unlikely to succeed if the lower rungs and departments do not understand and appreciate the complexities, advantages, and paradigm changes the cloud brings. Success criteria for cloud migration are multi-faceted. They range from technical benefits to cost benefits to legal compliance. So, all the teams need to align on cloud migration objectives. All teams in the organization should clearly understand the value proposition of cloud migration.

Some suggested steps in this stage of the roadmap are as follows:

1. Building a common understanding of cloud adoption use cases
2. Defining a cloud strategy aligned to IT's strategic goals

3. Defining the action steps to achieve goals

4. Formulating the migration principles based on readiness, priorities, legacy status, and vendor capabilities of applications

5. Understanding the data and metrics for usage

Some of the questions to be answered in this stage are listed here:

- *What is the current application landscape and hardware landscape of the organization?*

- *What are the expected business benefits and their priorities? Is the objective to achieve cost savings, to improve capacity management, to address workload volatility or a combination of these?*

- *What are the challenges involved? The challenges can be related to security, regulatory challenges, vendor lock-in, integration difficulties, and so on.*

- *What should be the target cloud environment? Should it be a private cloud, a public cloud, a community cloud, or a hybrid cloud model?*

- *What service model should be adopted? Should the organization adopt IaaS, SaaS, or PaaS?*

- *What should be the migration strategy?*

Gartner® suggests the framework shown in *Figure 9.3* for cloud adoption. All enterprise applications must be evaluated and placed into one of the four quadrants, and a cloud migration strategy should be chosen appropriately.

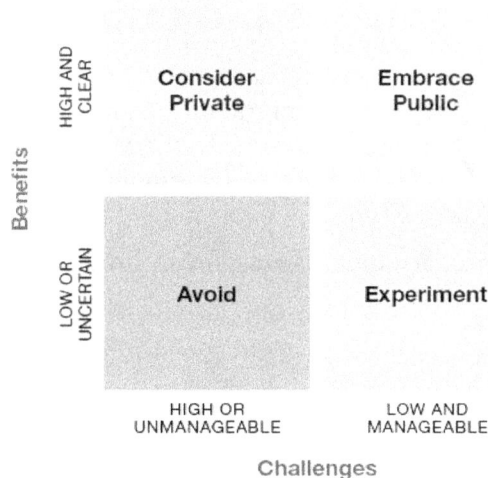

Figure 9.3: Gartner®'s framework for categorizing cloud service options

Developing an action plan

At this stage, the focus should be on identifying the sequence of steps needed for the desired end stage. Organizations either drive the adoption centrally or allow individual business units to migrate independently. Both approaches have advantages and disadvantages. Either way, some of the common steps in this stage are as follows:

1. Developing cloud competencies across the enterprise

2. Assessing different service providers (AWS, Google, Microsoft, and the like).

3. Building protections against cloud-specific risks.

4. Identifying viable investments in networking, security, and identity architectures, and tools.

Preparing for execution

This stage is predominantly about building cloud applications, and deploying and optimizing workload placement. The chosen migration strategy is vital in determining the steps needed here, and it drives the project plans and task assignments for individual teams. The tasks that are typically implemented here are listed here:

- Identifying workloads for migration

- Establishing cloud management workflow

- Adopting best practices for implementation

- Analyzing workloads pre- and post-migration

Establishing governance and mitigating risk

This stage involves establishing robust technical and business processes to minimize business disruptions arising from cloud migrations. Cloud migration is internal to an organization. End users are typically not concerned with the hosting of applications. It is the organization's responsibility to ensure that cloud migration does not cause inconvenience to the end users. The tasks that are typically implemented are as follows:

- Prioritizing data discovery, monitoring, and analytics

- Establishing security controls using appropriate tools

- Developing cloud governance life cycle

- Automating workflows to embed adherence to governance principles

Optimizing and scaling

This stage is in line with the Check and Act stages of the Deming Cycle, also known as the **Plan-Do-Check-Act cycle**. The purpose of this stage is to evaluate the cloud footprint, make corrections and incremental improvements, and prepare for the next stage of cloud migration. This stage is a critical component of continuous improvement for organizations. Lessons learned from each iteration are gathered at this stage and are incorporated into the next iteration. The typical activities undertaken at this stage are as follows:

- Prioritizing investments to advance existing cloud strategies

- Creating customer-centric shared objectives for cross-functional teams

- Iterating to optimize and evolve the cloud footprint

When detailing the mentioned stages, organizations should consider their resources, business needs, and IT capabilities. Short- and long-term needs must be kept in mind when deciding between trade-offs. Some common challenges faced during migration are as follows:

- **Incompatible infrastructure between the data center and cloud**: This happens in the case of OS or hardware configurations that might not be available with the CSP. Differences between required and available operating systems and APIs can result in performance issues or, in the worst case, abandoning the lift-and-shift migration of that application.

- **Incompatible security policies between organization and cloud**: A private data center offers complete freedom for designing security policies. CSPs might not always offer the same level of freedom. Some efforts must be spent in redesigning cloud security policies. For example, your application source code may be on a Git server in a private data center. Security policy can be specified to permit access to it only from within the company's intranet. The same restriction might not be easy to enforce after migration.

- **Migrating apps with dependencies**: It is not always possible to lift and shift entire data centers and apps. A phased or wave-like migration is preferred to allow room for process improvement and minimize disruptions. This results in applications being distributed across the cloud and data center, and latency is inevitable in such scenarios.

- **Cost of refactoring applications**: Teams tend to underestimate refactoring efforts, perhaps because the myriad dependencies between applications are not always clearly visible. As a result, refactoring tends to get underestimated.

- **Lack of strategic planning**: Not documenting the cloud strategy seriously jeopardizes the chances of a successful migration. As discussed earlier, strategic planning is the most critical part of the cloud journey.

- **Resource skill gaps**: An organization's in-house resources might not be well-versed with CSP features. Identifying and bridging this skill gap is vital for the optimal utilization of the cloud.

Migration life cycle

Like all projects, migration projects also have a life cycle. They have three stages: plan, build, and migrate. Each stage has several interrelated steps.

Planning

The planning stage determines the resource requirements for the networking, security, and other computing resources required to support the application requirements. It also includes understanding the CSP functionalities, analyzing data center workloads, analyzing the enterprise network, preparing the CSP's storage and network resources, and setting up a network communication between the data center and the CSP.

Building

This stage is used to build the **Software Defined Data Center** (**SDDC**), **software-defined network** (**SDN**), fail-over zones, enterprise-wide security policies, and the like, using the information prepared in the planning stage.

Migrating

This stage is the actual migration, and it involves creating cloud identities and resources and moving data, applications, and so on. Migration, either by wave or as a one-shot, happens at this stage. Migration of applications, data, and networks is all subtly different. Project plans should focus on these details and must be coordinated for a seamless user experience. A brief period of downtime, called **cutover**, is scheduled at the end of migration. Original data center applications and data are marked as read-only during this cutover. After this cutover, users start using the cloud applications, and their operations remain seamless. The original data center remains read-only for a while and then shuts down. There is no fixed rule on the cutover duration. Depending on the business use case, it can be less than a minute or longer than a weekend.

Application migration

Migrating applications follows the 5R/6R strategies discussed earlier. It is recommended to migrate low-risk, high-impact applications before migrating high-risk applications. Seamless user experience is the most important aspect during application migration. A thorough test of the impact of migrating applications with dependencies should be done carefully. If the dependencies are not part of the migration, rigorous testing should be done on performance latencies, and users must be prepared regarding the impact.

Data migration

Data migration happens in a slightly different manner compared to applications. Even within a migration wave, data migration might require multiple iterations. This is especially the case when the data volumes are high. For this, a snapshot of the data is migrated in the first iteration. In subsequent iterations, the data created during the previous iteration is migrated. The number of iterations varies with the data volume created and the time taken to migrate the same. It is necessary to perform as many iterations as needed until the iteration time is less than the downtime for cutover. After the cutover, users will access the data and should not see anything amiss. Take a look at *Figure 9.4* for an illustration of such a migration, which illustrates how an application hosted in a private data center is migrated to a cloud. Data is migrated in three iterations for this single application. The application itself might be part of a larger group of migrated applications in the given wave.

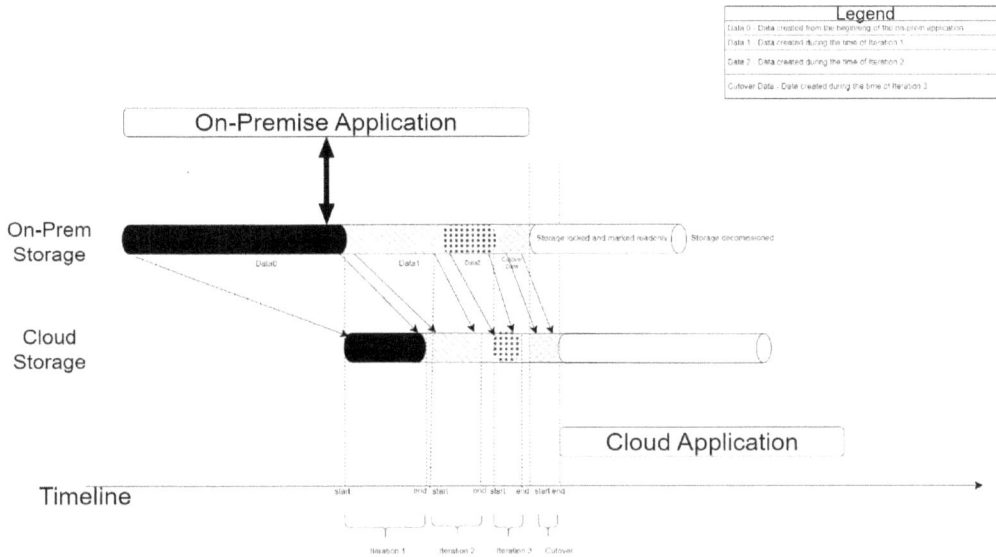

Figure 9.4: *Phased data migration*

Network migration

Strictly speaking, a network is not migrated. It is recreated on the cloud using SDN. When discussing migration, the focus is on applications and data, and the network is slightly overlooked. However, improper planning of networks can cause problems like high latency or high costs, negating the advantages of cloud migration. Proper analysis of bandwidth quotas, limits, and scaling is necessary to ensure optimal utilization of the cloud. Network modeling tools can help discover network topologies and their utilization in the private data center.

Security

As mentioned earlier, security is one of the most common challenges in cloud migration. It is common to encounter incompatibilities in security policies between private data centers and the cloud. In such cases, a thorough analysis of the gaps should be performed, and it is suggested to get approval from the management regarding the changes. Getting buy-in from legal teams regarding the gaps and changes is also advisable.

Billing

Most CSPs have a pay-as-you-go model for billing. This means you will be billed for the number of resources used by the organization. As discussed in previous chapters, this offers great cost benefits to organizations. At the same time, any mistake in setting up the cloud resources will run up the organization's charges. So, proper care should be taken when setting up the cloud resources to track each resource's costs. All CSPs offer cost-tracking mechanisms, which must be incorporated from the initial get-go on a cloud.

Some CSPs also allow organizations to cap costs during the billing period. Once the limit is reached, CSPs will automatically stop the VMs or networks. Employing limits is helpful for an organization to control costs. They should be monitored carefully and regularly, and alerts should be raised if they are being breached.

Identity and access migration

Identity migration is one of the initial steps when migrating to the cloud. The moment a contract is signed, identity management begins for administrator accounts. CSPs provide identity management in their environment, as discussed in the previous chapters. Identity migration is not likely to end with a complete retirement of the organization's homegrown IAM system. Cloud identities offer fine-grained control over access policies. An organization's IAM services are used for multiple purposes apart from cloud login. It is not advisable to rely completely on CSP's IAM for the organization's users.

So, the IAM migrations generally follow a four-stage process. In the first stage, CSP's IAM and the organization's IAM (via Active Directory or equivalent) are segregated. Users maintain two different login credentials for enterprise and cloud access. In the second stage, an SSO is provided between on-premises IAM and cloud IAM, with the access management system being on-premises. At the third stage, on-premise applications are authenticated using cloud identities. In the fourth stage, the access management system is moved to the cloud. This process is elaborate and not always the norm. Stages 3 and 4 are optional, and some CSPs do not support them.

Support

Cloud operates a shared responsibility model. IT teams have complete control of the application when they are running in private data centers. So, the distribution of responsibilities must be considered, and service-level agreements should be revisited during a migration. Support SLAs should be revisited when performing migrations. For example, a private data center might have a 99% SLA for uptime. Most CSPs have a much higher SLA to the tune of 99.9999%. The other aspect that should be kept in mind is the technical support SLAs. CSPs functionalities also suffer from bugs; they maintain SLAs to fix them and answer technical queries. Technical and priority support is a source of revenue for CSPs. Organizations should evaluate the cost-benefit of the available support tiers and purchase appropriate plans. This affects the turnaround time offered by organizations for their customers. So, it would be beneficial for the organization to revisit its SLAs, keeping the CSP's SLAs in view.

Conclusion

In this chapter, we learned the necessity of understanding cloud migration, the types of migration, and the strategies available for them. We also learned about the migration life cycle and the specific details of migrating different components of enterprise applications.

The next chapter will discuss orchestrating cloud applications. We will discuss automation, orchestration, and run book management strategies.

Glossary

- **Cutover**: A term indicating a change from old IT systems to new ones
- **Deming Cycle**: A technique used for improving organizational processes that is used to identify and address problems; contains four steps: Plan, Do, Check, and Act; named after Edward Deming, the proponent of the technique
- **PDCA cycle**: Another name for Deming Cycle
- **SDDC**: Software-defined data center

Practice questions

S. No.	Questions		Answers
1	**Which of the following is not a type of migration?**		B
	A) Physical-to-virtual	B) Virtual-to-static	
	C) Virtual-to-physical	D) Physical-to-physical	
2	**Which of the following is a migration strategy?**		D
	A) Reduce	B) Reuse	
	C) Recycle	D) Retire	
3	**Which of the following strategies is called the lift-and-shift strategy?**		A
	A) Rehost	B) Rehire	
	C) Reassign	D) Re-platform	

S. No.	Questions		Answers
4	An organization is performing cloud migration. The migration team commissioned VMs with the same configuration as the machines in their private data center and installed the necessary applications on the VMs. What migration strategy is this?		D
	A) Refactor	B) Replace	
	C) Revise	D) None of them	
5	An organization is migrating their cloud application from one CSP to another. The migration team makes a list of cloud components being used by their application and lists equivalent components provided by the new CSP. They ask the development team to modify the source code to call the new APIs and keep the UI as-is. What migration strategy is this?		A
	A) Replace	B) Rebuild	
	C) Revise	D) Re-platform	
6	In public SaaS, who is responsible for maintaining the data upkeep?		A
	A) CSP	B) Neither	
	C) Client	D) Both	
7	In public SaaS, who owns the data created by the application?		C
	A) CSP	B) Neither	
	C) Client	D) Both	
8	Consider a scenario: An organization is working on building a cloud application. The application is hosted on virtual machines in CSP 1. The application uses machine learning APIs provided by CSP 2. The application stores data in CSP3. Who is responsible for data management activities?		A
	A) Organization	B) CSP 1	
	C) CSP 2	D) CSP 3	
9	Consider a scenario: An organization is working on building a cloud application. The application is hosted on virtual machines in CSP 1. The application uses machine learning APIs provided by CSP 2. The application stores data in CSP3. Who is responsible for the upkeep and availability of application servers?		A
	A) Organization	B) CSP 1	
	C) CSP 2	D) CSP 3	

S. No.	Questions		Answers
10	Consider a scenario: An organization is working on building a cloud application. The application is hosted on virtual machines in CSP 1. The application uses machine learning APIs provided by CSP 2. The application stores data in CSP3. Who is responsible for the availability of storage space?		D
	A) Organization	B) CSP 1	
	C) CSP 2	D) CSP 3	
11	Consider a scenario: An organization is working on building a cloud application. The application is hosted on virtual machines in CSP 1. The application uses machine learning APIs provided by CSP 2. The application stores data in CSP3. Who is responsible for the upkeep and availability of VMs?		B
	A) Organization	B) CSP 1	
	C) CSP 2	D) CSP 3	
12	Consider a scenario: An organization is working on building a cloud application. The application is hosted on virtual machines in CSP 1. The application uses machine learning APIs provided by CSP 2. The application stores data in CSP3. Who is responsible for application functionality provided to users?		A
	A) Organization	B) CSP 1	
	C) CSP 2	D) CSP 3	
13	Consider a scenario: An organization is working on building a cloud application. The application is hosted on virtual machines in CSP 1. The application uses machine learning APIs provided by CSP 2. The application stores data in CSP3. Who is responsible for scaling the ML services as per demand?		C
	A) Organization	B) CSP 1	
	C) CSP 2	D) CSP 3	
14	Which of the following is a commonly used approach for tracking costs after migration?		C
	A) Tagging	B) Pay-as-you-go	
	C) Chargeback	D) Limits	

S. No.	Questions	Answers
15	An organization is considering migrating to the cloud. They have the following three options to track the expenses. Order the approaches in increasing order of effort. i. Separate CSP accounts for applications, data, security and so on. ii. Individual CSP accounts for each business unit in the organization. iii. Tagging of resources and chargeback based on tagging. A) i, iii, ii B) iii, ii, i C) ii, i, iii D) i, ii, iii	D
16	What stages of IAM migration are optional for CSPs? i. IAM for Cloud login ii. Single sign-on for cloud applications and on-premises applications iii. Authenticate on-premises applications with cloud login credentials iv. Access management system in the cloud A) i and ii B) I and iv C) iii and iv D) ii and iii	C
17	An enterprise is migrating an on-premises application to the cloud. After which step will the users be working in the cloud environment? A) Production rollout B) Retiring the on-premises application C) Advertising campaign D) Cutover	D
18	Which of the following migrations requires multiple iterations to be considered complete? A) Network B) Data C) Security D) Identity	B

Join our Discord space

Join our Discord workspace for latest updates, offers, tech happenings around the world, new releases, and sessions with the authors:

https://discord.bpbonline.com

CHAPTER 10
Orchestrating Cloud Applications

Introduction

As a rule, human beings detest doing repetitive, boring work. It is always preferable to transfer such repetitive activities to machines. This allows human beings to focus on activities that require a uniquely human trait of creativity. Computers, built to reduce human workloads, are perfect candidates for performing repetitive tasks, and cloud computing is no exception to this. Widespread adoption of the cloud by enterprises has brought in many repetitive activities to be performed by cloud administrators. This made cloud automation a necessary skill for administrators to save time and effort.

We will discuss cloud automation and orchestration in this chapter; there is a subtle difference between the two.

Objectives

This chapter focuses on the automation and orchestration aspects of a cloud application. We will start from the basics of automation, like scripting, and proceed to advanced topics like orchestration and run book management. Application orchestration is an important topic for cloud administrators and developers alike. The CVO-003 exam places an appropriate level of focus on this topic, and it cannot be ignored by anyone aiming to gain expertise in cloud application development.

Structure

We will cover the following topics in this chapter:

- Automation
- Orchestration
- Runbook management

Automation

Automation was an important skill required for systems administrators even before cloud adoption. Even simple activities like onboarding a new employee to an organization need a list of tasks to be completed in the system. Repeating these tasks manually is a waste of effort for administrators. So, administrators created automation tools that perform repeated activities. The automation tools started with shell scripting, where a series of commands were written into a file and executed as needed. Scripts are an indispensable component in a system administrator's repertoire. So, when the cloud was adopted by enterprises, it was only logical that system administrators required automation tools to support their activities.

Cloud automation use cases

Cloud administrators have several repetitive activities daily; many of these activities can be automated. The following is an example list of activities that can be automated; note that this list is only representative and is not exhaustive:

- Creating, sizing, and provisioning of virtual machines
- Load balancing
- Setting up network topographies in SDNs
- Data management activities like archival
- Security policy verifications
- Deploying applications onto virtual machines across development and production environments
- Integrated version control in CI/CD and other DevOps activities

Automation enables administrators to perform manual activities and can even enable the self-servicing of requests. A classic example is resetting passwords for users who got accidentally locked out of the system. In the olden days, users had to contact system administrators to reset their passwords. It is now common to have such requests handled routinely via an email or a web page created for such purposes.

Benefits of cloud automation

It is important to understand that automation is not meant to perform activities that cannot be done manually. Quite to the contrary, automation is only for reducing the effort in performing manual activities. All the individual steps in an automated task can be performed manually. However, laborious and manual repetition often leads to errors and requires troubleshooting efforts. So, automation is always preferred instead. The benefits of automation can be summed up as follows:

- Improved productivity
- Speed of delivery and scalability
- Improved security
- Improved IT compliance

Types of automation activities

Cloud automation activities can generally be arranged into two groups. The first group is activities performed by system administrators or cloud administrators. They are required for data center maintenance to meet the enterprise policies and legal standards regarding data management. It can also be for maintaining the network infrastructure, such as setting up the SDN, checking security compliance, and the like.

The second group of activities is for supporting the development activities for cloud applications. This includes creating and provisioning virtual machines, configuring and tuning load balancers, scaling servers, and rolling out application code.

There are other activities that are automated in the cloud, but these two form the largest groups.

Scripting

As mentioned earlier, using scripts is a common way to write automation tasks. Unix ecosystem has a wide range of shells, such as **c-shell (csh)**, **Korn-shell (ksh)**, **Bourne shell (bsh)**, **z-shell (zsh)**, and the more recent **Bourne Again Shell (bash)** for this purpose. Windows has batch files with the .bat extension for this purpose. Microsoft has introduced PowerShell in the recent past for enhanced capabilities.

It is necessary to understand how automation is made possible for different cloud models. This is because the logistics of automation are very different for SaaS users from PaaS or IaaS users.

SaaS users require automation of activities performed using the user interface. The end goal of their automation is not to affect a series of user interface interactions. In other words, the automation's purpose is not to simulate a few mouse clicks and keyboard strokes but to effect a change in the data or system. To make this possible, SaaS providers release a library or package containing API calls. These APIs can be called from high-level programming languages like Java, Python, and the like. A customized workflow is presented to the user, and the series of actions is affected by calling the APIs.

PaaS applications like Jenkins, Git, and the like can be automated using command-line utilities. Interacting with PaaS requires either command-line tools or programming libraries, so automation is a given for PaaS.

Automation for IaaS uses various tools to perform **Create, Read, Update, and Delete (CRUD)** operations on virtual machines and other virtual resources.

Infrastructure as Code

Extensive automation capabilities for IaaS have given rise to the concept called **Infrastructure as Code (IaC)**. In IaC, the provisioning and management of virtual resources are performed using programming code instead of interactive configuration tools. This provides great benefits to administrators in fine-tuning the virtual resources and ensuring their error-free reproducibility. The biggest advantages of IaC are in controlling costs, improving the speed of deliverables, and mitigating risks.

The programming code for maintaining infrastructure can be maintained in source code management systems to achieve version and quality control. The ability to treat IaC and use software development tools for developing the infrastructure offers significant agility to software developers for developing and deploying applications.

IaC is managed in two different approaches: imperative and declarative. Both these approaches aim to provide a virtual machine that meets the user's needs. They differ in their approach to provisioning the machine. Let us see how:

- **Imperative**: In this approach, the steps to attain the target configuration should be explicitly specified by a sequence of commands. Examples are Shell scripts and power shell.
- **Declarative**: In this approach, the final state of the VM is specified, including the properties, configuration, and so on. The IaC software will figure out the commands that need to be executed in order to reach the specified state. Terraform is a good example of a declarative approach.

IaC tools

Many open-source and commercial software are available for automating IaaS tasks and for IaC. They are created mainly to cater to the needs of **Continuous Configuration Automation (CCA)**. Examples are Puppet, Ansible, Terraform, Otter, Chef, and the like. Software like Terraform supports multiple CSPs, whereas software like Amazon's CloudFormation is dedicated to a single CSP.

Orchestration

Cloud orchestration is the process of automating cloud operations. Orchestration technologies integrate automation tools and business processes into a single workflow to perform specific business functions. It is important to note that orchestration is not the same as automation.

Orchestration uses programming to connect workloads and automation tasks in a cloud environment into a single cohesive business function. Orchestration technology typically works with heterogeneous systems like public and private clouds.

Orchestration software can oversee the interaction between multiple components that make up an application or automation solution. They provide dashboards for centralized viewing and managing the communication between components.

Automation vs. orchestration

We often hear the word orchestration along with automation in the enterprise context. These two are very closely related concepts with one significant difference. Orchestration is a superset of automation; it is about combining multiple automation tasks and processes into a single workflow to achieve a specific business function.

Here is a simplified scenario. Consider a business requirement where a system administrator has to archive data older than two months on a weekly basis. This is achieved using multiple steps, like running a job or process every week, identifying files that have not been modified in the past 2 months, moving those files into lower-tier storage, and indexing them.

Each of the steps described is an automation activity. Putting them together into a single workflow is orchestration.

If each of the automation steps creates its own VM, it might result in VM sprawl, which is a common problem in cloud environments. Orchestration can help address such problems. Orchestration and automation work together to provide value to organizations. Orchestration is not possible without automation, and automation without orchestration yields limited benefits.

Benefits of orchestration

Cloud orchestration is embraced by teams adopting DevOps for their enterprise cloud application development. A cloud orchestrator automates the management of complex IT systems. Orchestration is a good way to control VM sprawl, and it offers the following benefits to organizations:

- Reduction of costs

- Improvement of the speed of delivery
- Standardization of processes by using templates
- Improved security
- Centralized dashboards for viewing the information relevant to administrators

Cloud orchestration models

Cloud orchestration models allow a fully prepared cloud environment to be deployed on a CSP. As can be imagined, using a single CSP for all cloud needs is a simpler scenario. However, it is not uncommon for organizations to have multiple CSPs to meet their organization's needs. They may have email on Microsoft 365 (SaaS), CRM data on Salesforce (SaaS), data stored on Oracle Compute Platform (PaaS), and machine learning workloads running in Google Cloud (IaaS). Cloud orchestration tools can work across clouds to automate the deployment process.

Generally, orchestration is used to provision servers, acquire storage and other resources, deploy application software, and start the servers. They can even incorporate policies and permissions for compliance and security.

Event orchestration

Event orchestration is about identifying incidents of interest as they occur in real-time. For this, orchestration software relies on the log files generated by firewalls, routers, servers, applications, and other resources. Such logfiles are gathered in real-time, parsed, and analyzed using various rules. If any events are observed that match a predetermined pattern, then an incident is considered to have occurred. The incident can be a server using higher memory than usual or an unknown IP address trying to access the system. Depending on the incident severity, appropriate action is taken by the orchestration software.

Runbook management

A runbook is a sequence of procedures or steps to be implemented for the purpose of completing a given task. The important item to note is that all the procedures should be written down in a single document. Runbooks form a crucial aspect of an organization's IT protocols. They provide contextual information regarding incidents to both experienced and novice IT professionals. They provide a step-by-step guide on troubleshooting and incident responses. The steps contained in runbooks can be entirely manual, entirely automated, or a combination of both.

Two categories of runbooks are used in enterprises:

- **General**: These are for routine operations like auditing, data backup, and so on.

- **Specialized**: These are for special scenarios like application troubleshooting, disaster recovery, DevOps activities, and so on.

The contents of a runbook are very specific to the business function for which they were written. There is no industry standard format either. Runbooks can vary from a Word document to an Excel sheet. However, certain content can be observed to repeat across runbooks. The following sections are generally seen in runbooks:

- Overview
- Key personnel or roles with access to the runbook
- Process steps
- Monitoring system information
- Disaster recovery plans
- Technical documentation

Irrespective of the category, it is important for the runbook to contain all the information that is needed to address the incident. It is not advisable to keep relevant information out of the runbook. A good runbook document is up-to-date, accessible in times of need, contains action items for the incident, and is the only runbook for the incident. A thumb rule is to check whether the runbook can be followed by a complete novice user. If such a user can address the incident based on the runbook, then it is good enough.

Multiple runbooks

Sometimes, a single runbook is not sufficient to address an incident, especially in the case of business continuity and disaster recovery; there can be multiple runbooks related to different business functions. Such a combination of runbooks is referred to as a **playbook**.

Runbook automation

Runbook automation is the process of automating the steps mentioned in a runbook. This includes triggering the runbook to report that a runbook was run and to report the status of items. Runbook automation is highly helpful in improving system reliability. It can improve metrics like **Mean Time To Recover** (**MTTR**) and **Mean Time Between Failures** (**MTBF**). Commercial software is available for runbook automation.

Runbook life cycle

A runbook has the same life cycle as any other project. It is created, improved, and retired. The term runbook life cycle refers to a different life cycle. It refers to the evolution of a runbook from fully manual to fully automated. *Figure 10.1* illustrates the life cycle of a runbook:

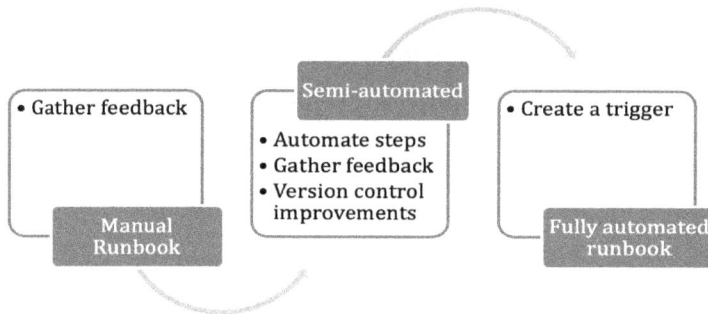

Figure 10.1: Runbook lifecycle

Conclusion

In this chapter, we discussed automation needs for cloud environments. We started by discussing the advantages of automation and moved on to explore how it is different from orchestration and how orchestration is achieved using runbooks and playbooks. We finally discussed the lifecycle of a runbook and runbook automation. Automation and orchestration together form the backbone of scalable and resilient cloud operations. In the next chapter, we will discuss troubleshooting cloud applications. Starting with CompTIA's troubleshooting methodology, we shall discuss troubleshooting approaches for cloud administrators, cloud application developers, and the best practices for cloud application development.

Glossary

- **CCA:** Continuous Configuration Automation
- **IaC:** Infrastructure as Code
- **MTBF:** Mean Time Between Failures
- **MTTR:** Mean Time To Recover
- **Orchestration:** Process of automating cloud operations
- **Playbook:** A combination of multiple runbooks
- **Runbook:** A sequence of procedures or steps to be implemented for the purpose of completing a given task
- **Shell Script:** A command-line interpreter for performing operations like file manipulation, program execution, and administrative activities
- **Shell scripts:** A computer program designed to be run at a shell's command prompt

- **VM Sprawl:** A situation where the VMs created by the organization grow beyond control; this typically happens when the processes are not clearly defined to decommission or reuse VMs

Practice questions

S. No.	Questions		Answers
1	**Which of the following is an approach for IaC?**		A
	A) Imperative	B) Descriptive	
	C) Intuitive	D) None of the above	
2	**Which of the following is not a use case for cloud automation?**		D
	A) Setting up SDN	B) Verification of security policies	
	C) Improving DevOps effectiveness	D) Authenticating users	
3	**Which of the following is an advantage of cloud automation?**		C
	A) Reducing the paperwork for creating a VM	B) Improving the VMs performance	
	C) Improve infrastructure consistency	D) Managing VM sprawl	
4	**Which of the following organizational activities gains a direct benefit from automation?**		B
	A) Customer support	B) Software development	
	C) Employee satisfaction	D) None of the above	
5	**The Dockerfile used in Docker software follows which approach to IaC?**		A
	A) Imperative	B) Descriptive	
	C) Declarative	D) None of the above	
6	**A newly joined system administrator is looking for information on how to perform a backup task. Where should they look for this information?**		C
	A) Guidebook	B) User manual of backup software	
	C) Runbook	D) None of the above	
7	**When reviewing the instructions for deploying a new software version, the administrator found that they are spread across multiple files. What is this file called?**		B
	A) Runbook	B) Playbook	
	C) Both	D) None of the above	

S. No.	Questions		Answers
8	When reviewing the infrastructure of their organization, a cloud administrator identified that many VMs were created for specific purposes but were not deleted. What is this situation called?		B
	A) VM surplus	B) VM sprawl	
	C) VM explosion	D) None	
9	What is the full form of YAML?		D
	A) Yet Another Markup Language	B) Your Automation Markup Language	
	C) Yuse Anywhere Markup Language	D) YAML Ain't Markup Language	
10	Which of the following is a container management tool?		C
	A) Docker	B) Ansible	
	C) Kubernetes	D) Chef	
11	Which of the following is not a tool used for orchestration?		C
	A) Puppet	B) Ansible	
	C) Kubernetes	D) Chef	

Join our Discord space

Join our Discord workspace for latest updates, offers, tech happenings around the world, new releases, and sessions with the authors:

https://discord.bpbonline.com

CHAPTER 11
Troubleshooting in Cloud

Introduction

It takes a lot of effort to build a complex system, and it takes an equal amount of effort to keep it running. Systems encounter many problems during their runtime, which were not anticipated during design. This necessitates fixing the issues **on the fly**. The activity of identifying and fixing the problems while the system is in operation is called **troubleshooting**.

Cloud applications can be complex. Consider applications like *Facebook, Gmail*, or *Microsoft 365*. The sheer number of features built into the application, not to mention the volume of users, makes them very complex applications. Troubleshooting them can be a challenge. It is important for developers and administrators to be familiar with the tools and techniques available for troubleshooting cloud applications.

Structure

We will cover the following topics in this chapter:

- CompTIA's troubleshooting methodology
- Troubleshooting for administrators
- Resource allocations on host machines

- Troubleshooting for developers
- Application development best practices

Objectives

This chapter will discuss the various troubleshooting tools and techniques available for cloud applications. We will start with a discussion on CompTIA's suggested troubleshooting methodology and then discuss the common problems encountered by cloud administrators and how CompTIA's methodology can be applied to troubleshoot those problems. We will also look at the common problems encountered by cloud developers and apply CompTIA's methodology for solving them. We will familiarize ourselves with the issues encountered by cloud application developers and the approaches available for triaging and addressing them. Finally, we will discuss best practices for cloud application development.

CompTIA's troubleshooting methodology

CompTIA has established a six-step approach for troubleshooting issues. At first glance, these steps might seem logical and obvious. When adopted as a formal process, the methodology is very efficient and helpful. Much of this section's information is quoted from CompTIA's official blog, written by *Damon M. Garn,* and can be found at:

https://www.comptia.org/blog/troubleshooting-methodology. Refer to *Figure 11.1* for the troubleshooting methodology suggested by CompTIA:

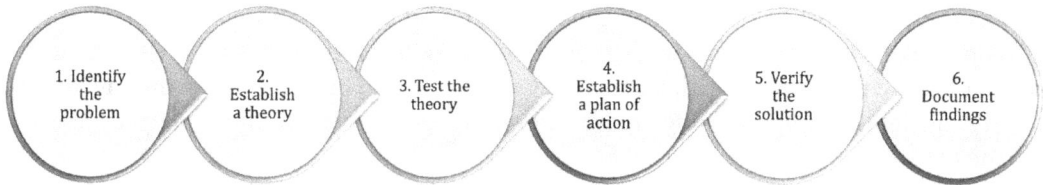

Figure 11.1: CompTIA's troubleshooting methodology

The steps involved in the methodology are listed as follows:

1. Identify the problem
2. Establish a theory of probable cause
3. Test the theory to determine the cause
4. Establish a plan of action and implement the solution
5. Verify full system functionality and implement preventive measures
6. Document findings

Sometimes, it is a practice to include an additional step called **Research** between steps 1 and 2. Some of the other steps can be named slightly differently.

Note: **The methodology is only for guidance. CompTIA does not mandate the adoption of the methodology in any organization. Even in organizations that do adopt it, an "as-is" implementation is not necessary. It is acceptable to tailor the methodology to suit the organization's needs.**

Identify the problem

To fix a problem, it must first be identified. However, identifying problems is not easy. Most of the time, the problem is reported by the users. It is very important to remember that users generally report symptoms they see and not the root cause. The purpose of step 1 of the methodology is to identify the root cause of the problem based on the reported symptoms. Several steps might be required to identify the root cause. These steps include the following:

- Gathering information from log files and error messages
- Interviewing users
- Identifying symptoms
- Determining recent changes
- Duplicating the problem
- Approaching multiple problems one at a time
- Narrowing the scope of the problem

Establish a theory of probable cause

After identifying a probable cause, a theory must be established to explain why the symptoms result from the cause. This is very much comparable to a medical professional saying that a broken bone is a cause for the pain being experienced in the form of symptoms. If the broken bone is in the right leg and the pain is reported in the left, then the probable cause might not be valid. This stage requires significant research by the technicians and the involvement of **Subject Matter Experts** (**SME**). The steps involved in this stage are as follows:

1. Questioning the obvious
2. Considering multiple approaches

Test the theory to determine the cause

Once the theory is established, it must be verified for confirmation. It behoves the administrators or SMEs to confirm or reject the theory before establishing a plan of action. At this stage, it is often seen that many theories do not stand scrutiny, and the troubleshooting team often must revert to step 1, that is, identifying the problem. In that sense, the methodology between steps 1 and 3 is not necessarily linear but iterative.

Establish a plan of action and implement the solution

Once the root cause is known, it can be addressed. However, it should not be done in haste. The pros and cons of the solution should be considered thoroughly before implementing it. For example, the solution might require restarting a suite of applications or servers. Such downtime should be planned and communicated well in advance. It is not uncommon to see trigger-happy teams rush into implementations and create additional problems for themselves. The age-old proverb *Haste makes waste* is aptly applicable here.

Verify full system functionality and implement preventive measures

Has the solution indeed fixed the problem? Was the user who reported the issue satisfied with the solution? These questions need to be answered at this stage. There are two aspects to this: the stability of the system itself, and the user who reported the problem. The plan of action suggested might, at times, not be sufficient for the user. So, it is necessary to consider the problem reporter when answering this question.

Consider a hypothetical example. A user mistyped their password and is blocked from logging in. The investigating team looked at the health dashboard and realised that the active directory server had crashed and planned to restart it. However, this plan of action does not solve the reporter's problem. They are still blocked because they mistyped their password. This is a hilarious example, but similar situations are encountered by users and IT teams.

The plan of action depends on the root cause of the problem. It is possible that the runbooks already describe the situation and have a solution. If that is not the case, it is advisable to have a **rollback** plan. Rollback plans are needed for scenarios where the devised solution does not solve the problem, and the system is not in a stable state. They describe the actions to be taken to restore the **status ante**, that is, the system state before starting the solution implementation.

It is sometimes seen that the rollback plans do not completely restore the status ante. This is indeed a troublesome scenario and requires escalation to support teams or management.

Document findings

Documentation is a topic of contention. There is a unanimous consensus that documentation is helpful. However, there are varying opinions on the amount of documentation needed. We will steer clear of that debate and stick to the necessity and advantages of documentation:

- Documenting the action plan and theories (proposed and discarded) helps in avoiding communication failures. It also helps save time when newer SMEs are to be included in the research process. Referring to the documentation can help avoid reinventing the wheel.

- Documenting the steps taken for troubleshooting could be a useful starting point when the issue recurs in the future.

- A well-documented sequence of steps is easier to reverse in case of a rollback.

Troubleshooting for administrators

So far, we have discussed the troubleshooting methodology. We will now discuss some of the most common troubles encountered in cloud environments. We will discuss the common problems for two separate groups, that is, administrators and developers. Both these groups are involved in the troubleshooting process, and they have very different paradigms of working in an organization and encounter very different problems.

Cloud computing administrators encounter distinct troubleshooting challenges due to the intricate and ever-changing nature of cloud environments. They must promptly identify and resolve issues with virtual machines, storage, and networking to minimize downtime and ensure optimal system performance. Troubleshooting in the cloud necessitates a thorough understanding of cloud architecture, as well as the capability to analyze logs and metrics for diagnosing problems. Administrators must also collaborate effectively with multiple vendors and platforms, as cloud environments often incorporate a variety of services and tools. Effective troubleshooting in cloud computing demands a combination of technical expertise, problem-solving skills, and meticulous attention to detail to resolve issues efficiently and successfully.

Resource allocations on host machines

This section is applicable for administrators working for public **Cloud Service Providers** (**CSP**) or for administrators working on private clouds.

Administrators working with virtualization hosts often encounter problems with computing resources. Compute resources here are CPU, RAM, Storage, network, and peripherals. It is a primary requirement for cloud administrators to ensure that the compute resources are optimally utilized. The compute resources should neither have long idle times nor should the VMs contend for resources. In other words, over-subscription without over-commitment is the goal for administrators. This is a fine balance to achieve.

When customers or applications adopt auto-scaling, they expect unlimited amounts of computing resources to be available to them whenever needed. This is not always feasible, especially when using private clouds. The problem is not so sharp with public CSPs, but it does exist. CSPs have a limited amount of physical hardware to share with customers, and they cannot scale it at a moment's notice. It is also not advisable for customers because the pay-as-you-go model will result in exorbitant charges. So, CSPs often place restrictions on the amount of computing resources available to applications. These restrictions are termed quotas and limits.

Quota is the highest amount of compute resources that can be made available to the application. These quotas are agreed upon as a contract between CSP and the application. Limits, on the other hand, are the levels offered by CSP. Quotas can be changed by raising a support request to the CSP. Limits are technical limitations arising out of the CSP's internal architecture and cannot be changed.

Quotas can be imposed as either hard restrictions or soft warnings. When the quota amount is breached, a hard restriction will prevent the application from further use of the resource. A soft restriction might permit a higher amount of the resource to be used, but with reduced efficiency or with a warning message sent to the application owner.

A good analogy to understand quotas and limits is to think of internet speeds offered by the **Internet Service Provider** (**ISP**). The fibre optic cable connecting your home to the internet highway might have a capability of 1 Gbps, but your internet plan might be for only 100 Mbps. Here, 1 Gbps is the limit, and 100 Mbps is your quota. You can ask for a higher quota *on demand*, but the limit cannot be changed unless the ISP rearchitects its infrastructure.

When multiple customers or applications are competing for computing resources, performance is bound to degrade. To avoid this, applications can reserve compute resources. When computing resources are reserved, a portion of the resource is set aside exclusively for that application or customer. Reservations are good for ensuring that computing resources are always available for applications. However, they can also be expensive. Customers will have to pay for reserved resources even if the actual use is significantly less.

Resource pooling is another technique adopted by administrators to ensure performance. Resource pooling is a technique in which computing resources from a single host or a cluster of hosts are logically combined into a single pool. Applications are allocated resources from this pool, which helps in maintaining the overall allocations across applications.

When troubleshooting performance issues, administrators must consider the quotas, limits, and reservations on the host hardware and hypervisors.

Licensing

Licensing is an area of concern for administrators, who must keep track of the number of licenses purchased and their actual usage. Autoscaling of VMs will increase the number of licenses required for OS and other commercial software. Attaching a license to a VM that does not use it is a waste of licenses. Alternatively, there is no over-subscription available for licenses. So, maintaining the licenses and installations requires close monitoring.

Some vendors distribute licenses using a dongle. It is a physical device to be connected to the computer (either to a USB, parallel, or serial port), and the software checks for its presence. At times, the dongle is configured to the MAC address of the computer where it should run. In these scenarios, attaching a dongle to a VM is a tricky proposition. Administrators need to work with the CSP to handle these special cases.

A similar challenge exists if edge computing or IoT devices need to be connected to virtual machines.

Performance degradation of memory

Administrators are often required to optimize the performance of the system. Performance degradation can be due to multiple reasons, like CPUs or memory being over-committed or applications not coping with workloads. Either way, administrators will have to be involved in addressing the issues along with development teams.

CSPs use techniques like **memory ballooning** and **disk space swapping** when overcommitting compute resources. These techniques are described as follows. They can sometimes adversely impact the VMs and cause performance degradation. It is advised for cloud administrators to familiarize themselves with these topics and configure the VMs accordingly.

- **Memory ballooning**: This is a technique adopted by CSPs to artificially enlarge their memory pool. Host machines install a special-purpose memory driver named **balloon driver** on the guest OS. When invoked, the balloon driver artificially consumes the unused memory on the VMs and releases it back to the host. While this helps the hosts address oversubscription, VMs may end up having insufficient RAM for their own needs.

- **Disk space swapping**: This problem is not exclusive to cloud environments. Whenever applications use more RAM than is available, operating systems use a certain portion of hard disk space in lieu of RAM. This is called **swap space** in Linux and **pagefile** in Windows. If the RAM requirement is much larger than the allocated swap space, then the OS runs into a problem called thrashing. Refer to the *Random Access Memory* section in *Chapter 3, Managing Virtual Machines*, for details. Thrashing results in performance degradation.

Memory ballooning and disk space swapping together can cause significant performance problems. Administrators should configure the swap space allocations and monitor the balloon driver to ensure that VMs and enterprise applications do not suffer performance degradation.

Performance degradation of CPU

CPU wait time is a metric of the time a program or thread spends waiting in the queue for execution. It is very important to calculate the wait times. Longer wait times mean that the CPU is over-committed and CPU demand is much higher than its availability. This inevitably degrades performance. Administrators should familiarise themselves with the tools and techniques to triage the CPU wait time problem. Multiple techniques are available to address this issue. We shall look at some of them here:

- **CPU affinity**: CPU affinity is a technique in which processes or threads are attached to a particular CPU. All subsequent requests from that process or thread are always executed on the same CPU. The advantage is that the CPU cache does not need to be refreshed every time, which avoids performance degradation. The drawback is that the process cannot be moved to another idle CPU. CPU affinity configuration should be done sparingly and after significant testing.

- **CPU anti-affinity**: This is the converse of CPU affinity. Processes and threads are marked to never be executed on a given CPU. CPU affinity and anti-affinity techniques are often used together. Some CPU-intensive processes are marked to be executed on high-performance CPUs only, and all other processes are marked not to run on those CPUs.

- **Scale out and scale up**: Sometimes, the application is CPU intensive and requires more computing capacity. In such cases, it might be prudent to add either more hardware of the same type or higher-grade hardware. Adding more CPUs of the same configuration is called **scale out** or **horizontal scaling**. Replacing the CPU with higher CPU hardware is called **scale-up** or **vertical scaling**. In the case of virtual machines, a VM's configuration is upgraded in vertical scaling. More VMs are spawned in horizontal scaling, and it results in server farms.

Performance degradation of storage

In cloud environments, the physical CPUs are typically decoupled from the storage systems. As we learned from *Chapter 4, Managing Storage*, SAN, and NAS are used to centralize storage management. The approach separates applications and storage. However, as virtualisation increases, multiple VMs depend on the same storage facilities for their needs. This can cause performance problems and needs to be monitored.

Multiple metrics are available for storage administrators to monitor the storage performance. We discussed them in *Chapter 4, Managing Storage*:

- Disk performance
- Disk tuning
- Disk latency
- I/O throttling
- I/O tuning

Cloud administrators using cloud storage should consider different metrics, such as the following:

- SLAs provided by CSP
- IOPS
- Metadata performance
- Storage tier usage to optimize costs

Performance degradation of network

Network administrators need to monitor the performance of network speeds. There are multiple parameters that should be monitored to ensure network performance. These parameters were discussed in *Chapter 5, Networking Fundamentals*. Network administrators in a private cloud need to monitor the following parameters to ensure that performance does not degrade:

- Bandwidth
- Throughput
- Latency
- Multi-pathing

Cloud administrators using public CSPs should monitor the following issues to ensure the optimal performance of their applications:

- Dropped network traffic
- Hop counts between the cloud application's region and the user's location
- Network configurations, including VPCs, firewalls, NAT, and PAT schemes
- DNS resolution issues
- Network SLAs of the CSP

Troubleshooting utilities

Cloud administrators must monitor the physical or virtual resources running in their data centres while troubleshooting. Doing so requires special-purpose tools. Unlike a physical machine, a virtual machine cannot be seen or touched. This makes troubleshooting them challenging. There are multiple tools available to access the machines. We will cover the most popular tools among them.

Remote access tools

It is difficult to investigate the issue being faced by the VM if administrators can not access it. A VM can be accessed using the remote access tools that are available on operating systems. For example, Microsoft offers Remote Desktop Tool for enterprise customers. This tool can be used to log in and access a remote computer by using its IP address. The remote computer can be either a physical or virtual machine.

- **Accessing hypervisors**: As discussed earlier, Type 1 hypervisors do not have an operating system between the hardware and VMs. So, traditional remote access software does not work for them. Hypervisor providers also supply special-purpose software that can be used to connect and monitor multiple hypervisors from a single central location.

- **Remote desktop protocol**: It is a proprietary protocol developed by Microsoft. Remote desktop client is the software using this protocol. A remote desktop client can log in to any physical or virtual machine using the appropriate credentials, and administrators can centrally access and manage the remote system.

- **SSH**: As discussed in the *Networking protocols* section in *Chapter 6, Managing Networks*, SSH can be used to log in to any host machine. It is a very popular tool for Unix-based machines, and administrators often use it.

Utilities

Several utilities are available for each operating system to monitor the performance of the machine. We will not discuss the commercial utilities here. We will discuss utilities that are either natively available or open-source.

Utilities for Linux OS:

- **arp**: Used to view and add content to the kernel's ARP table

- **curl, wget**: Used for downloading files from the internet through CLI

- **dig, nslookup**: Domain Information Groper; performs a DNS lookup to query the DNS name server and is used to troubleshoot DNS-related issues

- **host**: Displays the domain name for a given IP address and the IP address for a given hostname

- **hostname**: Used to view and set the hostname of a system

- **ifconfig**: Used to initialize an interface, configure it with an IP address, and enable or disable it; also used to display the route and the network interface

- **mtr**: Combination of ping and traceroute

- **netstat**: Provides statistical figures about different interfaces, which include open sockets, routing tables, and connection information

- **ping**: Stands for Packet Internet Gopher. Checks for the network connectivity between two nodes

- **route**: Displays and manipulates the routing table

- **tcpdum**: Captures the traffic that is passing through the network interface and displays it

- **traceroute**: Used to detect the delay and determine the pathway to the target machine; provides the names and identifies every device on the network path, follows the route to the destination, and reports the network latency at each device on the path

- **whois**: Used to fetch the registration and ownership information related to a website

Utilities for Windows OS:

- **Component services**: View and configure all Component Object Model services running on the local computer

- **Computer management**: Single app for launching all the various administrative options available for Windows machines

- **Event viewer**: Displays the events, errors, and additional information about the operating system

- **iSCSI initiator**: Used to connect to an external iSCSI storage

- **Performance monitor** : Used for an overview of memory usage, network usage, and disk usage

- **Registry editor**: A graphical tool for editing the configuration settings required for efficient computer operation

- **Resource monitor**: Used for viewing the usage of system resources

- **System configuration**: Used for customizing bootup settings and enabling/disabling device drivers and other services

- **System information**: Gives a comprehensive view of hardware, system components, and software environment

- **Windows memory diagnostic**: Used to diagnose problems with the system's RAM

In addition to the mentioned issues, administrators should always look out for the physical failure of devices. For example, there is always a possibility of network interface cards, CPUs, or RAM modules failing. Discussing their troubleshooting is out of scope for the purpose of the CVO-003 exam.

Troubleshooting for developers

Troubleshooting applications is of paramount importance to developers. Any application having a bug will result in an unsatisfied customer. So, application developers spend time debugging and fixing bug reports. Compared to administrators, developers need a much more detailed view of their application performance. After all, there are no off-the-shelf utilities available to triage the problem in code. So, developers need to build some additional facilities to help themselves with debugging the application. These additional facilities should be built into the applications from the very early days of application development.

Logging

Logs are textual records of all events that are occurring in the application or system. Logs are the first place to look for information when debugging the system. There is no standard format for the information being logged, but certain best practices have emerged over time.

- **Log levels**: Information is written into the logs based on preconditions. Developers categorize the message as information, warning, or error. This helps developers filter out unwanted information and also helps in not writing sensitive information in customer-facing logs.

- **Log contents**: Information in the log includes a timestamp and additional information like input values, function calls, stack trace, exceptions, system calls, and the like. Logs traditionally have been text files, but structured or binary log files are used too.

- **Centralizing the logging output**: Storing log information to a local file of a VM adds little value to debugging. If the VM is decommissioned, then the local info is irretrievably lost. So, it is necessary to store the logs in a centralized location.

Log files tend to grow and consume storage space. So, a recurring job should be maintained to delete log files older than a certain age.

Metrics

Metrics are numerical values of selected parameters. The value is calculated over a fixed time and is a crucial indicator of the parameter's health. For example, CPU utilization on a machine is a parameter that is often of interest to developers while troubleshooting application performance. The metric is CPU utilization on a minute basis. This can be plotted on a graph or can be stored in a database for further analysis.

Traces

Trace is a record of the start-to-end journey of a request or transaction in the application. The transaction could be a job started within the system, either by a user action or by a built-in mechanism. Irrespective of the trigger, a trace records the information of every activity that occurs during the execution of that transaction. Bottlenecks in the system performance can be identified by inspecting traces.

Observability

Observability is a property of the system. It is the extent to which a system's internal state can be measured by inspecting the outputs. A system is considered **observable** if its current state can be estimated using only its outputs. Observability is a highly desirable aspect of modern systems and cloud applications. It enhances visibility into system internals for the developers and administrators, allows them to effectively monitor the system, and performs root cause-effect analysis. Logs, metrics, and traces are considered the three pillars of observability. Implementing them does not guarantee observability, but they lay down a solid foundation upon which observability can be built into the systems.

Observability vs. monitoring

Observability is a property of the system, and monitoring is an activity performed on the system. There is a significant difference between the two. Monitoring requires prior knowledge of what properties should be measured, whereas observability allows for looking at the outputs over time and determining the parameters of interest. A good analogy is that of an ICU in a hospital. An ICU has a number of sensors and other equipment to monitor the vital signs of a patient. This is strictly monitoring. Observability allows the doctors to analyze the patient's breath output, body discharges, voice, and other outputs of the body to determine which organs might be unhealthy. Observability depends on monitoring to a certain extent.

Application development best practices

This section focuses on best practices to be followed during application development. These practices have evolved over time and have been recognised to reduce the need for troubleshooting to a considerable extent. We shall touch upon these topics lightly. A detailed discussion of best practices is beyond the scope of this book.

Requirement analysis

Requirements are the first question to be answered when building a cloud application. Unless there is clarity on what should be built, the end goal remains vague, and developers will not be able to direct their efforts. The requirements should be analyzed regarding the following topics:

- Software
- Hardware
- Network requirements
- Integration with other applications or systems
- Budgetary constraints
- Compliance
- **Service-level agreement (SLA)**
- User and business needs
- Security

Environments

It is highly recommended to maintain dedicated environments for each stage in the software development lifecycle. This allows application developers to build features incrementally and test them thoroughly before releasing them.

- **Development environment**: This is the most frequently modified environment and is the least stable. White box testing should happen in this environment.

- **Quality assurance** (**QA**): This is where testers perform black box testing of the application.

- **Staging**: This is a mirror of the production environment. Users can get a preview of the features in this environment. Some teams perform load testing here, whereas other teams prefer the QA environment.

- **Production**: This is the environment where the end users access the final released product.

Testing techniques

QA teams employ multiple strategies and techniques when performing testing. Some of the important techniques are listed as follows:

- Functional testing is a technique that validates the application behavior against approved requirements.

- Usability testing refers to evaluating the ease of use of the product with regard to the intended users.

- Regression testing is a black-box testing technique. It is used to confirm that a code change does not negatively impact the existing functionality.

- Penetration testing is a security testing technique in which the system's vulnerabilities are explored, and hacking is simulated.

- Performance testing, also called **load testing**, is a technique in which the system's health parameters are verified under simulated loads.

Secure coding

The concept of secure coding has arisen from the realisation that security needs to be built into the software development life cycle. It is not sufficient to run penetration testing at the end of the coding cycle and fix the bugs. Security needs a comprehensive focus and should be integrated into every stage of the life cycle. Secure coding has a few best practices, which we will discuss here:

- **Avoiding hardcoded passwords**: Cloud applications have multiple components that need to interact with other cloud services. Authentication is required for access, and it is tempting to hardcode the username and password into the code itself. However, this makes the system vulnerable if the attacker gains access to source code using disassembling techniques.

- **Use of individual service accounts**: This follows the principle of least privilege. This topic was discussed in *Chapter 8, Identity and Access Management*. Using individual service accounts is the cloud-native way of implementing the access principles discussed in that chapter. In cloud environments, instead of giving full access to all applications, individual service accounts are created for each operation, like reading/writing a database, managing backups, and so on. Applications that need to perform these actions connect to the service account rather than directly communicating with the database. This can also be considered as driving a high level of fan-in for critical activities.

- **Password vaults**: If an application is using multiple service accounts, it is likely to need multiple authentications. These usernames and passwords need to be stored somewhere for future reference. Storing passwords in plain text poses a security challenge. So, applications are recommended to store passwords using a vault. Password vaults help in managing, retrieving, and rotating database credentials, API keys, and other secrets throughout their life cycles. The advantage of such vaults is that passwords are stored centrally, and changing them does not require redeployment of the application.

- Key-based authentication is another way of authenticating services without revealing usernames and passwords. Key-based authentication uses public key cryptography, which we discussed in *Chapter 7, Managing Security*. A public and private key pair is generated for the account and registered with the service and the application. When attempting a login, the service encrypts a value with the public key and sends the cipher text to the application. The application uses the private key to decrypt it and sends the plain text back to the service. If the received plain text information matches the original information, then the application is authentic.

Deployment

Once the application code is tested and verified to be acceptable, it needs to be deployed to production environments. Deployment can be done in multiple strategies. Each strategy has pros and cons and needs to be chosen after due discussion with stakeholders. Refer to *Table 11.1* for the deployment strategies and their pros and cons:

Strategy	Description	Pros	Cons
Basic deployment or one-shot deployment	In this strategy, all nodes are updated with the latest code version simultaneously.	Simplicity of deployment	Any failure will impact all nodes and all users. Either everyone or no one is moved to the new version. The risk is very high.

Strategy	Description	Pros	Cons
Rolling deployment	Nodes are updated one at a time.	Ease of rolling back deployment	Nodes with updated code and older code must co-exist. This adds to the development and testing effort.
Blue-Green Deployment	Two separate environments are maintained: one with the older version and the other with the newer version. Users are redirected to the newer environment at the time of cutover, and the older environment is not used.	Simplicity, ease of implementation and ease of rolling back	The cost of replicating the production environment can be high.
Canary deployment	The newer functionality is released to small increments of users at a time. For example, the initial iteration will provide the new functionality to 5% of users, the second iteration will be for another 10% of users, the third iteration will be for 25%, and so on.	Allows the functionality to be tested with real users and identify problems early on without widespread impact Least risky of all approaches	Deployment runbooks must be repeated multiple times. This can be complicated. Monitoring the production might require complex and special-purpose instrumentation.
Dark Launch or silent launch	The new code is released to a select group of users without any information to them. That is the reason for calling **dark** or **silent** launch. The choice between new and older code base is controlled by developers using **feature flag** or **feature toggles**.	Feedback from users regarding the problems and challenges is very beneficial Widespread impact is avoided	Both older and newer features must coexist. This can add to the development effort.

Table 11.1 Application deployment strategies

Conclusion

We started this chapter with a discussion on CompTIA's troubleshooting methodology. We discussed the common problems encountered by cloud administrators and cloud application developers. We then discussed monitoring, observability, and the three pillars of observability. We also looked at application development best practices, secure coding practices, development environments, testing strategies, and deployment strategies.

In the next chapter, we shall discuss disaster recovery and high availability systems. We will discuss the importance of backups, backup and recovery strategies, business continuity in case of disasters, and recovery metrics. We shall also discuss building and maintaining high availability systems.

Glossary

- **CPU affinity**: A technique in which processes or threads are attached to a particular CPU

- **CPU anti-affinity**: A technique in which processes or threads are never attached to a particular CPU

- **Deployment strategy**: The approach adopted for rolling out a new version of the application code into the production environment

- **Disk space swapping**: A fraction of the hard disk space used by the OS, like RAM

- **Horizontal scaling**: Another name for scale-out

- **Limit**: The quantity of computing resources the CSP can provide to customers

- **Memory ballooning**: A technique adopted by CSPs to artificially enlarge their memory pool

- **Password Vault**: A program that securely stores usernames and passwords; in the cloud, vaults are used for the secure coding of applications

- **Quota**: The highest amount of computing resources that can be allocated to a component or system

- **Rollback plan**: A sequence of steps to be taken in case the original plan of action fails; intended to restore the system to the state before the action plan was initiated

- **Scale-out**: A way of improving performance by adding multiple machines of similar configuration and splitting the application to run on them simultaneously

- **Scale up**: A way of improving performance by replacing the infrastructure with a higher-grade infrastructure

- **SME**: Subject Matter Expert

- **Vertical Scaling**: Another name for Scale Up

Practice questions

S. No.	Questions		Answers
1	Consider a scenario: An enterprise application is used by users across the globe. For performance reasons, the application is run on different servers specific to each geography. When releasing a new application version, the product team adopted the following approach. The application is released to a small %ge of users without any official announcement. Based on their feedback, the application will be expanded to a higher number of users. What type of deployment strategy is this?		A
	A) Dark launch	B) Canary	
	C) One shot	D) Rolling deployment	
2	Consider a scenario: An enterprise application is used by users across the globe. For performance reasons, the application is run on different servers specific to each geography. When releasing a new application version, the product team adopted the following approach. The application is released to a small %ge of users in the first iteration. In each subsequent iteration, it is released to a larger number of users. What type of deployment strategy is this?		B
	A) Dark launch	B) Canary	
	C) One shot	D) Rolling deployment	
3	Consider a scenario: An enterprise application is used by users across the globe. For performance reasons, the application is run on different servers specific to each geography. When releasing a new application version, which deployment strategy is the least expensive in terms of infrastructure cost?		C
	A) Blue green	B) Rolling	
	C) One shot	D) Canary	
4	Which of the following environments is best suited for load testing?		D
	A) Development	B) QA	
	C) Production	D) Stage	
5	Which of the following environments is modified least frequently?		B
	A) Development	B) Production	
	C) QA	D) All of the above	

S. No.	Questions		Answers
6	**Which of the following pieces of information is most helpful for developers when troubleshooting a bug in an application's business logic?**		C
	A) RAM metrics	B) CPU metrics	
	C) Traces	D) Logs	
7	**Which of the following is a tool useful for accessing a windows VM?**		A
	A) Remote desktop	B) PUTTY	
	C) SSH	D) Hypervisor console	
8	**Which of the following is a tool useful for accessing host machines for Type 1 hypervisors?**		D
	A) Remote desktop	B) PUTTY	
	C) SSH	D) Hypervisor console	
9	**Which of the following disk performance tuning utilities is needed for HDDs but not for SSDs?**		B
	A) Disk formatting tool	B) Disk defragmentation tool	
	C) Disk partition tool	D) None of these	
10	**An enterprise application was receiving complaints for its high turnaround time in completing activities. The development team decided to replace the VM'd four-core CPU with an eight-core CPU. What type of scaling is this?**		B
	A) Horizontal scaling	B) Vertical scaling	
	C) Diagonal scaling	D) None of these	
11	**An enterprise application was receiving complaints for its high turnaround time in completing activities. The development team decided to double the number of VMs on the server farm. What type of scaling is this?**		A
	A) Horizontal scaling	B) Vertical scaling	
	C) Diagonal scaling	D) None of these	
12	**What is another name for horizontal scaling?**		B
	A) Scale up	B) Scale-out	
	C) Scale down	D) Scale in	
13	**An enterprise is adopting the cloud for hosting its internal applications. One of its applications uses legacy software, which is licensed using a dongle device. The software vendor configures the dongle to recognise a particular CPU only. Which feature of cloud computing can the organisation use to allow the VMs to use this software?**		A
	A) CPU affinity	B) CPU anti-affinity	
	C) CPU downtime	D) Mac binding	

S. No.	Questions	Answers
14	A cloud application is receiving frequent complaints about speed. The team investigating the problem identified that the VM was thrashing very often. Upon closer investigation, the team identified that the available RAM is less than what was subscribed from the CSP. What could be the reason for this?	C
	A) Cloud application is using more memory than anticipated B) VM is not being allocated enough memory by CSP	
	C) CSP is using memory ballooning techniques D) All of the above	

15	What is the correct sequence of steps for troubleshooting in CompTIA's suggested methodology?
	
	    i. Establish a theory of probable cause
	    ii. Identifying the problem
	    iii. Establish a plan of action and implement the solution
	    iv. Test the theory to determine the cause
	    v. Document the findings
	    vi. Verify full system functionality and implement preventive measures
		D

	A) i,iii,v,ii,iv,vi B) ii,iv,vi,i,iii,v	
	C) vi,v,iv,iii,ii,i D) ii, i, iv, iii, vi, v	

Join our Discord space

Join our Discord workspace for latest updates, offers, tech happenings around the world, new releases, and sessions with the authors:

https://discord.bpbonline.com

CHAPTER 12
Disaster Recovery and High Availability

Introduction

This chapter discusses the disaster scenarios that can impact a cloud application, the need for business continuity, and the methods for withstanding and recovering from disasters. Disasters are inevitable, and computing systems should be resilient enough to withstand them. Business continuity planning is needed to address such situations. Such plans should be carefully planned, tested, and practiced. We will discuss all this in this chapter.

Structure

We will cover the following in this chapter:

- Backups and recovery
- Business continuity
- Disaster recovery
- DR and cloud
- High availability
- Incident response

Objectives

Planning for **disaster recovery (DR)** is an important part of the job for cloud administrators and engineers. Business continuity planning requires all levels of the organization to be involved, and it is important for administrators and engineers to support their needs. Accordingly, CVO-003 places much emphasis on DR and high availability. We will learn about backups, business continuity, RPO, RTO, and other metrics, DR planning, preparation, and resolution. We will also understand high-availability systems and how building a high-availability system can help in DR.

Backups and recovery

A backup is a copy of the organization's data. There are many good reasons to back up data on computers regularly. These can be as simple as inadvertent deletion or as complex as the failure of storage devices. Legal regulations might also require retaining data. We briefly discussed backups in *Chapter 4, Managing Storage,* and will discuss them in detail here.

As discussed earlier, DR refers to restoring operations and data in case of adverse events. Recovery happens from backups. This makes a backup strategy very vital for recovery activities. The data recovery process changes based on the backup strategy. Several backup strategies are used in the industry. We will see them here.

Full backup

This is exactly what the term says: a full copy of the entire data. They offer the best protection for data. All data stored in the disk is copied onto a secondary disk as is. This is very time-consuming and costly in terms of disk space. So, organizations perform full backups on a less frequent basis.

Incremental backup

Incremental backups only back up the data that has been modified since the previous full or incremental backup. For example, if a full backup is performed on Sunday, the incremental backup on Monday only is for the data changed on Monday. Incremental backup on Tuesday will be only for data modified on Tuesday.

Incremental backups reduce the backup time and storage space needed. However, restoration is a time-consuming process. Restoring backup on Wednesday needs Sunday's full backup to be restored first, then Monday's incremental backup, and then Tuesday's incremental backup. This increases the time needed for restoration. Also, the risk of data loss is higher. The entire process will fail if either Monday's or Tuesday's incremental backups are lost.

Differential backup

Differential backup is like incremental backups with one difference. In differential backups, the data modified since the previous full backup is included in the latest backup. This consumes more time and storage than incremental backups, but reduces the complexity of the restore process. Also, the restore process depends only on the latest full backup and the latest differential backup.

Synthetic full backup

Synthetic full backups are not created from the original data. They are assembled from existing backups. A synthetic full backup combines the latest full backup and subsequent incremental backups, resulting in a single aggregated backup. The advantage is a full backup created without having to work on the original data. Administrators use this approach to reduce the time spent creating full backups from the original data. Instead, the original data only gets incremental backups. Synthetic full backups are performed on backup files separately, reducing the CPU load on original data.

Figure 12.1 illustrates full, differential, incremental, and synthetic full backups:

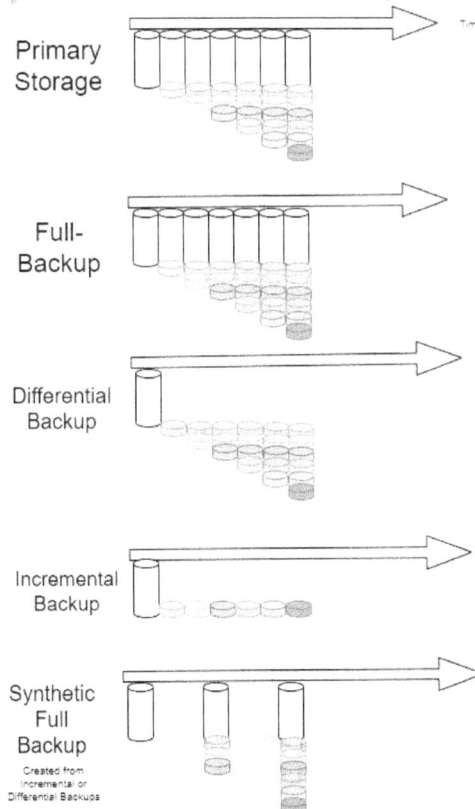

Figure 12.1: *Full, differential, incremental and synthetic full backups*

Mirror backup

Mirror backup is like a full backup, with the difference that the entire hard disk is backed up. Unlike full backups, where the backup process is limited to select folders or files, mirror backup is performed on the entire storage device.

Snapshot backup

Snapshot backup is a copy of data at a given point in time, including settings. Snapshot backups are very common when working with virtual machines. They are extremely useful in restoring the past behavior of VMs. By restoring the snapshot backup and the corresponding mirror or full backup, the VMs can work as they did earlier.

3-2-1 backup

3-2-1 backup is not a backup technique by itself. It is an effective guideline for maintaining healthy backups for DR. The rule says that all data should be stored in three copies, on two different media, and one offsite location to minimize the risk of data loss. This can be remembered as follows:

- Production data (Copy 1, media 1)
- Backup data on another storage media (Copy 2, media 2)
- Disaster recovery off-site (Copy 3)

Grandfather-father-son backup

Grandfather-father-son is another guideline for maintaining healthy backups for DR. In this approach, a full backup is stored offsite and is called **Grandfather**. A more frequent full backup is stored locally and is called **father**. Regular incremental backups are called **son**.

- **Grandfather**: A full backup, performed less frequently than father and usually stored offsite.

- **The father**: A full backup performed more frequently compared to Grandfather and usually stored on a local device.

- **The son**: Incremental backup and usually stored locally.

This might look similar to the 3-2-1 strategy at first glance, but there are a few differences. 3-2-1 is applicable to both incremental and full backups. In other words, even incremental backups can be stored in other media and offsite as well. In GFS, generally, only Grandfather is stored offsite. As an example, Grandfather backup is performed once a month, father is performed weekly, and incremental can be daily. If the primary data center is impacted and the father and son are lost, RPO becomes 1 month.

Archives

Archives are different from backups. Archive refers to chronologically old data that is not used frequently. This could be data retained for regulatory purposes, but has only occasional or no usage. For example, banks do not delete the record of financial transactions in an account. At the same time, it makes little sense to keep years-old transaction records on expensive storage media. Such data can be rolled off to inexpensive storage media even if such media is slower. Such inexpensive media is called archives. This is not a backup of the original data.

Recover vs. restore

It is a common misunderstanding in the IT industry to use the words recover and restore interchangeably. However, they have very different meanings and purposes. Both recovery and restoration are done in the event of failure. Recovery is for specific files. If a file is deleted by accident, only that file is recovered. Restoration is for the entire data backup.

Business continuity

The intention of BC is to ensure that adverse events do not result in undue impact on the organization. Whatever the adverse event, the business should continue with as little disruption as possible, hence BC.

The adverse event could be anything. It can be a cyberattack, a loss of power supply, a terrorist attack, a war, or an earthquake. Whatever might be the cause, critical business functions should not suffer adversely. This is of primary importance to the organization and its users.

Consider a bank that has fully computerized its operations. With hundreds of transactions happening every minute on the server, the database carries information that is critically important for healthy financial transactions. *What happens if the server suffers an internet link failure?* The customers would be irate at delayed transactions. There will be a reputation loss for the bank. *What if the hard disk containing the database fails? What if the data backups are lost either in a fire or other natural calamity?* The loss of the financial records will be cataclysmic and can lead to punitive legal actions. These are the kinds of scenarios where BC is required.

As can be inferred by these examples, **business continuity planning** (**BCP**) is an organizational approach to prevent and recover from adverse situations when potential threats materialize. BCP covers both assets and people who are protected and aims to get them functioning quickly when disasters occur.

Business continuity planning

We will briefly discuss the salient aspects of BCP in this section. A detailed discussion of BCP practices and approaches is out of the scope of CVO-003. The typical steps involved in creating a BCP are listed here:

- Identify the risks to your business

- Analyze their impact on the business

- Plan the recovery steps

- Train the support teams on the recovery plans

- Iteratively improve the BCP

Depending on the nature of the business, businesses have various risks to be considered. Not every business process is of the same importance. It is typical for organizations to perform BCP only for critical processes. In the example of the bank, maintaining the financial transaction data is a critical operation and requires an elaborate BCP. However, onboarding a new customer is a lower-priority process at the time of disaster. Disruptions to financial data management are inconceivable under any circumstances. However, in case of a disastrous event like a cyclone or earthquake, delaying the addition of a customer by a couple of days is acceptable. Many organizations had their business continuity plans tested during the recent COVID-19 pandemic when lockdowns were announced in many parts of the world.

The disasters themselves can be of multiple types. They can be systemic, like equipment failure; man-made events like cyberattacks and terrorist attacks; local events like a power loss in the location of the data center; force-majeure disasters like earthquakes or cyclones; country-wide events like wars or global events like the recent pandemic.

Disaster recovery

DR is very similar to BCP, with one significant difference. DR is limited to systems and data, while BCP covers personnel as well. For CVO-003, we will discuss DR extensively. We will focus on the planning needed for DR, metrics used for DR preparedness, and how DR differs in the cloud world, particularly with public CSPs.

DR planning

DR begins with documents and guidelines. Corporate-level documents like **business impact analysis** (**BIA**) results are inputs for DR planning. DR planning aims to resolve data loss and restore the bare-minimum system functionality critical for the organization's existence.

As discussed earlier, not all business processes are critical to the organization. As part of the DR planning process, a BIA document is created. It contains an inventory of the organization's business processes, and their criticality and financial impact in case of process failure. Processes are grouped as per their criticality. The processes whose failure will result in irrecoverable damage to an organization's existence are called **existence-critical processes** or tier-0 processes. Processes whose failure will cause significant hardship to employees or users but will not threaten the organization's existence are called mission-critical or tier-1 processes.

DR adds to the complexity and cost of IT systems significantly, so it is generally planned for tier-0 and tier-1 processes only. A one-size-fits-all approach does not work for DR. DR should be planned for each business process, depending on its tier. A risk assessment, the likelihood of risk, and the financial impact should be evaluated, and DR should be planned accordingly. DR playbooks should be periodically revisited. Mock drills should be performed to ensure that the plans are relevant, DR objectives are met, and the organization is trained to follow them.

Multiple metrics are relevant for DR planning. Some of the important metrics are as follows:

- **Recovery Point Objective (RPO)**
- **Recovery Time Objective (RTO)**
- **Mean time between failure (MTBF)**
- **Mean time to recovery (MTTR)**
- **Service-level agreement (SLA)**
- **Recovery Service Level (RSL)**

We will discuss each of these metrics in detail now.

Recovery Point Objective

RPO is the maximum amount of data loss that is tolerable for the organization when a disaster occurs. If a disaster were to happen this instant, *how much data loss would be acceptable when the system is back online?* In the example of a bank, if the data center suffered an earthquake, *how many hours or minutes' worth of loss of past transaction data is acceptable for the bank?* That duration is called RPO.

RPO determines the frequency of backups made to the system. The lower the RPO, the higher the frequency of backups. If the organization is tolerant of a loss of 1 hour worth of data, taking backups every hour is sufficient. If data loss tolerance is 1 minute, backups should happen every minute.

Recovery Time Objective

RTO is the target duration for an organization to recover from disaster and resume tier-0 and tier-1 operations. RTO answers the question, *once a disaster occurs, in how much time should the tier-0 and tier-1 operations be restored? Figure 12.2* illustrates RPO and RTO:

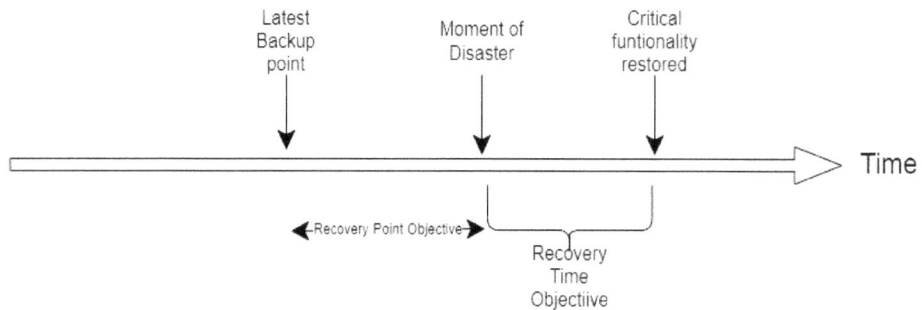

Figure 12.2: *Illustration of RPO and RTO*

It is important to remember that RPO and RTO are target values. The actual values are visible only during an actual disaster and are represented using **Recovery Point Actual (RPA)** and **Recovery Time Actual (RTA)**. An ideal DR plan is one where RPO and RTO match RPA and RTA.

Mean Time Between Failure

We discussed MTBF in the chapter on storage. It refers to the average number of hours a device can be used before failure. MTBF should be considered for all system components when evaluating the risk of failure for servers and critical information systems.

Mean Time to Recovery

This metric is also called **Mean Time to Repair** (**MTTR**). It refers to the time taken to repair or replace a component that has failed. MTTR is typically part of maintenance contracts for IT systems. System vendors should maintain spares of components to ensure that MTTR values are met for their customers.

Service-level agreement

SLA is a commitment given to customers by service providers regarding the services provided and the standards the provider is obligated to meet. For example, before widespread computerization, it was common for banks to display a commitment to process withdrawals in 15 minutes. Success or failure to meet SLAs has immense impact on customer satisfaction.

Recovery Service Level

RSL is measured as a %. It refers to the amount of computing power needed to run the DR processes as compared to a normal full workload of the organization. It gives a view into the amount of tier-0 and tier-1 business processes in the organization for which DR is being planned.

DR and cloud

A prevalent misunderstanding among layman users is that once an application is hosted on the public cloud, there is no need for DR. This cannot be further from the truth. Public CSPs take responsibility for only a few kinds of failures. For example, they take responsibility for equipment, and equipment failure is typically invisible to cloud users. A failed hard disk or network card will not impact cloud users. However, other adverse events like natural disasters, terror attacks, war, cyberattacks, pandemics, and the like impact the CSPs just the same as private data centers. Moreover, CSPs will have downtime too. Cloud is a complicated IT system. No matter how many redundancies are added, the probability of a cloud being unavailable is always non-zero.

Consider this example. Suppose the CSP is using a host machine that is guaranteed to work 90% of the time in the year. This means the probability of downtime is 10% or 0.1. If the CSP adds another machine for redundancy, the probability of both machines collapsing simultaneously is 0.1 X 0.1 = 0.01, which is 1%. This is 3.65 days per year. Adding a third host will reduce the probability to 0.0001, that is, 0.01%, which is nearly 1 hour per year. Combined with various factors like computing, network, internet, storage, CSP's internal applications, and the like, the probability is never zero. Applications requiring resilience against such events should still plan for DR. We will discuss this in detail in this section.

A traditional DR in private data centers generally contains a dedicated secondary facility with all the necessary IT infrastructure. Idle capacities of computing, storage, network, and internet bandwidth are maintained for it to be used at short notice. Many organizations invested heavily in private data centers before the cloud became mainstream. So, they often prefer to reuse their investments for DR. However, an intelligent combination of private investments with public CSPs can offer significant savings in costs.

As mentioned earlier, DR adds cost and complexity to IT systems. Maintaining idle computing capacities can be expensive. The pay-as-you-go model of cloud computing makes it well-placed to control such costs. Well-orchestrated cloud implementations can bring up the tier-0 and tier-1 IT processes in a cloud environment and ensure BC.

The nature of DR changes considerably with the introduction of the cloud. We shall discuss each component of IT systems in this section and look at how DR should be planned for them in the context of the cloud.

Cloud DR types

Whether the organizations use a private cloud, a public CSP, or dedicated DR-as-a-Service providers, there are three approaches to cloud-based DR:

- Cold DR typically involves storing backups and VM snapshots in the cloud. Cold DR sites do not have any active processes, and the usage is mostly for storage. When a disaster occurs, the organization has to follow playbooks to bring up the

VMs, restore the data backups, and set up the network before resuming business operations. This approach has the least complexity and expenses, but a high RTO is unavoidable.

- Warm DR has computing machines (VMs, storage, network) ready in the cloud. Storage is continuously replicated from primary storage into the cloud, but the VMs do not perform any operations in normal situations. When a disaster occurs, the applications/users need to be redirected to the new IP address. Business operations shall resume with minimal downtime.

- Hot DR is the most expensive approach and has the highest complexity. In this approach, the DR site and the original site both perform business operations under normal situations. A hot DR is a live, parallel deployment of business workloads. This approach provides zero downtime, and customers will not notice any disruption at all.

Storage

DR for storage consists of two steps:

1. **Restore data**: Data backed up to the cloud storage must be restored in this step. Restoration starts with the latest full backup and proceeds till the latest differential or incremental backup. Based on the backup strategy, GFS or 3-2-1 strategy, the source data must be restored to the target disks.

2. **Recovery of databases**: This is an extra step needed for databases. Simple restoration of database backups is insufficient. Databases should typically be recovered to the point in time. This also requires transaction logs to be restored. So, the backup strategy of databases should include backing up the transaction logs as well. The exact recovery procedure depends on the database software.

Network

Software-Defined Networking and Network Virtualization were discussed in *Chapter 6, Managing Networks*; they can be used to spin up networks in the cloud in case of DR. DR for the network requires setting up the load balancers, service mesh, DNS, and VPC networks. A well-orchestrated DR script can quickly spin up the required VMs and cloud resources with appropriate network infrastructure. If the main DNS is updated with the IP address of the cloud VM, then the user traffic will be rerouted, and BC will be achieved.

Many CSPs offer **Application Delivery Controllers** (**ADCs**). ADCs work like load balancers and also offer features like content-based routing, URL translation, and hybrid cloud support. These features help in routing incoming traffic on the cloud and control network usage in DR scenarios.

CSP SLAs

We have briefly mentioned SLAs in reference to uptime in the *Support* section of *Chapter 9, Migrating to the Cloud*. We will discuss this in a little more detail here. No CSP can offer 100% uptime for their offering; they can and will fail. CSPs advertise their uptimes and agree on them in contractual obligations. The downtime of a CSP based on their SLA can be calculated and has been provided as follows:

SLA	Maximum downtime in a year
99%	Nearly 3 days and 16 hours
99.9%	Nearly 8 hours, 46 minutes
99.95%	Nearly 4 hours, 22 minutes
99.99%	Nearly 52 minutes
99.999%	Nearly 5 minutes

Table 12.1: Downtime as per SLAs

If public CSPs breach their SLAs, they set off a fraction of the cloud expenses to the next billing cycle as compensation. Not only is this procedure long, it is also not commensurate with the loss suffered by the organization. So, organizations needing resilience should consider cloud service outages as well in their DR.

Geographically distributed systems

Traditional DR relied on maintaining a secondary data center in an alternate location. Public CSPs rely on this approach as well. They also offer this as a facility to their customers, which can be used in DR planning. This functionality of clouds is called **regions**. CSPs maintain multiple data centers in different parts of the globe. In addition to DR, it improves responsiveness and meets legal constraints.

Organizations can use geographically distributed data centers to replicate their data and IT infrastructure; this is called **georedundancy**. Public CSPs have built an impressive list of geographic regions:

- Regions are geographic locations and represent a wide area. Data centers in a region are designed to be isolated from data centers in any other regions to ensure the best possible fault tolerance and stability.

- Availability zones are one or more data centers within each region. All data centers in one availability zone have in-built redundancies and are interconnected. Together, they offer higher resilience and fault tolerance to customers than a single data center.

Figure 12.3 illustrates how regions and availability zones work in Microsoft's Azure cloud. The image is taken as is from **https://learn.microsoft.com/en-us/azure/reliability/availability-zones-overview**.

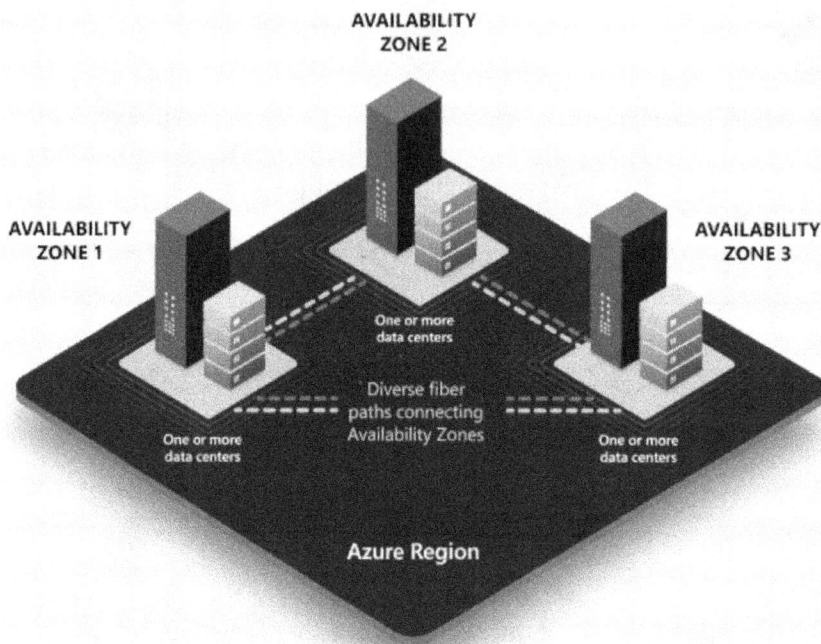

Figure 12.3: Azure's regions and availability zones

Geo-clustering

Geo clustering is a technique of hiding geographically distributed computers behind a single public name/IP address. The entire cluster appears as a single entity to the outside world, but internally, there can be multiple redundant computers that can be spread widely. This protects the computers from location-specific issues and provides a high degree of resilience to enterprises. In clouds, geo-clustered sites can be distributed to a single region, multiple regions, or even multiple CSPs.

High availability

High availability (**HA**) is a characteristic of systems that are available without downtime for prolonged time periods. HA is not a technical feature of any hardware system; it is a characteristic of a system that can be achieved by implementing rigorous fault tolerance approaches and building resiliency in systems. Techniques for implementing high-availability systems have a significant overlap with techniques for DR. For example, increasing the MTBF to a very large value will improve DR and make the system highly available. However, it is important to remember that HA is for avoiding downtime when disasters occur. On the other hand, DR is for recovering after a disaster has occurred.

HA systems require fault tolerance. For example, an enterprise data center with a single internet service provider will experience an outage if the ISP fails. Such a system cannot be considered fault-tolerant. The same holds for power connections, storage devices, CPUs, GPUs, RAM modules, and so on. A fault-tolerant system is one where an unexpected failure of a critical component will not result in an outage of the entire system. We discussed HA, fault tolerance, and redundancy in *Chapter 4, Managing Storage*.

Multipathing is another way to achieve fault tolerance. This is a specialized application of redundancy used particularly in networking or in SANs. Multiple communication routes are maintained between each pair of devices. This helps in tolerating the failure of one communication path. Mesh networks discussed in *Chapter 5, Networking Fundamentals*, are a good example of multi-pathing.

Incident response

No matter how much one wishes for a foolproof system, the architects, administrators, and developers are only human. Unwanted incidents happen, and disasters are inevitable. It is important for an organization to be prepared for incidents. Appropriate planning is needed for handling incidents. The best time to plan for an incident is before its occurrence. For this section, we will discuss incidents in general terms. An incident can be anything. All kinds of disasters are severe incidents. Other events, like internet failure, can be a lower priority if redundancies are available.

Procedures and planning

As mentioned earlier, incidents require proper planning. Planning includes the following activities:

- Incident listing is a brainstorming activity where all possible incidents are listed.

- Incident classification assigns the priority for the incident when it occurs. The likelihood of the incident and its impact are identified at this stage.

- Incident response procedure lists the series of steps to be taken when the incident occurs. Depending on the incident, the procedure can detail granular instructions.

- Incident handling roles and responsibilities explain who should be informed about the incident, what information should be provided, and the responsibilities of each person or team.

Testing the recovery plan

It is not sufficient to have a plan. It is important to test it as well. Organizations should periodically perform mock exercises for the incident response plans. Mock exercises serve multiple purposes. They help the incident response team to be familiar with the steps to be taken when incidents occur, and they help in identifying and improving the drawbacks of the plan. After all, what use is it to purchase a fire extinguisher after the house is burnt?

Post-mortem analysis

It is also important to perform post-mortem analysis after an incident is handled. Incidents provide valuable lessons that sometimes cannot be identified in mock drills. Such lessons learned should be identified and incorporated into incident response procedures.

Conclusion

We started this chapter by understanding backups and recovery approaches. We learned how such techniques are necessary for BCP and DR, and then discussed the metrics used for DR planning. We discussed how DR changes in a cloud environment and looked at how to handle DR for storage, network, and SLAs offered by CSPs. We then learned how public CSPs offer regions and availability zones, and how they should be used for DR planning. Finally, we briefly discussed incident management and response.

In the next chapter, we shall discuss the topic that was added to CV0-004's syllabus, called DevOps. Starting with a history of DevOps, we shall discuss DevOps culture, team roles, source control strategies, and Infrastructure as Code in detail. We shall also discuss the relevance of DevOps for the CV0-004 exam.

Glossary

- **ADC**: Application Delivery Controller
- **Archive**: Chronologically old data that is not used frequently
- **Availability Zone**: One or more interconnected data centers set up by the CSP in a given region
- **BCP**: Business Continuity Planning
- **BIA**: Business Impact Analysis
- **Cloud Region**: Geographic locations where CSP has set up interconnected data centers that are isolated from all other regions
- **DR**: Disaster recovery
- **Geo-Clustering**: A technique of hiding geographically distributed computers behind a single public name/IP address
- **MTBF**: Mean Time Between Failures
- **MTTR**: Mean Time To Recover
- **RPO**: Recovery Point Objective
- **RSL**: Recovery Service Level
- **RTO**: Recovery Time Objective
- **SLA**: Service Level Agreement

Practice questions

S. No.	Questions		Answers
1	**Which of the following is the best protection for data by way of backups?**		A
	A) Full backup	B) Incremental backup	
	C) Differential full backup	D) Synthetic full backup	
2	**When setting up a daily backup strategy for the data center, a storage administrator specified this approach: a full back up every Sunday, and backup limited to changes done to data from the previous Sunday till date on all other days. What approach is this?**		B
	A) Incremental backup	B) Differential backup	
	C) Synthetic backup	D) 3-2-1 backup	
3	**Which of the following statements is true?**		C
	A) In the 3-2-1 strategy, only the third tier is a full backup	B) In the 3-2-1 strategy, only incremental backups are taken on tier 1 storage.	
	C) In the 3-2-1 strategy, at least one data backup should be maintained offsite	D) In the Grandfather-Father-Son strategy, only Grandfather is a full backup	
4	**Which of the following data is a good candidate for storing on tape media?**		D
	A) Log files generated by an application	B) Newspaper headlines of the day	
	C) Shares traded on Sensex the previous day	D) Financial transactions of a customer from the previous financial year	
5	**Which of the following statements is true?**		B
	A) BCP addresses DR of systems only	B) DR addresses DR of IT infrastructure only	
	C) DR addresses DR of IT systems and people	D) All of the above	
6	**When analyzing their DR processes, an organization concluded that they could afford to lose 1 hour worth of data, and downtime should not exceed 6 hours. Considering this, which of the following is correct?**		C
	A) RPO is 6 hours, RTO is 1 hour	B) RPO and RTO are 6 hours	
	C) RPO is 1 hour, RTO is 6 hours	D) RPO and RTO are 1 hour	

S. No.	Questions		Answers
7	When analyzing their DR processes, an organization concluded that they can afford downtime but cannot accept data loss. What DR approach would you suggest to them?		A
	A) A cold DR with 321 strategy	B) A hot DR with 321 strategy	
	C)A hot DR with GFS strategy	D) All of the above	
8	Which of the following DR types is the most expensive?		D
	A) Cold DR	B) Frozen DR	
	C) Warm DR	D) Hot DR	
9	An organization lost its primary data center in a disaster. They failed over to a backup data center. After restoring the primary data center, they are now trying to switch the workload back to the primary data center. What is this process called?		B
	A) Failover again	B) Failback	
	C) Fail after	D) Fail harder	
10	A cloud administrator configures the primary and secondary data centers. They specify the synchronization policy requiring a data write request to be completed in both data centers before applications can make the next request. What is this synchronization policy called?		B
	A) Asynchronous replication	B) Synchronous replication	
	C) Mirroring replication	D) Snapshot replication	
11	A cloud administrator needs to take a backup of a VM, including its disk and memory state. What approach should they use for this?		A
	A) Snapshot	B) Imaging	
	C) Mirroring	D) None	
12	A cloud administrator received a request to create a VM with the same configuration as another. Which approach best suits them?		B
	A) Mirroring	B) Cloning	
	C) Duplicating	D) Template-based creation	
13	Which of the following approaches will not help in achieving HA for a data center?		A
	A) Single point of failures	B) Fail-safe infrastructure	
	C) Redundancy	D) Fault tolerance	
14	Which of the following parameters should have a large value in order to achieve a HA data center?		C
	A) RTO	B) RPO	
	C) MTBF	D) All of the above	

CHAPTER 13

DevOps

Introduction

DevOps is a set of practices that combines **software development** (**Dev**) and **IT operations** (**Ops**) aimed at shortening the systems development life cycle and providing continuous delivery with high software quality. It emphasizes collaboration and communication between developers and IT professionals, automation of processes, and continuous monitoring. By integrating these functions, DevOps aims to improve efficiency, increase deployment frequency, and achieve faster time-to-market. The main components include continuous integration, continuous delivery, and **Infrastructure as Code** (**IaC**). DevOps often leverages tools such as Jenkins, Docker, and Kubernetes to automate and streamline workflows.

Structure

In this chapter, we will cover the following topics:

- Overview of DevOps
- History of DevOps
- DevOps culture
- DevOps team roles
- DevOps and CV0-004

- GrafanaDevOps topics
- Source control

Objectives

This chapter explores the origins and evolution of DevOps, exploring its cultural foundations and the critical roles within DevOps teams. We will also discuss the DevOps lifecycle, including the CompTIA CV0-004 certification, and cover fundamental DevOps topics such as continuous integration, continuous delivery, and IaC. Finally, we will highlight the importance of source control in maintaining code quality and enabling seamless collaboration.

The topic of DevOps is newly added to Cloud+ certification's syllabus from version 004. CV0-003 did not discuss DevOps as a separate topic. The fact that CV0-004 added DevOps as a standalone topic is an indication of the importance of this discipline in the software development world. That said, the CV0-004 exam does not deal with advanced DevOps topics like GitOps, AIOps, and the like. Only the basic aspects like source control, CI/CD, automation, IaC are included in CV0-004's purview. These topics shall be discussed thoroughly in this chapter.

Overview of DevOps

DevOps is a cultural and professional movement that emphasizes the collaboration and communication between software developers and IT operations professionals while automating the process of software delivery and infrastructure changes. The core principles of DevOps include:

- **Collaboration and communication**: Breaking down silos between development and operations teams to work towards common goals.

- **Automation**: Automating repetitive tasks such as testing, integration, and deployment to increase efficiency and reduce human error.

- **Continuous integration and continuous delivery (CI/CD)**: Ensuring that code changes are automatically tested and deployed to production environments, facilitating faster and more reliable releases.

- **Infrastructure as Code (IaC)**: Managing and provisioning computing infrastructure through machine-readable configuration files, rather than physical hardware configuration or interactive configuration tools.

- **Monitoring and logging**: Continuously monitoring applications and infrastructure for performance and issues and maintaining logs to identify and resolve problems quickly.

DevOps aims to create a more agile and responsive development environment where software can be delivered rapidly, reliably, and safely. This approach improves overall productivity, reduces time to market, and enhances the ability to respond to customer needs and market changes.

History of DevOps

Let us discuss the history and origins of DevOps very briefly here:

- **Early 2000s**: The initial ideas that led to DevOps began to take shape. The Agile software development movement, which started in the early 2000s, laid the groundwork for DevOps by emphasizing iterative development, collaboration, and customer feedback.

- **2008**: The term *DevOps* was coined by *Patrick Debois*, a Belgian consultant, who organized the first DevOpsDays event in *Ghent, Belgium*. This event brought together developers and operations professionals to discuss the challenges of agile operations.

- **2010s**: DevOps gained significant traction, with more organizations adopting its principles and practices. Tools and technologies that support DevOps, such as Jenkins (for continuous integration), Docker (for containerization), and Kubernetes (for container orchestration), became popular.

- **2014**: The creation of the DevOps Enterprise Summit helped to further popularize DevOps in larger enterprises, showcasing successful case studies and best practices.

- **Present**: DevOps has become a mainstream practice, with organizations of all sizes adopting its principles to improve their software development and delivery processes. The DevOps ecosystem continues to evolve, incorporating new methodologies like GitOps, DataOps, and AI/ML-driven operations.

DevOps has fundamentally changed the way software is developed and delivered, fostering a culture of collaboration, continuous improvement, and rapid innovation.

DevOps culture

DevOps culture is centered around collaboration, communication, and integration between software development (Dev) and IT operations (Ops) teams. The goal is to create a culture of shared responsibility, transparency, and continuous improvement to deliver high-quality software quickly and reliably. The key aspects of DevOps culture include:

- **Collaboration and communication**: Encouraging open communication and collaboration between development, operations, and other stakeholders. This breaks down silos and fosters a team-oriented mindset.

- **Shared responsibility**: Both development and operations teams share responsibility for the software lifecycle, from development to deployment and maintenance. This includes shared accountability for performance, stability, and security.

- **Continuous improvement**: Emphasizing iterative improvements and learning from failures. Teams continuously seek ways to optimize processes, reduce waste, and enhance performance.

- **Automation**: Automating repetitive and manual tasks to increase efficiency, reduce errors, and free up time for more strategic work.

- **Customer-centric focus**: Prioritizing the needs and feedback of end-users to ensure that the software delivers value and meets customer expectations.

It is important for the readers to note that the discussion on DevOps culture is not in scope for CV0-004 examination. It is generally expected in the industry for DevOps practitioners to be familiar with the culture. Hence, the preceding discussion is included for completeness. It has no direct relevance to the examination itself.

DevOps team roles

A DevOps team typically consists of various roles that work together to ensure seamless integration, continuous delivery, and efficient operations. Some common roles are listed in the following table:

Role	Activities generally performed
DevOps Engineer	Responsible for automating and streamlining operations and processes. Builds and maintains CI/CD pipelines. Bridges the gap between development and operations teams.
Site Reliability Engineer (SRE)	Focuses on reliability, availability, and performance of applications. Works on incident response, monitoring, and capacity planning. Often writes code to automate operational tasks.
Release Manager	Manages the release process, ensuring smooth deployment of new features and updates. Coordinates between development, QA, and operations teams. Oversees the release schedule and ensures compliance with release policies.
Automation Architect	Designs and implements automation frameworks and tools. Works on automating infrastructure provisioning, configuration management, and application deployment. Ensures that automation practices align with organizational goals.
Security Engineer	Integrates security practices into the DevOps pipeline (DevSecOps). Conducts security assessments and vulnerability scans. Ensures compliance with security standards and regulations.

Role	Activities generally performed
QA/Test Engineer	Focuses on testing and quality assurance within the CI/CD pipeline. Develops automated tests and integrates them into the build process. Ensures that software meets quality standards before deployment.
Infrastructure Engineer	Manages and maintains the underlying infrastructure (servers, networks, storage). Works on IaC to provision and manage resources programmatically. Ensures infrastructure scalability, reliability, and performance.
Monitoring and Logging Engineer	Implements and manages monitoring and logging solutions. Ensures that systems are monitored for performance, availability, and security. Analyzes logs and metrics to identify issues and optimize performance.
Product Owner/Manager	Represents the customer's interests and ensures that the development aligns with business goals. Prioritizes features and enhancements based on customer feedback and market demands. Collaborates with the DevOps team to ensure timely and successful delivery.

Table 13.1: Roles and responsibilities of DevOps personnel

These roles are not rigid and can overlap depending on the organization's size and structure. The key is to foster a collaborative environment where team members work together to achieve common goals and deliver high-quality software efficiently.

DevOps and CV0-004

DevOps has become an essential aspect of modern IT practices, making it a critical topic for the CompTIA CV0-004 certification exam. With 10% of the exam questions dedicated to DevOps fundamentals, understanding these concepts is crucial for aspiring IT professionals. This new chapter reflects the evolving demands of the industry, emphasizing the importance of collaboration, automation, and efficiency in software development and IT operations. By mastering DevOps principles, candidates will be better equipped to meet the expectations of today's dynamic and fast-paced IT environments. This chapter aims to provide the foundational knowledge necessary to excel in the DevOps-related portions of the CV0-004 exam.

CompTIA stated the following objectives for the CV0-004 exam in this link here: **https://partners.comptia.org/docs/default-source/resources/comptia-cloud-cv0-004-exam-objectives-(1-2)**

- Explain source control concepts.
- Explain concepts related to **continuous integration/continuous deployment (CI/CD)** pipelines.

- Explain concepts related to the integration of systems.

- Explain the importance of the tools used in DevOps environments.

DevOps lifecycle

The DevOps lifecycle is a sophisticated framework that comprises eight distinct phases, each representing the essential processes, capabilities, and tools required for development and operations. This lifecycle is often illustrated using an infinity loop to emphasize the continuous and iterative nature of DevOps practices. In this professional discourse, we will delve into the intricacies of the DevOps lifecycle, highlighting the critical elements that facilitate seamless collaboration and communication between development and operations teams.

Eight phases of the DevOps lifecycle

The DevOps lifecycle is bifurcated into two primary domains: development, represented on the left side of the loop, and operations, depicted on the right. Each phase within this lifecycle is crucial for maintaining alignment, velocity, and quality throughout the software development and delivery process. The phases are as follows:

- **Plan**: Establish project goals, requirements, and timelines through collaborative planning sessions.

- **Code**: Develop and manage source code, ensuring adherence to coding standards and version control practices.

- **Build**: Compile source code into executable artifacts, managing dependencies and creating packages.

- **Test**: Validate code quality through automated testing, identifying and rectifying defects.

- **Release**: Coordinate the deployment of new features and updates, ensuring compliance with release policies.

- **Deploy**: Automate the deployment process, managing configurations and IaC.

- **Operate**: Monitor and manage the application in production, ensuring performance, stability, and security.

- **Monitor**: Continuously track application and infrastructure metrics, gathering insights to inform future development.

The DevOps life cycle is represented as an infinity loop, as shown in *Figure 13.1*. The infinity loop is a powerful symbol in the DevOps paradigm, illustrating the perpetual cycle of improvement and collaboration that defines this methodology. Although the phases may appear to flow sequentially, the loop underscores the necessity for ongoing interaction and iterative enhancement across all stages of the lifecycle. This continuous approach ensures that teams remain agile, responsive, and aligned with organizational objectives. This is observed in the following DevOps lifecycle:

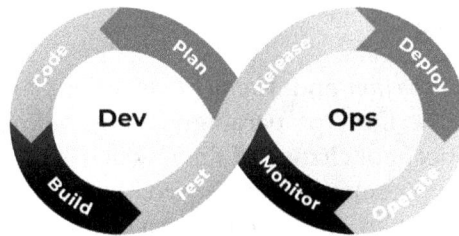

Figure 13.1: *DevOps lifecycle*

The DevOps lifecycle is a dynamic and continuous process that encapsulates the essential phases of software development and operations. By leveraging the infinity loop as a visual representation, practitioners can appreciate the interconnectedness and iterative nature of these phases.

DevOps frameworks

DevOps is more than just a set of practices; it encompasses a philosophy and framework that guide practitioners in implementing these practices effectively and efficiently. This report explores key DevOps frameworks and methodologies that are instrumental in optimizing the development and operations continuum, ensuring that the principles of DevOps are embedded deeply within organizational processes. The CV0-004 exam syllabus does not explicitly mention anything about DevOps frameworks. However, it is suggested that the readers familiarize themselves with the information provided here for completeness of DevOps topics.

CALMS framework

The CALMS framework, introduced by *Jez Humble* in *The DevOps Handbook*, serves as a foundational guide for implementing DevOps principles. CALMS is an acronym that stands for culture, automation, lean, measurement, and sharing. The following list explains each of these:

- **Culture**: Emphasizes the importance of fostering a collaborative and open environment.
- **Automation**: Focuses on automating repetitive tasks to enhance efficiency and reduce human error.
- **Lean**: Advocates for continuous improvement and waste reduction in processes.
- **Measurement**: Stresses the need for metrics to assess performance and inform decision-making.
- **Sharing**: Encourages knowledge sharing and transparency within and between teams.

This framework encapsulates the core values of DevOps and provides a comprehensive approach to implementing its principles.

Team Topologies

In *Team Topologies*, *Matthew Skelton* and *Manuel Pais* articulate a structured approach to team organization within the DevOps paradigm. They define four fundamental team types and introduce the concept of **change of flow**, which is crucial for understanding the dynamics of DevOps teams. A common anti-pattern identified is the superficial renaming of teams or roles to include *DevOps,* such as creating a *DevOps Team* or appointing a *DevOps Engineer,* without any substantive change in practices.

The Team Topologies framework helps organizations understand how their practices and tools fit into the broader organizational context, promoting a more holistic and integrated approach to DevOps.

Team structures

Effective team structures are essential for accelerating DevOps practices. It is important to recognize that not all software teams share the same goals or utilize the same practices and tools. Structuring teams appropriately can significantly impact the success of DevOps implementation. This section explores various ways to organize teams to enhance collaboration, streamline workflows, and align objectives with DevOps principles.

DORA metrics

DevOps Research and Assessment (DORA) has developed four key metrics that are critical for measuring the efficacy of DevOps practices. These metrics provide valuable insights into the performance and efficiency of the development and operations processes, such as:

- **Lead time for changes**: Measures the time taken for code changes to move from check-in to production. Short lead times indicate efficient processes and faster delivery of features.

- **Deployment frequency**: Assesses how often and how quickly code is deployed to production. Higher deployment frequencies suggest a more agile and responsive development process.

- **Time to restore service**: Evaluates the duration taken to remediate and restore service after an incident is detected. Shorter restoration times reflect robust incident management and recovery processes.

- **Change failure rate**: Tracks the frequency of deployment failures that require immediate remedy or rollback. Lower failure rates signify more reliable deployments and stable production environments.

These metrics are indispensable for DevOps practitioners, providing a quantifiable means to gauge the effectiveness of their practices and identify areas for improvement.

By adhering to these frameworks, organizations can ensure that their DevOps practices are not only efficient and effective but also aligned with the broader goals of collaboration, continuous improvement, and operational excellence.

DevOps tools

In this section, we shall look at the various tools used in each phase of DevOps life cycle. The tools can be broadly classified into the following categories:

- Pipeline
- Test automation
- CI/CD
- Monitoring
- DevSecOps

An example listing of tools in each phase of the lifecycle can be seen in the following *Table 13.2:*

Phase	Purpose	Activities	Tools
Plan	Define project goals, requirements, and specifications.	• Collaborative planning sessions. • Creating user stories and tasks. • Prioritizing features and setting timelines.	Jira, Trello, Azure Boards.
Code	Write and manage the source code.	• Source code development. • Code review and version control. • Branching and merging strategies.	Git, GitHub, GitLab, Bitbucket.
Build	Compile the source code into executable artifacts.	• Automated builds. • Dependency management. • Packaging and artifact creation.	Maven, Gradle, Jenkins, Travis CI.
Test	Validate the code and ensure it meets quality standards.	• Automated testing (unit, integration, functional, performance). • Continuous testing in the CI/CD pipeline. • Identifying and fixing bugs.	Selenium, JUnit, TestNG, SonarQube

Phase	Purpose	Activities	Tools
Release	Deploy the application to production or staging environments.	• Release management. • Versioning and tagging. • Coordinating with stakeholders for deployment timelines.	Jenkins, CircleCI, Azure DevOps, Bamboo.
Deploy	Move the code to production environments.	• Automated deployment. • Configuration management. • IaC	Ansible, Chef, Puppet, Terraform, Kubernetes.
Operate	Manage and operate the software in production.	• Monitoring and logging. • Incident management and response. • Performance tuning and optimization.	Nagios, Prometheus, Grafana, Splunk, ELK Stack.
Monitor	Continuously monitor the application and infrastructure.	• Real-time monitoring. • Log analysis. • User behavior tracking and feedback collection.	New Relic, Datadog, Dynatrace.
Continuous Feedback Loop	Gather insights and feedback to inform future development.	• Collecting metrics and user feedback. • Analyzing performance data and usage patterns. • Using feedback to prioritize and plan new features.	Google Analytics, UserVoice, Sentry.
Continuous integration and continuous delivery (CI/CD)	Integrate code changes frequently and deliver them to production quickly and reliably.	• Merging code changes into a shared repository multiple times a day. • Automatically building, testing, and deploying each code change. • Ensuring that the software is always in a deployable state.	Jenkins, CircleCI, GitLab CI/CD, Travis CI.

Table 13.2: Tools and activities in DevOps

The following listed tools are explicitly mentioned in CV0-004 exam objectives for DevOps. So, the readers are advised to familiarize themselves with the basics of these tools.

• Ansible and Terraform

• Docker, Kubernetes

- **Elasticsearch, Logstash, and Kibana** (**ELK**) stack
- Git, GitHub actions, Jenkins

GrafanaDevOps topics

In this section, we will discuss the main topics that are generally discussed as DevOps topics. DevOps encompasses a lot more than the topics listed here. However, no discussion of DevOps can be considered complete without a thorough understanding of these topics.

Automation

Automation in the context of DevOps refers to the use of technology to perform tasks with minimal human intervention, aiming to enhance efficiency, consistency, and speed in the software development and deployment processes. It encompasses various activities such as automated testing, CI/CD, and infrastructure provisioning. By automating repetitive and manual tasks, teams can reduce human error, accelerate release cycles, and ensure consistent environments across development, testing, and production. Tools like Jenkins, Ansible, Terraform, and Kubernetes are commonly used to facilitate automation in DevOps. Automation also supports the principles of CI/CD, enabling rapid and reliable delivery of software updates. Ultimately, it fosters a more agile and responsive development pipeline, aligning with the core objectives of DevOps.

Jenkins

Jenkins is a popular open-source automation server widely used for CI/CD in software development. Jenkins automates the building, testing, and deployment of software projects. It allows developers to integrate code changes frequently and detect issues early in the development process. It operates through a series of interconnected steps that form a comprehensive automation pipeline. It begins by integrating with version control systems like Git or Subversion to manage source code. The system can be configured to initiate builds based on various triggers, such as code commits or scheduled times. Once triggered, Jenkins executes the build process, which typically involves compiling code, running tests, and generating reports. After a successful build, Jenkins manages the resulting artifacts, storing them for future use or deployment. Finally, it can automatically deploy these builds to staging or production environments, completing the automation cycle from code change to live application.

Jenkins has some very important functionalities that are of immense use for developers. The following is a very brief listing of some key features of Jenkins.

- **Extensibility**: Jenkins supports hundreds of plugins, allowing integration with various tools and services.
- **Distributed Builds**: It can distribute build and test loads across multiple machines.

- **Pipeline support**: Jenkins Pipeline allows defining complex workflows as code.

- **Easy configuration**: Web interface for easy setup and configuration.

- **Monitoring**: Provides real-time monitoring of builds and tests.

- **Notifications**: Can send alerts via email, Slack, and other channels.

CI/CD

Continuous integration (CI) and **continuous delivery/deployment (CD)** are key practices in the DevOps methodology that aim to improve software development and delivery processes. Here is a brief introduction to each of those practices.

Continuous integration

CI is a practice where developers frequently commit code changes to a shared repository, typically multiple times a day. Each commit triggers an automated build and testing process. The main goals of CI are as follows:

- **Early detection of issues**: By integrating code frequently, teams can detect and address issues early in the development process.

- **Improved collaboration**: CI encourages collaboration among team members, as they are integrating their work continuously and resolving conflicts early.

- **Automated testing**: Automated tests run with each build ensure that new code does not break existing functionality.

- **Fast feedback**: Developers receive quick feedback on their code, enabling them to make improvements rapidly.

Continuous delivery

Continuous delivery is an extension of CI that ensures code changes are automatically prepared for a release to production. It focuses on making sure the software can be reliably released at any time. The key aspects include:

- **Automated deployment pipelines**: Code changes pass through various stages of testing and validation via automated pipelines.

- **Consistent releases**: Ensures that releases are consistent and less prone to errors, as the deployment process is fully automated.

- **Frequent releases**: Enables frequent and smaller releases, which reduces the risk associated with large, infrequent updates.

Continuous deployment

Continuous deployment goes a step further than continuous delivery by automatically deploying every change that passes the automated tests to production. This practice requires a high level of confidence in the automated testing and deployment processes. The benefits include:

- **Faster time to market**: New features and fixes are delivered to users quickly.

- **Immediate feedback**: Real-time feedback from users can be gathered faster, allowing for quicker iterations and improvements.

- **Reduced manual intervention**: Minimizes human error and reduces the need for manual deployment steps.

CI/CD pipeline

A CI/CD pipeline is a series of steps that code changes go through from development to production. Typical stages in a CI/CD pipeline include:

1. **Source Code Management**: Integrating changes into a shared repository.

2. **Build**: Compiling the code and creating executable artifacts.

3. **Testing**: Running automated tests to validate the code.

4. **Deployment**: Deploying the code to staging/production environments.

5. **Monitoring**: Observing the deployed application to ensure it is running smoothly.

CI/CD in DevOps offers multiple benefits to practicing organisations. The benefits include, but are not limited to, Improved Code Quality, Reduced Risk, Enhanced Collaboration, and Faster Delivery. By implementing CI/CD practices, organizations can achieve more efficient and reliable software delivery, ultimately leading to better software products and higher customer satisfaction.

Source control

Source control, also known as **version control**, is a system that tracks changes to files over time in software development. It allows multiple developers to work on a project simultaneously, maintaining a history of modifications. Key features include the ability to revert to previous versions, create branches for experimentation, and merge changes from different contributors. Popular source control systems include Git, **Subversion (SVN)**, and Mercurial. Source control helps teams collaborate effectively, manage code conflicts, and maintain a reliable record of project evolution. It is essential for tracking bugs, implementing new features, and ensuring code integrity in both small and large-scale software projects. Among these, Git is a recent introduction and has revolutionized the source control approach followed in enterprises. It has almost become the standard for version control. So, CV0-004 exam places a certain emphasis on familiarity with Git and its usage.

Git

Git is a **distributed version control system (DVCS)** created by *Linus Torvalds* in 2005. It was developed to manage the source code of the Linux kernel with efficiency and reliability. The history of Git is closely tied to the development of the Linux operating system. *Linus Torvalds*, the original creator of Linux operating system, started Git in 2005 after a dispute with the developers of BitKeeper, a proprietary version control system previously used by the Linux community. Within a few weeks, the first version of Git was released. It was designed to be fast, scalable, and fully distributed. Over time, Git has become the de facto standard for source code management in open-source projects and is widely used in the industry.

Benefits

The following are the benefits of Git:

- **Distributed system**: Each developer has a full copy of the repository, including the entire history of changes, allowing offline work and ensuring data redundancy.

- **Performance**: Git is optimized for speed. Most operations are performed locally, which makes them very fast.

- **Branching and merging**: Git's branching model is robust and flexible, enabling developers to create, merge, and delete branches with ease.

- **Data integrity**: Git stores data in a way that ensures the integrity of the source code. Every change is checksummed before it is stored, and it is identified by that checksum.

- **Collaboration**: Git enhances collaboration by enabling multiple developers to work on the same project simultaneously without interfering with each other's work.

Key features

The following are the key features of Git:

- **Branching and merging**: Git allows for easy branching and merging, providing an efficient workflow for managing feature development, bug fixes, and experiments.

- **Staging area**: The staging area (or index) allows developers to prepare changes before committing them, offering more control over the commit process.

- **Distributed nature**: Every clone of a Git repository is a full-fledged repository with complete history and full version tracking capabilities.

- **Lightweight**: Git repositories are compact and efficient in terms of disk usage and network performance.

- **Commit history**: Git maintains a detailed history of changes, allowing developers to revert to previous versions and understand the evolution of the codebase.

- **Rewriting history**: Advanced users can rewrite history using commands like rebase to clean up commits and maintain a linear project history.

- **Hooks**: Git supports hooks, which are scripts that run automatically at certain points in the Git workflow. These can be used to enforce policies, run tests, or perform other custom operations.

Automation support

Git plays a crucial role in automation, particularly in the context of DevOps. Here are some ways in which Git is integrated into automated workflows:

- **CI/CD**: Git repositories are often integrated with CI/CD pipelines (e.g., Jenkins, GitLab CI, Travis CI, CircleCI) to automate the process of building, testing, and deploying code. Changes pushed to a Git repository can trigger automated builds, tests, and deployments, ensuring that code changes are quickly and reliably integrated into the main codebase.

- **Infrastructure as Code (IaC)**: Git is used to version control infrastructure configurations (e.g., Terraform, Ansible playbooks). This allows teams to track changes to their infrastructure and roll back if necessary. Automated pipelines can provision and configure infrastructure based on the state defined in the Git repository.

- **Automated code reviews**: Tools like GitHub Actions, GitLab CI, or custom scripts can be used to automate code review processes. These tools can check for code style, run static analysis, and enforce coding standards before changes are merged.

- **Deployment automation**: GitOps is a paradigm where Git repositories are the source of truth for the desired state of the system. Changes to the Git repository automatically trigger deployments to the target environment. Tools like ArgoCD and FluxCD watch Git repositories and apply changes to Kubernetes clusters based on the repository's state.

- **Issue tracking integration**: Git can be integrated with issue tracking systems (e.g., Jira, GitHub Issues) to link code changes with tasks, bugs, or feature requests. This integration helps in tracking the progress and context of development work.

Common Git commands

A detailed discussion of Git commands is out of scope for the purposes of this book. However, a basic knowledge of Git commands is necessary for CV0-004 exam. Some common Git commands are listed here for easy reference for the readers.

- **git clone [repository URL]**: Creates a local copy of a remote repository on local machine.

- **git commit**: Records changes to the repository with a descriptive message explaining what was changed.

- **git push**: Uploads local repository content to a remote repository.

- **git pull**: Updates local repository with changes from the remote repository.

- **git branch**: Lists, creates, or deletes branches, allowing parallel development work.

- **git fetch**: Downloads objects and references from a remote repository without integrating them into local working files.

Git is a powerful and versatile tool that has transformed the way software development and collaboration are managed. Its distributed nature, efficient branching and merging capabilities, and robust history management make it an essential tool for modern software development. Furthermore, Git's integration with automation tools and CI/CD pipelines makes it a cornerstone of DevOps practices, enabling teams to deliver high-quality software efficiently and reliably.

IaC

IaC is a key practice in modern IT operations and cloud computing. It is an approach to infrastructure management where systems, networks, and other IT resources are provisioned and managed using machine-readable definition files, rather than physical hardware configuration or interactive configuration tools. IaC treats infrastructure configuration as software code. This means that the same principles used in software development - version control, testing, small deployments, continuous integration, and Delivery - can be applied to infrastructure management.

Virtual machines (**VMs**) and IaC complement each other in modern IT environments. IaC can be used to define, provision, and manage VMs automatically, specifying their configurations, resource allocations, and network settings in code. This approach allows for rapid deployment and consistent replication of VM environments across development, testing, and production stages. By treating VM configurations as code, teams can version control their infrastructure, easily roll back changes, and maintain identical environments across different cloud providers or data centers. The combination of VMs and IaC enhances scalability, reduces manual errors, and supports the agile and DevOps principles of frequent, reliable deployments.

IaC is guided by several key principles and offers numerous benefits while adhering to best practices. The approach favors declarative specifications over imperative instructions, focusing on describing the desired end-state rather than step-by-step procedures. It emphasizes idempotency, ensuring that repeated applications of the same configuration yield consistent results, and promotes modular design for reusable components. These principles contribute to the significant benefits of IaC, including enhanced consistency that reduces human errors, improved speed and efficiency in deployments, robust version control for tracking and auditing changes, built-in documentation through the code itself, easy scalability, and overall cost reduction through automation. To maximize these advantages, practitioners follow best practices such as utilizing version control for all IaC files, implementing thorough code review processes, creating modular and reusable code components, conducting proper testing before deployment, integrating with CI/CD pipelines, and adhering to security best practices, including the encryption of sensitive data. By following these principles and practices, organizations can fully leverage the power of IaC to streamline their infrastructure management and support agile development processes.

IaC is a cornerstone of DevOps practices, enabling closer collaboration between development and operations teams. It allows for treating infrastructure with the same agility and frequency of updates as application code.

Conclusion

In this chapter, we have seen an introduction to DevOps fundamentals as they are needed for CV0-004 examination. It is critical to note that DevOps is a vast topic, and the exam covers only the fundamentals of DevOps. A more detailed discussion of DevOps topics is out of scope for the purposes of this book. This chapter started with an overview of DevOps, its history, culture, and various topics of DevOps.

The next chapter provides practice questions for the CVO-004 examination. This chapter provides a mock test to prepare you for the actual examination.

Glossary

- **Agile**: A software development methodology emphasizing iterative development, collaboration, and flexibility.

- **CI/CD:** Continuous integration and continuous delivery/deployment. Practices that automate the building, testing, and deployment of applications.

- **Configuration management:** The process of maintaining systems, servers, and software in a desired state.

- **Containerization**: Packaging an application and its dependencies together in a *container* to ensure consistent operation across different environments.

- **Docker:** A popular platform for containerizing applications.

- **IaC**: Managing and provisioning infrastructure through code instead of manual processes.

- **Kubernetes**: An open-source container orchestration platform for automating deployment, scaling, and management of containerized applications.

- **Microservices:** An architectural style where applications are composed of small, independent services.

- **Monitoring**: The practice of observing and tracking the performance and state of systems, applications, and infrastructure.

- **Orchestration:** Automating the deployment, management, scaling, and networking of containers.

- **Pipeline:** An automated series of steps that code changes go through from development to production.

- **Version control**: A system that records changes to files over time, allowing for collaboration and rollback capabilities (e.g., Git).

Practice questions

S. No	Question		Correct Answer
1	**What is DevOps?**		A
	A) A methodology combining software development and operations	B) A programming language	
	C) A database management system	D) A software testing tool	
2	**Which of the following is a key principle of DevOps?**		B
	A) Manual deployment	B) Continuous integration and continuous deployment (CI/CD)	
	C) Waterfall development	D) Isolated development and operations teams	
3	**What does CI/CD stand for in a DevOps context?**		C
	A) Continuous integration and continuous development	B) Continuous improvement and continuous delivery	
	C) Continuous integration and continuous deployment	D) Continuous initialization and continuous debugging	
4	**Which tool is commonly used for Continuous Integration in DevOps?**		A
	A) Jenkins	B) Photoshop	
	C) Microsoft Word	D) AutoCAD	

S. No	Question		Correct Answer
5	**What is Infrastructure as Code (IaC)?**		A
	A) A process for managing infrastructure using code and automation	B) A manual method for configuring servers	
	C) A type of hardware used in cloud computing	D) A programming paradigm	
6	**Which of the following is a popular containerization tool used in DevOps?**		A
	A) Docker	B) GitHub	
	C) Jenkins	D) Selenium	
7	**What is the role of configuration management tools in DevOps?**		B
	A) To automate the deployment of applications	B) To manage and maintain the consistency of configurations over time	
	C) To write code for applications	D) To perform manual testing	
8	**Which of the following is not a DevOps practice?**		D
	A) Continuous Monitoring	B) Continuous Testing	
	C) Continuous Deployment	D) Continuous Debugging	
9	**Which of the following tools is used for monitoring and logging in DevOps?**		A
	A) Nagios	B) Jenkins	
	C) Git	D) Docker	
10	**What is the main benefit of using version control systems in DevOps?**		B
	A) To improve the aesthetic of the code	B) To track and manage changes to code	
	C) To automate the deployment process	D) To perform manual code reviews	

Join our Discord space

Join our Discord workspace for latest updates, offers, tech happenings around the world, new releases, and sessions with the authors:

https://discord.bpbonline.com

CHAPTER 14
Vendor Specific Solutions

Introduction

As discussed in the previous chapters, cloud services have become the mainstay in any organisation's tech stack. Even hardcore sceptics of cloud computing have come to accept that cloud computing is the new normal and are integrating it into their portfolios. Whether it is a private cloud, public, or hybrid, the benefits of cloud computing can no longer be denied. Even organizations that have invested heavily in private data centres are finding business cases where some kind of public cloud usage is beneficial for agility and cost efficiency. For smaller organisations and start-ups, public clouds have become the go-to approach.

Considering this, it is beneficial for students to be familiar with cloud offerings from the major cloud players. This information is complementary to the CV0-004 exam's body of knowledge. It is neither necessary nor expected that students be familiar with all the services, their similarities, and differences. This chapter serves as a reference to students on CSP offerings. For example, if they want storage for their cloud application, this chapter provides the names of the services that are available from popular CSPs, which might meet their requirement.

As of 2022, AWS is the undisputed market leader, and Azure is the second with a significant gap [1]. Interested readers can see more details of the market share distribution at this link from **statista.com**. The following figure can be seen on *www.statista.com* at the given link:

https://cdn.statcdn.com/Infographic/images/normal/18819.jpeg

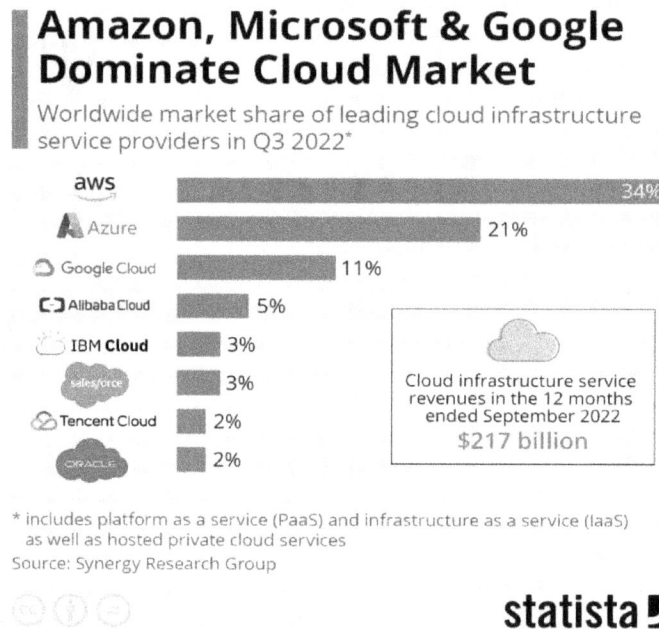

Figure 14.1: Statista infographic on CSP market share

We shall not be comparing the relative advantages or disadvantages of the individual services. Nor shall we discuss pricing. These topics are completely out of scope for the current book and for CV0-004 exam as well.

Objectives

The objective of this chapter is only to familiarize the readers with the names of the different cloud offerings from major CSPs. The list provided here is neither complete nor comprehensive. This list is only for the reference of the readers and is not part of the exam syllabus. This chapter covers only the cloud offerings from AWS, Azure, and Google. Other major CSPs include IBM Cloud, Oracle Cloud, Alibaba Cloud, and Huawei Cloud. Combined, these CSPs command a market share of more than 80%.

Structure

This chapter contains the following topics:

- Compute services

- Storage services
- Networking services
- Management services
- Identity and Security services

Compute services

In *Table 14.1*, we will list various compute services offered by CSPs along with a brief description for each of them:

Service Offering	Purpose	AWS	Azure	GCP
Virtual Servers (IaaS offering)	For hosting virtual machines	Amazon EC2	Azure Virtual Machine	Compute Engine
Bare Metal Server services	For renting physical machines in cloud which are not shared with any other clients	Amazon EC2 Bare Metal Instance	Azure Bare Metal Servers	Bare Metal Solution
Virtual Dedicated Hosts		Amazon EC2 Dedicated Hosts	Azure Dedicated Host	Sole Tenant Node
		AWS Nitro Enclaves		
High-Performance Computing		High-Performance Computing	Azure High-Performance Compute	High-performance Computing
		AWS ParallelCluster		
		Elastic Fabric Adapter		
		NICE DCV		
Container Services	For managing Containers	Amazon **Elastic Container Service (ECS)**	Azure Container Registry	Artifact Registry
		Amazon **Elastic Kubernetes Service (EKS)**	**Azure Kubernetes Service (AKS)**	Kubernetes Engine
		Red Hat Openshift on AWS	Azure Container Instances	
		Bottlerocket	Azure Red Hat OpenShift	

Service Offering	Purpose	AWS	Azure	GCP
Serverless Computing	Allows developers to run code without having to manage backend or infrastructure.	AWS Fargate	Azure Container Instances	Google Cloud Run
		AWS Proton	Azure Container Apps	
Micro Services Development		AWS Lambda	Azure Service Fabric	Google Cloud Functions
			Azure Functions	EventArc
			Event Grid	

Table 14.1: Listing of compute services from major CSPs

Storage services

In *Table 14.2*, we will list various storage services offered by CSPs along with a brief description for each of them:

Service Offering	Purpose	AWS	Azure	GCP
Virtual Machine Disk Storage	Raw block storage to be attached to compute instances	Amazon **Elastic Block Storage** (EBS)	Azure Page Blobs / Premium Storage	Persistent Disk
			Managed Disks	
File Storage	Filestorage compatible with SMB using CIFS	Amazon **Elastic File System** (EFS)	Azure Files	File Store
Long Term Cold Storage	High latency, low-cost long-term storage	Amazon S3 Glacier	Azure Archive Storage	Cloud Storage
			Azure Cool Storage	

Service Offering	Purpose	AWS	Azure	GCP
Databases	Fully managed RDBMS	Amazon Aurora	Azure SQL Database	Cloud SQL
		Amazon RDS	SQL Server Stretch Database	Cloud Spanner
			Azure Database for MySQL	
			Azure Database for PostgresSQL	
			Azure SQL Database Edge	
	Non-Relational Database Management Service	Amazon DynamoDB	Azure CosmosDB	Cloud Datastore
		Amazon **DynamoDB Accelerator (DAX)**	Table Storage	Cloud Firestore
		Amazon DocumentDB (with MongoDB compatibility)	Azure Time Series Insights	
		Amazon Keyspaces (Apache Cassandra)		
	Timeseries Database	Amazon Timestream	Azure Time Series Insights	Cloud Bigtable
	In-Memory Data Store	Amazon ElastiCache	Azure Cache for Redis	Cloud MemoryStore
		Amazon MemoryDB for Redis		
	Data Warehousing	Amazon Redshift	Azure Synapse Analytics	BigQuery

Table 14.2: Listing of storage services from major CSPs

Networking services

In *Table 14.3*, we will list various networking services offered by CSPs along with a brief description:

Service Offering	Purpose	AWS	Azure	GCP
Networking and Content Management	Virtual Networking to setup secure private networks within the cloud	Amazon VPC	Azure VNet	Virtual Private Cloud
	Virtual network connectivity for peering networks	AWS Transit Gateway	Azure VNet Peering	Google VPC Peering
		AWS VPC peering		
	Network Gateway	AWS Site-to-Site VPN	Azure VPN Gateway	Cloud VPN
		AWS Client VPN		
	Content Delivery Network	Amazon CloudFront	Azure CDN	Cloud CDN
			Azure Front Door	
	Networking & Content Delivery	Amazon Route 53	Azure DNS	Cloud DNS
	Private Connectivity	AWS Direct Connect	Azure Express Route	Cloud Hybrid Connectivity
		AWS Private Link	Azure Private Link	
	Load Balancers	Elastic Load Balancing	Azure Load Balancer	Cloud Load Balancing

Table 14.3: Listing of networking services from major CSPs

Management services

In *Table 14.4*, we will list various services offered by CSPs to manage cloud applications, VMs and other resources deployed in the cloud:

Service Offering	Purpose	AWS	Azure	GCP
Management Tools	Cloud Deployment Templates/ Infra as Code	AWS CloudFormation	Azure Resource Manager	Cloud Resource Manager
		AWS OpsWorks	Azure Building Blocks	Cloud Deployment Manager
	Logging & Monitoring of cloud applications	Amazon CloudWatch	Log Analytics	Google StackDriver
		AWS CloudTrail	Azure portal	Monitoring
		AWS X-Ray	Application Insights	Logging
				Error Reporting
				Trace
				Debugger
	Cloud Management Tools	AWS Command Line Interface	Azure Command Line Interface	Cloud Shell
		AWS CloudShell	Azure Powershell	Cloud Console
		AWS Management Console	Azure Management Console	Billing API
		AWS Console Mobile Application	Azure Cloud Shell	Cloud APIs
		AWS Tools & SDKs		

Table 14.4: Listing of cloud management tools from major CSPs

Identity and Security services

In *Table 14.5*, we will list various services offered by CSPs to manage identity and access in cloud. We will also list services provided for ensuring security for cloud resource:

Service Offering	Purpose	AWS	Azure	GCP
Security, Identity and Compliance	Identity & Access Management	AWS **Identity and Access Management (IAM)**	Azure Active Directory	Cloud IAM
				Cloud Identity-Aware Proxy
	Cloud Security Assesment Service	Amazon Inspector	Azure Security Center	
		Guard Duty		
	Key Management Services	AWS Secrets Manager	Azure Key Vault	Cloud Key Management Service
	Directory Services	AWS Directory Service	Azure Active Directory	Cloud IAM
			Azure Active Directory B2C	Cloud Identity-Aware Proxy
			Azure Active Directory Domain Services	Security Key Enforcement
			Azure Active Directory Multi Factor Authentication	
	DDos Protection Service	AWS Shield	Azure DDoS Protection	Cloud Armor
	Security & Compliance Service	AWS WAF	Azure WAF	
		AWS Firewall Manager	Azure Firewall Manager	
		AWS Network Firewall		

Table 14.5: Listing of IAM and Security services from major CSPs

DevOps tools

In *Table 14.6*, we will list various DevOps tools and services offered by CSPs along with a brief description:

Tool Offering	Purpose	AWS	Azure	GCP
Continuous integration and continuous delivery (CI/CD)	Securely store and version source code and automatically build, test, and deploy the application.	AWS CodePipeline, AWS CodeBuild AWS CodeDeploy	Azure Pipelines	Cloud Build
Microservices	Building and deploying a microservices architecture using containers or serverless computing.	Amazon Elastic Container Service AWS Lambda	Azure Kubernetes Service Azure Functions Azure Container Apps	Google Kubernetes Engine Cloud Run
Infrastructure as Code	Provision, configure, and manage cloud infrastructure resources using code. Monitoring and enforcing infrastructure compliance.	AWS CloudFormation AWS OpsWorks AWS Systems Manager		Cloud Deployment Manager Terraform on Google Cloud
Monitoring and Logging	Recording logs and monitoring application and infrastructure performance.	AWS Config Amazon CloudWatch AWS X-Ray AWS CloudTrail Amazon DevOps Guru	Azure Monitor Application Insights	Cloud Operations
Platform as a Service	Deploying web applications without provisioning the infrastructure.	AWS BeanStalk		
Version Control	Private code hosting	AWS CodeCommit	Azure Repos	Google Cloud Source Repositories

Table 14.6: Listing of IAM and Security services from major CSPs

Conclusion

As mentioned earlier, this chapter contains information that is complementary to CV0-004 exam. The contents of the chapter need not be memorized for the exam. It should be noted that the listing provided above is neither comprehensive nor complete. Moreover, CSPs are continuously innovating new services and deprecating existing ones to ensure better support for customers. So, the lists above should be treated as a starting point. The next chapter will cover practice questions along with their corresponding answer key.

References

https://www.statista.com/chart/18819/worldwide-market-share-of-leading-cloud-infrastructure-service-providers/

Join our Discord space

Join our Discord workspace for latest updates, offers, tech happenings around the world, new releases, and sessions with the authors:

https://discord.bpbonline.com

CHAPTER 15

Practice Questions

Introduction

This chapter is for providing you with practice for the actual exam. Choose any 85 questions from the MCQs and both the performance-based questions. Finish them in 2 hours and 30 minutes and check your performance against the answer key. This simulates the exam for you closely.

Multiple choice questions

1. **Which of the following service models would be used for an ERP in the cloud?**

    A. IaaS

    B. PaaS

    C. SaaS

    D. FaaS

2. **What is Serverless computing also called?**

    A. IaaS

    B. PaaS

    C. SaaS

    D. FaaS

3. A VDI administrator received a complaint from users that the virtual desktops seem to be sluggish even though the memory usage is low. What should the administrator check for?

   A. Storage

   B. CPU

   C. Network

   D. Memory Ballooning

4. An administrator is reviewing the Disaster Recovery plans of the organization. He needs to revisit all the possible scenarios that can impact the organization. Where should he look for this information?

   A. Business Requirements

   B. Risk Register

   C. SLA

   D. Legal agreements

5. A cloud engineer has configured multiple VMs in the cloud. After an OS upgrade on the VMs, one of the VMs was not reachable over RDP. Cloud management console has shown that the VM has an IP address of 169.254.11.12. What can the administrator infer from this information?

   A. The VM failed to obtain an IP address from DHCP server

   B. The VM was isolated by hypervisor due to anomalous activity

   C. Firewall has blocked access to the VM

   D. All the above

6. A news organization has been receiving complaints about slow access to their news website. Upon inspection, they realized that most of the complaints were from users residing in foreign countries. What should they do to resolve this situation?

   A. Increase bandwidth on cloud

   B. Setup a CDN

   C. Increase CPU of their VMs

   D. Setup QoS rules

7. An organization is considering migrating its on-prem hosting to public cloud. Legal requirements require that the server hardware running their mission critical application should not run any other application. What options do they have for moving the mission critical application hardware to cloud?

   A. Use Hybrid cloud

   B. Use Bare Metal Server services from the CSP

    C. Setup the server in regions outside the legal purview

    D. Continue with On-Prem hosting

8. **An organization is having many VMs within its cloud. They are looking for a way to track and manage the IP address space. Which solution can they use?**

    A. Private IP addresses

    B. IPAM

    C. IPv6

    D. Static IPs

9. **A system administrator is migrating virtual machines from an on-premise hypervisor to the cloud. What type of migration is the administrator performing?**

    A. V2V

    B. P2P

    C. P2V

    D. V2P

10. **An administrator is calculating the number of vCPUs, Memory and network requirements for his applications. He determined that the current configuration of vCPUs and RAM is too high and reduced them. Network bandwidth was increased. What is this process called?**

    A. Right sizing

    B. Scaling in

    C. Auto-scaling

    D. Scaling up

11. **An organization is reviewing workloads in its private data center. They identified that on weekends, there are a large number of in-house clean-up tasks which are CPU intensive. The currently installed CPU capacity is unable to meet them. So, they decided to use computing power in public clouds during the weekends and in-house capacity for rest of the week. What is this approach called?**

    A. Auto-scaling

    B. Multi-clouding

    C. Load balancing

    D. Cloud Bursting

12. **An organization has a load balanced web application. Five VMs are load balanced by a load balancer that routes incoming requests in a Round Robin fashion. Administrator is receiving complaints from users that they are having**

to login multiple times, sometimes within the same session. What can the administrator do to solve this problem?

    A. Reduce the number of VMs

    B. Implement stickiness on the load balancer

    C. Reconfigure the VMs to share the same storage

    D. Implement SSO

13. **A cloud administrator reviews the authentication and authorization mechanism implemented within the cloud environment. Upon review, the administrator discovers that file access is provided by individual owners to other users as they see fit. What is this approach called?**

    A. Mandatory Access Control

    B. Discretionary Access Control

    C. User level access control

    D. Attribute based access control

14. **A company developed a product using a cloud provider's PaaS platform and many of the platform-based components within the application environment. The CTO wants the application to be migrated to another cloud provider. Application development team is unable to do so because the target cloud provider does not offer some necessary features available with the current provider. What is this situation called?**

    A. Licensing

    B. SLAs

    C. Authentication providers

    D. Vendor Lock-in

15. **A systems administrator is trying to establish an RDP session from his desktop to a cloud server in the cloud. He is able to, but other users are unable to do so. What should the administrator check FIRST?**

    A. Firewall rules

    B. ACLs

    C. Subnets

    D. Authentication

16. **Which among the following RAID configurations offers maximum storage performance?**

    A. RAID 1

    B. RAID 5

C. RAID 0

D. RAID 6

17. A user working on a VM was able to traverse the virtualization layer and was able to access other VMs running on the same hypervisor. What is the name of this attack?

   A. VM escape

   B. Directory traversal

   C. Buffer overflow

   D. Heap spraying

18. A CTO has determined that in the event of a disaster, past 30 minutes worth of data can be lost, but the services should be available and running within 5 minutes. What are these metrics?

   A. RTO, RPO

   B. MTTF, SLA

   C. RPO, RTO

   D. RPA, SLA

19. An administrator has procured a new hard drive for his archive storage. The HDD manufacturer claims that once a failure occurs in the hard drive, the next failure shall not occur for another 365 days on average. What metric is the manufacturer referring to?

   A. SLA

   B. MTTF

   C. Uptime

   D. RTO

20. A cloud administrator has a large number of VMs to monitor his applications. He wants to centralize the logs generated by applications on to the VMs into a single location. Which is the best option to follow?

   A. Shared Storage

   B. Archive management

   C. Syslog forwarding

   D. FTP service

21. An administrator of the on-premises data center is receiving complaints of high latency of network communications within the data center. What approach can he try to improve network performance without investing additional budget? He has CPU power to spare on all devices in the network.

A. Setup QoS rules

B. Enable jumbo frames for internal traffic.

C. Oversubscribe the vNICs

D. Setup affinity rules

22. **Which of the following security controls will prevent the exfiltration of sensitive data?**

    A. WAF

    B. FIM

    C. ADC

    D. DLP

23. **An application development team has finished their application development and are rolling the new version to a small select group of users. After fixing any problems that arise, the new application shall be rolled out to larger number of users. What deployment approach is this?**

    A. Canary

    B. Beta

    C. Blue-Green

    D. Rolling deployment

24. **A web application which is heavy in database access is being migrated to public cloud. Administrator has to ensure that communication between application service and database service do not consume the internet bandwidth. Which is the best approach for achieving this?**

    A. Setup application VM and database VM as a subnet and specify security group rules

    B. Enable QoS rules between application VM and Database VM

    C. Setup affinity rules to run the database VM and application VM on the same hypervisor

    D. Setup application VM and Database VM on separate subnets and peer the networks

25. **A market research organization has agreements to place sensors in their users homes. The sensors transmit data to a cloud-based Database PaaS. They increased their survey sample size from 500 users to 10,000. They found that at any given point, data from only 2500 sensors is being stored. Which of the following best describes the reason for it?**

    A. Incorrect billing account

    B. API request limit

    C. Misconfigured auto-scaling

    D. Bandwidth limitation

26. **An organizations deals with highly sensitive government data. They do not want to take the risk of unknown malware from infecting their IaaS servers. Which of the below is the best way to guard against it?**

    A. Encrypt all applications that users should not access

    B. Set the execute filesystem permissions on the desired applications only

    C. Install an anti-virus on all IaaS instances

    D. Implement an application whitelisting policy

27. **An administrator is configuring VMs on a hypervisor. The CPU is a critical resource for the VM applications. Which storage options among the below will not add CPU cycles?**

    A. Thick provisioning

    B. Disk level encryption

    C. Thin provisioning

    D. Jumbo data frames

28. **When migrating from one CSP to another, which of the following is most needed for a lift-and-shift migration?**

    A. Licensing

    B. Identity management

    C. Feature compatibility

    D. SLAs

29. **A private cloud administrator is receiving complaints that video buffering is slow on the internal training application server. The remaining content is traveling fast on the network. What can he do to improve the video experience?**

    A. Increase bandwidth on the cloud

    B. Implement QoS rules

    C. Enable jumbo frames

    D. Isolate the server to a dedicated network

30. **A company has experienced a disaster and has failed over its data center to the backup site. Disaster was addressed, and now they want to move back to their primary location. What should the administrator first do for this?**

    A. Update documentation and lessons learned

    B. Restore backups

    C. Clean-up any artefacts

    D. Initiate a failback

31. **A finance organization has a very low RTO and zero RPO. Any loss of data can be catastrophic. What kind of process is required for them to write data.**

    A. Synchronous replication

    B. Real-time archives

    C. Asynchronous replication

    D. Fault-tolerant storage

32. **After replacing the firewall in a private cloud, all machines started showing incorrect times. What could be the most probable reason for this?**

    A. Firewall is infected with malware

    B. The firewall hardware is incompatible with machines

    C. The new firewall's configuration is incorrect and blocks the NTP

    D. Firewall's hardware clock is faulty

33. **An organization is considering purchasing an application for installation in its cloud servers. The application licensing costs are based on the number of processors on the physical machine where it is installed. What licensing model is this?**

    A. Per user licensing

    B. Socket based licensing

    C. Capacity-based licensing

    D. Volume-based licensing

34. **An organization is considering purchasing an application for its users. The application licensing costs are staggered as follows:**

1-10 users: 100 USD

10-50 users: 75 USD

50-100 users: 70 USD

100-500 users: 65 USD

>500 users: 60 USD

What licensing model is this?

    A. Per user licensing

    B. Socket based licensing

    C. Capacity-based licensing

    D. Volume-based licensing

35. An application development team has finished their application development and are ready to deploy the new version. Which of the following should the perform first?

   A. Change Management

   B. Capacity planning

   C. Backups

   D. End-user communication

36. When comparing CPUs for performance, which is the suggested sequence of parameters to choose the better CPU?

   A. Hyperthreading, Cache, clock speed

   B. Number of cores, cache, hyperthreading

   C. Number of Cores, Clock speed, Cache size

   D. Hyper threading, clock speed, number of cores

37. A storage administrator has configured a shared storage in such a way that it appears as a local disk to all the VMs it is attached to. What storage architecture is this?

   A. NAS

   B. SAN

   C. CIFS

   D. RAID

38. An application developer working on a VM accidentally got access to the host hypervisor's operating system. What kind of hypervisor is the VM running on?

   A. Type A

   B. Type Z

   C. Type 1

   D. Type 2

39. Which technology allows application developers to deploy their solution in isolated environments with high portability and lightweight resource footprint?

   A. Containers

   B. Infrastructure as Code

   C. Desktop virtualization

   D. Virtual Machines

40. A company has tasked an administrator to check its network for vulnerabilities. Administrator is asking his manager to provide him with a written approval

before he can start the testing. What kind of testing is the administrator tasked with?

    A. Load testing

    B. Vulnerability testing

    C. Penetration testing

    D. Regression testing

41. An application development team has rolled out a new version of its application to their users in canary mode. The initial set of users did not raise any concerns. When the application was rolled out to all users, there were a large number of complaints on application slowness. Which testing strategy was missing in the development cycle?

    A. Functional testing

    B. Load testing

    C. Beta testing

    D. Usability testing

42. A company is migrating from on-premises to a public cloud. The administrator has been tasked with ensuring that the cloud expenses are charged back to the appropriate department that has utilized them. What is the approach to achieving this?

    A. Show back

    B. Identity management

    C. ACL

    D. Tagging

43. An administrator has to configure the firewall to route HTTP traffic to HTTPS. Which rule should be set?

    A. port 80 to port 443

    B. port 21 to port 123

    C. port 443 to port 80

    D. port 80 to 21

44. A network administrator is tasked with ensuring that all traffic on the network is encrypted, irrespective of the application. Which is the best approach for this?

    A. Encryption as a service

    B. Upgrade all VMs to latest OS

    C. Implement IPsec

    D. Use HTTPS and TLS 1.3

45. Which of the following will provide a systems administrator with the most information about potential attacks on a cloud IaaS instance?

    A. FIM

    B. Network flows

    C. HIDS

    D. DDos Protection

46. An organization requires its data to be hosted on multiple regions. It also requires communications between the regions to be of low latency and to be secured. Which is the best approach for this?

    A. VPCs

    B. VPN

    C. MPLS

    D. Peering

47. Which of the following approaches is best for authenticating data in transit?

    A. Hashing

    B. Parity

    C. Encryption

    D. CRC bits

48. A storage administrator has received complaints about latency of a database. Upon review, he found that database is running on older storage technologies. What technology can he upgrade to?

    A. iSCSI

    B. iFC

    C. SSD

    D. SR-IOV

49. A Chief Security Officer has instructed the administrator to implement a new authentication policy. Users should be authenticated with *something they know* and *something they have*. What is the CSO referring to?

    A. Username, password

    B. Multi-factor authentication

    C. SSO

    D. Access cards

50. A systems administrator is concerned that developers might accidentally include sensitive application data along with system logs. Turning off logging is not an option. What solutions can the administrator implement?

A. Obfuscation

B. Log encryption

C. Log level management

D. Log scrubbing

51. **Which of the following requires analysis when rehosting applications from private data centers to the cloud?**

    A. Licensing

    B. Right-sizing

    C. SLAs

    D. Bandwidth limitation

52. **Which of the following is the best explanation of serverless computing?**

    A. A cloud-hosting service that utilizes infrastructure that is fully managed by the CSP

    B. Predictable billing and offering lower costs than VM compute services

    C. A scalable, highly available cloud service that uses SDN technologies.

    D. Application development paradigm where client-server architecture is avoided

53. **Which of the following is a best practice for securing new web servers?**

    A. Disable password authentication

    B. Disable the superuser/administrator account

    C. Restrict access on SSH port to the administrator's machine

    D. All the above

54. **An organization is setting up a cold site for its DR activities. Which among the following does a cold site guaranteed to have?**

    A. Personnel

    B. Systems

    C. Data

    D. Electric supply

55. **An organization has their employees user ids provisioned in their on-prem IAM system. Upon migration to cloud, they want their on-prem system to continue to be used. What should be enabled on the CSP for this?**

    A. Identity Federation

    D. LDAP

C. Digital certificates

D. Active Directory

56. An administrator is responsible for managing a cloud application that is distributed across multiple regions and availability zones. He has received complaints that some network communications are slower than others. He wants to evaluate the path taken by network packets across the cloud. Which command will help him for this?

A. ping

B. ifconfig

C. traceroute

D. arp

57. Which type of cloud service is best suited for cloud bursting?

A. PaaS

B. IaaS

C. SaaS

D. CaaS

58. A network administrator has to host 40 hosts in his network. Which subnet mask suits his needs with the least wastage of IP address space?

A. 255.255.255.128

B. 255.255.255.224

C. 255.255.255.240

D. 255.255.255.192

59. Users of a website hosted on a Linux server are unable to access it. Administrator suspects the server is compromised by a DoS attack. Which command can be run on the server to verify this?

A. netstat

B. ps

C. top

D. fstat

60. Users of a website that was operational for past 6 months are now complaining that they are getting an error message when visiting the site. No software changes have been made to the site. What is the most like cause of this?

A. Virus attack

B. OS has gone out of support

    C. Expired certificates

    D. Broken trust relationship

61. **A cloud administrator manages an organization's infrastructure in a public cloud. All servers are currently located in a single virtual network with a single firewall that all traffic must pass through. Per security requirements, production, QA, and development servers should not be able to communicate directly with each other. Which of the following should an administrator perform to comply with the security requirement?**

    A. Create separate virtual networks for production, QA, and development servers. Move the servers to the appropriate virtual network. Apply a network security group to each virtual network that denies all traffic except for the firewall.

    B. Create separate network security groups for production, QA, and development servers. Apply the network security groups on the appropriate production, QA, and development servers. Peer the networks together.

    C. Create separate virtual networks for production, QA, and development servers. Move the servers to the appropriate virtual network. Peer the networks together

    D. Create separate network security groups for production, QA, and development servers. Peer the networks together. Create static routes for each network to the firewall.

62. **A network administrator has moved a server VM to a new subnet of 100 Mbps bandwidth. After this, users started complaining of server slowness. Administrator investigated and found out that the server CPU and memory utilization are stable at 35% and 50%, respectively. The vNIC is showing download bandwidth ranging from 70-90 Mbps but the upload bandwidth is holding steady at 10 Mbps. What should the administrator infer from this information?**

    A. Memory should be scaled out

    B. CPU should be scaled up

    C. Some download bandwidth should be repurposed for upload

    D. Upload bandwidth has reached its quota. This needs to be adjusted.

63. **For performance reasons, an administrator should ensure that VMs have direct access to the hardware with near real-time performance. What can the administrator do to enable this?**

    A. SR-IOV

    B. hardware pass through

    C. GENEVE

    D. hyper virtualization

64. **After deploying a new application to cloud, application team started receiving error messages about databases servers. Which of the following is the most likely cause of the issue?**

    A. Incorrect IP address configuration

    B. Incorrect syslog configuration on the web servers

    C. Incorrect assignment group in service management

    D. Incorrect SNMP settings

65. **Which of the following is not a way to assign IP addresses to machines?**

    A. Static IP addressing

    B. CIDR

    C. Dynamic IP addressing

    D. IPAM

66. **Which of the below approaches does not increase storage efficiency?**

    A. Replacing spinning disk storage with SSD

    B. Deduplication

    C. Compression

    D. Encryption

67. **Which approach should be adopted to ensure high availability?**

    A. Redundancy

    B. Scale Up

    C. Load balancing

    D. Cold sites

68. **A developer is working on a local copy of code. He was informed that a colleague's code was submitted to source code repository. He needs to fetch the colleague's code changes to his local code base without losing his own changes. Which Git command can he use?**

    A. git push

    B. git commit

    C. git fetch

    D. git merge

69. **What is the best approach for preventing lateral moving malware from infecting the entire organization's servers?**

    A. WAF rules

    B. micro segmentation on the network

    C. EDR

    D. HIPS

70. **A Cloud administrator received a ticket that a user is unable to access a particular VM but can access other VMs. What should the administrator check first?**

    A. Network ACL rules

    B. Active Directory domain

    C. Firewall rules

    D. Security group rules

71. **An organization has 4 identical servers behind a load balancer running a web application. To meet additional demand, additional servers of higher compute capabilities were added. The administrator noticed that load balancer needs to be reconfigured to ensure the new hardware is utilized appropriately. What configuration should he choose?**

    A. Weighted scheduling

    B. Most Recently Used

    C. Round Robin

    D. IP Hash

72. **What are the benefits of Autoscaling? (choose two)**

    A. Low resource utilization

    B. Cost savings

    C. Physical server usage optimization

    D. Better handling of predictable workloads

73. **What is not the advantage of software-defined storage?**

    A. Data compression, Scalability, Replication

    B. Automated, policy-based storage provisioning

    C. Hyper convergence

    D. Separation of hardware and management software

74. A storage administrator configures data back-up to minimize downtime and maximize the reproduction of backup data. Which method should the choose?

    A. Incremental

    B. Snapshot

    C. Archive

    D. Synthetic full

75. A storage administrator has configured the backup strategy in such a way that the first full backup is taken from the original data, and subsequent full backups are created using incremental backups. He expects to minimize the downtime needed for backups and also restore time. What approach is this?

    A. Synthetic Full

    B. Synthetic Incremental

    C. Synthetic Differential

    D. Natural Incremental

76. Which of the following approaches is not useful for checking issues with Domain Name resolution?

    A. Checking whether clients can resolve names, and if not, check if resources can be reached with IP addresses.

    B. Checking proxy server's connectivity to the Internet.

    C. Checking DNS records for presence of destination resource.

    D. Checking correctness of DNS entries.

77. Which of the following does not ensure data integrity?

    A. Digital Signatures

    B. File Integrity Monitoring

    C. DLP

    D. Hashing

78. An organization noticed that it fell prey to a cybercrime. The activities of the perpetrator were identified by the response team. The CIO has instructed the systems administrator to track the potential evidence throughout the incident response processes. What is the CIO referring to?

    A. Evidence Acquisition

    B. Evidence preservation

    C. Evidence Isolation

    D. Chain of custody

79. **Which of the below storages is most suitable for data that is read many times but is not frequently modified?**

    A. Object storage

    B. File storage

    C. Block storage

    D. Distributed storage

80. **In which storage is data stored to media in fixed-size chunks with a unique address for each chunk?**

    A. Object storage

    B. Block storage

    C. File Storage

    D. Data base storage

81. **Which connector type is suitable for a SAN if the priorities are low cost and simplicity?**

    A. FCoE

    B. FC

    C. iSCSI

    D. CIFS

82. **Which solutions are useful for Disk encryption? (choose two)**

    A. Linux Unified Key Setup (LUKS)

    B. EFS

    C. ZFS

    D. Bit locker

83. **Which among the below is used to document traffic flow through the organization's software arrangements, switches, routers, and other network equipment?**

    A. Topology diagram

    B. Gantt chart

    C. Technology Stack

    D. Fish bone diagram

84. **An organization is considering implementing Disaster Recovery for its operations. They want to set up an alternate location containing the necessary space for a data center and business offices. The site shall also contain some computer and network hardware but will not actively maintain any data or computing. What is this site called?**

A. Cold Site

B. Warm site

C. Hot site

D. Duplicate site

85. Which of the following is the best way to monitor the utilization of cloud resources like CPU, GPU, memory, and network capacity including bandwidth and latency?

A. Packet capture analysis tool

B. Netstat

C. Cloud management console

D. Open SSL client

86. What should be considered as part of secrets management? (Choose two)

A. Public keys

B. Passwords

C. Private keys

D. API tokens

87. A network administrator wants to reduce the complexity of routing tables. Which of the below approaches shall help with it?

A. MPLS

B. IPv6

C. IP Security

D. Dynamic addressing

88. A team of developers is building a graphics intensive application on VMs. To ensure better performance, they are asking 100% access to GPU capabilities including processing power and graphics memory. What should the administrator do to address this request?

A. GPU offloading

B. GPU passthrough

C. GPU cluster

D. Distributed computing

89. A storage manager is tasked with setting up shared storage for his organization. The business requirements are for connecting to the shared storage and accessing files stored in it. Access controls are needed to manage permissions to the resources. Which approach should he choose?

    A. SAN

    B. Hybrid storage

    C. CIFS

    D. SCSI

90. **A network administrator is looking for tools that can exist between the network infrastructure and infrastructure security tools to gather information about the network. Which option must he choose?**

    A. Web proxies

    B. Block lists

    C. Data loss prevention (DLP)

    D. Network Packet Brokers (NPB)

91. **An organization is considering moving to public cloud. They want their cloud services in an isolated segment, and do not want to share any resources with other companies. What should they ask the CSP?**

    A. Virtual Private Cloud

    B. Community Cloud

    C. Multi-tenancy

    D. Bare metal servers

92. **An administrator wants to install a select set of security patches on the VMs he is responsible for. What should he look for?**

    A. Service Pack

    B. Rollups

    C. Hotfixes

    D. Signature updates

93. **What are the components of trend analysis? (Select all that apply)**

    A. Audits

    B. Anomalies

    C. Patterns

    D. Trends

94. **A network administrator wants to identify misconfigurations and unanticipated web apps on the network. What should he try?**

    A. Agent-based scan

    B. Network-based scan

    C. Vulnerability scan

    D. Service availability Scan

95. **A network administrator wants to review the performance of the network. He wants to refer to the known past performance first. What should he look for?**

    A. Baselines

    B. Anomalies

    C. Audits

    D. Patterns

96. **Which networking technique will help an administrator in segmenting user groups to control their access to the networks?**

    A. Data Deduplication

    B. VLAN

    C. Load balancing

    D. Peering

97. **How does high latency impact network?**

    A. Oversubscribes network

    B. Increases the hops between source and destination

    C. Reduces bandwidth

    D. Wastes IP address space

98. **Which of the below allows the transmission of encapsulated frames or packets from different types of network protocols over an IP network?**

    A. IPsec

    B. SR-IOV

    C. TLS

    D. GRE

99. **Which of the following is the best option for storing archive data?**

    A. Glacier storage

    B. Object storage

    C. File storage

    D. Block Storage

100. **Which of the following tools can be used to identify open ports on a machine?**

    A. Telnet

    B. nmap

C. ipconfig/ifconfig

D. ping

101. What is the primary purpose of a version control system?

A. To optimize code execution speed

B. To track changes in files over time

C. To automatically fix bugs in the code

D. To deploy applications to production servers

102. Which of the following is not a common Git command?

A. git commit

B. git push

C. git compile

D. git pull

103. What does the term *branching* mean in version control?

A. Splitting the code into multiple files

B. Creating a separate line of development

C. Combining two or more repositories

D. Deleting obsolete code

104. What is a *merge conflict* in Git?

A. When two branches have competing changes that can not be automatically resolved

B. When a repository exceeds its storage limit

C. When a user does not have permission to push changes

D. When a branch is created without a proper name

105. Which of the following best describes a *pull request* in the context of Git?

A. A request to download the latest changes from a remote repository

B. A proposal to merge changes from one branch into another

C. A command to force-push local changes to a remote branch

D. A method to revert the last commit in a repository

106. Which of the following is not typically a stage in a CI/CD pipeline?

A. Build

B. Test

C. Deploy

D. Refactor

107. **What is the main purpose of the *Build* stage in a CI/CD pipeline?**

     A. To review code changes

     B. To compile code and create artifacts

     C. To deploy the application to production

     D. To perform user acceptance testing

108. **In a CI/CD context, what does *fail fast* mean?**

     A. Quickly terminating the application in case of errors

     B. Identifying and reporting issues as early as possible in the pipeline

     C. Rapid deployment of new features

     D. Frequent rollbacks of production deployments

109. **Which of the following is a key benefit of implementing a CI/CD pipeline?**

     A. Eliminating the need for code reviews

     B. Reducing the frequency of releases

     C. Automating the software delivery process

     D. Increasing the cost of software development

110. **Which of the following best describes the concept of an API in systems integration?**

     A. A user interface for system administrators

     B. A set of rules and protocols for communication between software components

     C. A database management system

     D. A network security protocol

111. **In the context of systems integration, what is the primary purpose of middleware?**

     A. To provide a graphical user interface

     B. To manage database transactions

     C. To facilitate communication between different software applications or systems

     D. To optimize server performance

112. **Which integration pattern is best suited for real-time, event-driven communication between systems?**

     A. Batch processing

     B. Message queuing

     C. File transfer

     D. Remote procedure call (RPC)

113. **Which of the following is primarily used for container orchestration?**

    A. Docker

    B. Kubernetes

    C. Jenkins

    D. Ansible

114. **What is the main purpose of Terraform in a DevOps environment?**

    A. Continuous integration

    B. Infrastructure as Code

    C. Monitoring and Logging

    D. Container Management

115. **Which tool is commonly used for configuration management and automation in DevOps?**

    A. Git

    B. Puppet

    C. Gradle

    D. Splunk

116. **What is the primary function of Jenkins in a DevOps pipeline?**

    A. Database Management

    B. Continuous integration/continuous delivery

    C. Network Security

    D. Load Balancing

117. **Which of the following tools is best suited for monitoring and observability in a DevOps environment?**

    A. Maven

    B. Prometheus

    C. SonarQube

    D. Vagrant

Performance-based questions

1. An organization has its web application as shown in the following configuration. The organization wants to improve the performance of its application, but has tight constraints on budget. Suggest two changes the administrator can make to improve performance for their end users.

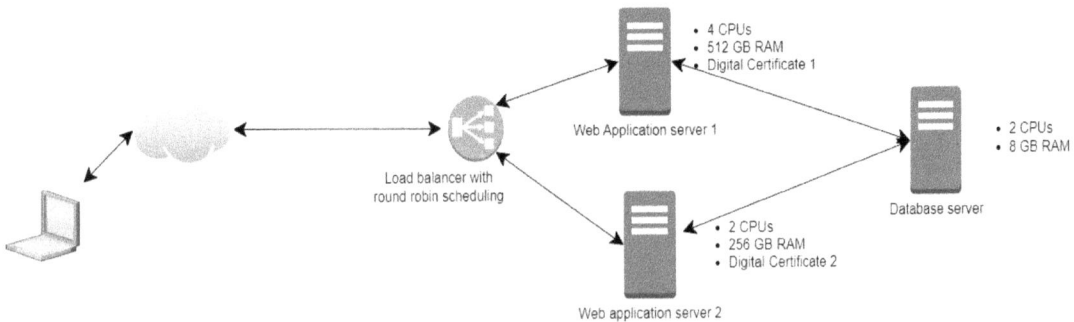

Figure 15.1: *Scenario one*

2. An organization has its cloud resources arranged as shown in *Figure 15.2*. The network administrator is receiving complaints of slow responses across all dev, test, and prod environments. All the VMs have their CPU and RAM utilization well below the threshold. Upon closer inspection, the administrator identified that the network bandwidth within the network is overwhelmed with data exchange between hypervisors. Administrator is looking for ways to reduce the network bandwidth consumption on the internal network. Suggest two ways for the administrator to achieve this.

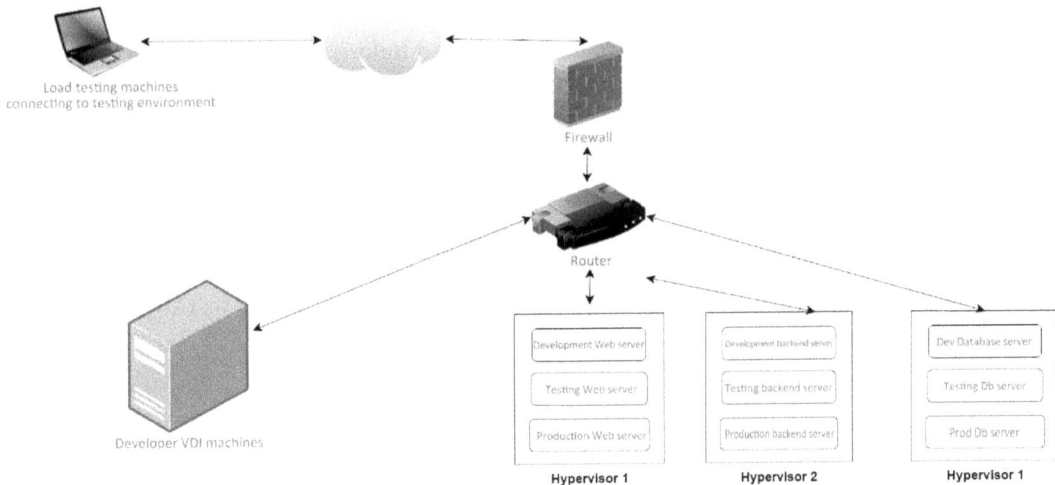

Figure 15.2: *Scenario two*

Answer key for multiple choice questions

1	2	3	4	5	6	7	8	9	10	11	12	13	14	15
C	D	D	B	A	B	B	B	A	A	D	B	B	D	A
16	17	18	19	20	21	22	23	24	25	26	27	28	29	30
A	A	C	B	C	B	D	A	C	B	D	A	C	B	D

31	32	33	34	35	36	37	38	39	40	41	42	43	44	45
A	C	B	D	A	C	B	D	A	C	B	D	A	C	B
46	47	48	49	50	51	52	53	54	55	56	57	58	59	60
D	A	C	B	D	A	C	B	D	A	C	B	D	A	C
61	62	63	64	65	66	67	68	69	70	71	72	73	74	75
B	D	A	C	B	D	A	C	B	D	A	B, D	C	D	A
76	77	78	79	80	81	82	83	84	85	86	87	88	89	90
B	C	D	A	B	C	A, D	A	B	C	B, D	A	B	C	D
91	92	93	94	95	96	97	98	99	100	101	102	103	104	105
A	B	B, C, D	D	A	B	C	D	A	B	B	C	B	A	A
106	107	108	109	110	111	112	113	114	115	116	117			
D	B	B	C	B	C	B	A	B	B	B	B			

Answer key for performance-based questions

1. These are the two changes the administrator can do to improve performance for their end users:

   A. Move the digital certificate to the load balancer.

   B. Change the load balancer configuration to weighted scheduling.

2. These are the two changes the administrator can do to improve performance for their end users:

   A. Move all dev servers to Hypervisor 1, test servers to Hypervisor 2and prod servers to Hypervisor 3.

   B. Configure rules on firewall to limit access of load testing machines to Hypervisor 2 only.

Join our Discord space

Join our Discord workspace for latest updates, offers, tech happenings around the world, new releases, and sessions with the authors:

https://discord.bpbonline.com

Index

www.ingramcontent.com/pod-product-compliance
Lightning Source LLC
Chambersburg PA
CBHW071959220326
41599CB00034BA/6886